POETICS OF VISIBILITY IN THE CONTEMPORARY ARAB AMERICAN NOVEL

POETICS OF VISIBILITY IN THE CONTEMPORARY ARAB AMERICAN NOVEL

MAZEN NAOUS

THE OHIO STATE UNIVERSITY PRESS
COLUMBUS

Copyright © 2020 by The Ohio State University.
All rights reserved.

Library of Congress Cataloging-in-Publication Data
Names: Naous, Mazen, author.
Title: Poetics of visibility in the contemporary Arab American novel / Mazen Naous.
Description: Columbus : The Ohio State University Press, 2020. | Includes bibliographical references and index. | Summary: "Redefines dominant perceptions of Arab Americans via an aesthetic analysis of Arab American novels, such as Diana Abu-Jaber's *Arabian Jazz* and *Crescent*, Rabih Alameddine's *Koolaids: The Art of War*, Laila Halaby's *Once in a Promised Land*, and Mohja Kahf's *The Girl in the Tangerine Scarf*, thereby launching transcultural possibilities by initiating visibility through poetics"—Provided by publisher.
Identifiers: LCCN 2019041562 | ISBN 9780814214299 (cloth) | ISBN 9780814277751 (ebook)
Subjects: LCSH: American fiction—Arab American authors—History and criticism. | American fiction—20th century—History and criticism. | American fiction—21st century—History and criticism. | Arab Americans in literature. | Marginality, Social, in literature. | Identity (Psychology) in literature.
Classification: LCC PS153.A73 N38 2020 | DDC 811/.50953—dc23
LC record available at https://lccn.loc.gov/2019041562

Cover design by John Barnett
Text design by Juliet Williams
Type set in Adobe Minion Pro

*For my mother, whose intellect, integrity,
and courage continue to inspire me*

CONTENTS

Acknowledgments		ix
INTRODUCTION	Poetics of Visibility, Visible Poetics	1
CHAPTER 1	The Disease as Queer Cure: Rabih Alameddine's *Koolaids: The Art of War*	13
CHAPTER 2	Blue Notes and Accented Rhythms: Diana Abu-Jaber's *Arabian Jazz*	55
CHAPTER 3	Sign after Sign: Mohja Kahf's *The Girl in the Tangerine Scarf*	87
CHAPTER 4	Anagrams of Identity: Laila Halaby's *Once in a Promised Land*	121
CHAPTER 5	Reframing Infidelity: Diana Abu-Jaber's *Crescent*	149
CONCLUSION	Arab American Polyphonics	189
Bibliography		195
Index		205

ACKNOWLEDGMENTS

Writing a book is not an easy endeavor. Writing a book on contemporary Arab American novels in the current climate of Arabophobia and Islamophobia is fraught with challenges, but it is also rewarding. I am fortunate to have crossed paths with extraordinary writers, scholars, musicians, poets, colleagues, and friends, whose thoughtfulness, kindness, and encouragement have accompanied me from the book's inception to its publication.

This book would not be what it is without the unwavering support of Suzanne Daly, who read multiple drafts of this book, provided incisive criticism, and offered invaluable advice. I am grateful to Cathy Schlund-Vials for her support of this project from its beginnings, and for steering me along the way. Thanks to Asha Nadkarni and Malcolm Sen for reading chapter drafts, and for their words of encouragement.

My colleagues in the English department at the University of Massachusetts Amherst have shown me unfailing support and kindness. Special thanks go to Joseph Black, Stephen Clingman, Martín Espada, Donna LeCourt, Marjorie Rubright, TreaAndrea Russworm, Joseph Skerrett, Jenny Spencer, Ron Welburn, and Adam Zucker. Randall Knoper, my department chair, and Julie Hayes, dean of the College of Humanities & Fine Arts, have offered invaluable guidance. I am grateful as well to the English department's administrative staff, who make sure everything runs smoothly. I would like to thank Brian Baldi, Mary Dougherty, Edwin Gentzler, Jim Hicks, A Yęmisi Jimoh, Miliann

Kang, Charles Schweik, James Smethurst, and Eve Weinbaum for fostering a sense of community at UMass that extends well beyond my department. My undergraduate and graduate students, who continue to impress me with their ideas, generosity of spirit, and achievements, deserve acknowledgment, as do the library staff at UMass Amherst and at Amherst College (particularly Blake Doherty, Dunstan McNutt, and Bilal Muhammad) for making the long hours I spent at the libraries productive and convivial.

My debts extend beyond the university and Western Massachusetts. For their time, energies, and intellectual camaraderie, I am grateful to Moustafa Bayoumi, Sylvia Chan-Malik, Moira Clingman, Martha Cutter, Carol Fadda-Conrey, Omar Dahi, Cynthia Franklin, Raymond Gunn, Joe Kraus, Charles Lemert, Gabriel and Samar Moushabeck, Michel Moushabeck, Vijay Prashad, Hiltrud Schulz, Nadine Sinno, and Rajini Srikanth. I would like to thank the novelists and critics whose writings have enriched and strengthened this intervention. Thanks also to my family and friends near and far—you know who you are—for good food, music, conversation, support, and long walks.

At The Ohio State University Press, I am deeply grateful to my editor Ana Jimenez-Moreno for her unwavering support of this project, timely advice, patience, expertise, and encouragement. I would also like to thank Editor-in-Chief Kristen Elias Rowley for her interest in my project. I am truly appreciative of my anonymous reviewers for their generous, engaged, and constructive reviews. Thank you to all of the editors and staff at the press involved in the production of this book.

An earlier version of chapter 2, titled "*Arabian Jazz* and the Need for Improvising Arab Identity in the US," was published in *MELUS*, volume 34, number 4, winter 2009, pp. 61–80. This article is adapted and reprinted by kind permission of Oxford University Press.

INTRODUCTION

Poetics of Visibility, Visible Poetics

In the 1990s, Arab American writers and critics spoke of their cultural, social, and political invisibility in the US.[1] As Nadine Naber argues in "Ambiguous Insiders: An Investigation of Arab American Invisibility," the condition of invisibility was produced by "factors both external and internal to the Arab American community." Externally, US government officials "classified Arabs and their descendants according to multiple and conflicting categories" (38). First labeled as Turks (because early Arab migrations originated from an Ottoman province, Syria) in the late nineteenth century, then as Syrians—with attendant conflations of Arabians, Armenians, Assyrians, and Turks—in the first half of the twentieth century, and most recently as Arabs-cum-Muslims post-1967, Arab Americans continued to slip through the cracks of the racial categories on which the US is organized. Not quite white and not in every respect a people of color, Arab Americans, "bereft of a [distinct] racial category, have often been left in obscurity within the academy and in the political

---

1. Arab Americans share this condition of invisibility with other groups in the US. These include Native Americans, African Americans, Asian Americans, Latinx Americans, LGBTQ Americans, and white working-class Americans. A comparative invisibility project is worthy of its own investigation. While this book is primarily concerned with the relationship between poetics and invisibility in contemporary Arab American novels, it addresses intergroup overlaps in poetics and invisibility when pertinent.

arena" (Saliba 305).[2] In other words, Arab Americans' racial indeterminacy has contributed to their invisibility across multiple registers.[3]

These external factors are compounded by the fact that Arab Americans have identified (and disidentified) in ways frequently informed by their disparate ethnicities, religions, cultures, languages, and political affiliations.[4] The heterogeneity of Arab American identifications and experiences has increased the difficulties of achieving visibility on Arab American terms. Despite this fact, and despite the shortcomings of the designation "Arab American," I concur with Carol Fadda-Conrey's view that it is "useful insofar as it denotes a minority collective whose members are connected not only through a shared cultural and linguistic Arab heritage but more importantly through a common investment in shaping and performing a revisionary form of US citizenship that alters the simplistic, binary constructs inherent in dominant understandings of the US nation-state" (*Contemporary* 10–11). I therefore speak not of one culture or one ethnicity in utilizing the term "Arab American," but of a minority collective of heterogeneities capacious enough to include those who disavow the term. In this sense, Arab Americans are transnational and transcultural citizens both within their own groups and within the US.[5]

Arab Americans' sense of social or cultural invisibility prior to 9/11 thus had to do with their histories, their heterogeneity, their lack of a cohesive group identity, and, in some cases, their ability to blend in or hide in plain sight. Many, however, experienced something akin to what psychologist Anderson J. Franklin terms "invisibility syndrome": the condition in which "one's talents, abilities, personality, and worth are not valued or even recog-

---

2. While the US Census Bureau currently classifies "a person having origins in any of the original peoples of Europe, the Middle East, or North Africa" ("Race") as white, Arab Americans are interpellated in various ways. In day-to-day interactions, darker-skinned Arab Americans and Muslim Arab Americans are unlikely to be perceived as white.

3. For more on Arab American invisibility please consult Nadia Abuelezam's "As an Arab Woman, I Feel Equally Visible and Invisible in the U.S.," Kristine J. Ajrouch and Toni C. Antonucci's "Social Relations and Health: Comparing 'Invisible' Arab Americans to Blacks and Whites," Louise Cainkar's "No Longer Invisible: Arab and Muslim Exclusion after September 11," Mervat F. Hatem's "The Invisible American Half: Arab American Hybridity and Feminist Discourses in the 1990s," Alia Malek's "Invisible Arab-Americans," and John Tehranian's *Whitewashed: America's Invisible Middle Eastern Minority*. These interventions are not comprehensive (and they do not include the texts I engage in this book), but they map the terrains of Arab American in/visibility.

4. For example, "Some Lebanese Americans actively combat this [designation of Arab American], preferring instead to remain *Lebanese* [. . .] Other Lebanese Americans, on the other hand, participate actively in Arab America" (Salaita, *Arab American* 56).

5. I discuss the terms "transcultural" and "cross-cultural" in detail on pages 7–8.

nized because of prejudice and racism" (761).⁶ The terrorist attacks of 9/11 threw the Arab and Arab American communities into sharp relief and brought with them the added responsibilities, which Arab American writers continue to carry, of denouncing extremism while engaging and challenging pernicious stereotypes and manifestations of Islamophobia in the US. After 9/11, Arab Americans came to "exist" in the US (despite their long history of immigration), yet their newly acquired hypervisibility proved more fraught than their previous invisibility; rather than being invisible, Arab Americans were perceived as a visible threat to the nation-state and the so-called American way of life. Michel Foucault contends, "Visibility is a trap," a situation of being an "object of information, never a subject in communication [. . . and this] impl[ies] a lateral invisibility" (200). In the case of Arab Americans, post-9/11 visibility is limited to security considerations, and it consequently enters a metonymic relationship with its opposite, invisibility, as a "guarantee of order" (Foucault 200). That is, the US security apparatuses' maintenance of order renders the heterogeneity and cross-cultural experiences of Arab Americans largely invisible or at best opaque. In "such a version [of metonymy] one feature of a group—attached to the group, so to speak—may come to represent the group as its quintessence. This is metonymy as a form of synecdoche—the part standing for the whole" (Clingman 12).⁷ In this formulation, nineteen terrorists who happen to be Arab come to stand in for all Arabs. The result is a crisis of representation, precipitated in considerable part by this conflation of an already problematic metonymy (terrorism associated with Arabs and/or Muslims) and synecdoche (terrorism as a stand-in for Arabs and/or Muslims). In his 2003 preface to the twenty-fifth anniversary edition of *Orientalism*, Edward Said states, "I wish I could say [. . .] that general understanding of the Middle East, the Arabs, and Islam in the United Sates has improved somewhat, but alas, it really hasn't" (xviii). Far from rendering Arab Americans visible, 9/11 and its consequent backlash against Arabs, Arab Americans, and Muslims placed members of these groups in the precarious position of what I call *hyper-in-visibility*: simultaneous visibility and invisibility that occasion the Arab American struggle for self-representation and visibility on Arab Ameri-

---

6. Franklin's model, the vast influence of which attests to its broad applicability, nevertheless draws on the uniquely dire experiences of African American men. The literature on invisibility as experienced by specific minority groups in the US spans several disciplines and is too vast to survey here. In literary studies, Ralph Ellison's 1952 novel *Invisible Man* (which Franklin cites) and Toni Morrison's *Playing in the Dark*, both of which theorize African Americans' racialized invisibility, have likewise strongly influenced subsequent studies of invisibility in other minority literatures.

7. Stephen Clingman suggests by contrast other possibilities in metonymy, which can also link syntactically through and across difference in its combinatory capacities.

can terms. Since the date of Said's preface, Arab American writers, artists, and intellectuals have established the field of Arab American studies, through which they continue to challenge the reductive, neo-orientalist, and racialized discourses of Islamophobia and anti-Arab racism in the US.

The past eighteen years have seen a proliferation of Arab American literature, often specifically designated as "Arab American writing." While these works frequently take up political issues, this fact should not preclude their being understood and analyzed as art. Unfortunately, both the classification and the critical reception of "Arab American writing" continue to place it in overdetermined sociopolitical matrices that prescribe certain readings, which tend to deemphasize the works' artistic significance. Arab American novels tend to be promoted as issues novels, as if Arab Americans are incapable of making sophisticated artistic interventions. This was true even before 9/11. In her well-known call to Arab American writers and critics in 1999, Lisa Suhair Majaj addresses this issue: "Literary criticism also has a crucial role to play in highlighting not just the cultural and the sociological, but the literary dimension of our writing, reminding us that we are, first and foremost, writers" ("New Directions" 72). Steven Salaita echoes Majaj's call in 2007 and adds that "emphasis on literature's aesthetic integrity is not only the best moral option available to critics, but also the most strategically viable one for critics interested in supplementing their criticism with a broader disciplinary purpose" (*Arab American* 53). In 2011, Salaita returns once again to this limitation, maintaining that "literature is ultimately a form of art. Good art can do many things simultaneously, and its consumers do themselves a delightful favor when they attempt to access as many of its affections as they can" (*Modern* 10). Furthermore, Fadda-Conrey asks in 2014, "To what extent do these texts' rebuttal of simplistic labels and exclusionary US citizenship relegate them to a position of constant retaliation that limits innovative forms of aesthetic creation or thematic exploration?" (*Contemporary* 156). The necessity of repeatedly reminding critics, writers, and readers that Arab American literature is a form of art that has or should have aesthetic integrity is telling. In this book, I argue that Arab American fiction does many things simultaneously and that its aesthetic, formal, and political elements—its poetics—are symbiotic and cogenerative. *Poetics of Visibility* investigates this relationship as a poetic manifestation of Arab American diversity, heterogeneity, and transculturality. Through these elements, I draw attention to the novels' creative representations of largely unrecognized subjects in the Arab American communities, who are rendered invisible by Islamophobia's singular and reductive representation of Arabs and Muslims (and the conflation of Arabs and Muslims). These include LGBTQ communities, complex Muslim characters, Muslim women and feminists, Christian Arabs, Druze Arabs, and secular Arabs. In my archive of novels, poetics and visibility are mutually constitutive.

Poetics of Visibility engages the distinct yet intersecting fields of Arab American literary studies and American studies. My interventions in these fields, particularly in relation to the burgeoning field of Arab American literary studies, are interdisciplinary, transcultural, and transpoetic. My analyses of Diana Abu-Jaber's *Arabian Jazz* and *Crescent,* Rabih Alameddine's *Koolaids: The Art of War,* Laila Halaby's *Once in a Promised Land,* and Mohja Kahf's *The Girl in the Tangerine Scarf* are shaped by a commitment to examining their formally and linguistically innovative aspects, exploring the relationship between politics and aesthetics, and foregrounding underrecognized subjects. In setting out to identify and interpret the novels' poetics of visibility and transcultural possibilities on Arab American terms, I necessarily privilege the literary, cultural, and political criticism of Arab and Arab American writers. Arab American fiction as a genre draws on and combines cross-cultural aesthetics and forms to create protean interart and transcultural possibilities, which build upon the richness and contradictions of Arab American experiences. In the novels, the use of vignettes and billboard signs; music as motif and counterlanguage; intertexts including *A Thousand and One Nights, Othello,* and *The Odyssey*; Arab oral storytelling traditions; crises of signification; and formal experimentation all enter into varying, energetic combinations. *Poetics of Visibility* examines the poetics of Arab American writers before and after September 11, 2001, as they move from conditions of invisibility to hyper-in-visibility. The literature of Arab Americans is emerging from years of neglect in the US academy, where it was not readily admitted alongside other literatures of migration and exile. This book aims both to secure a space for the contemporary Arab American novel as serious art and to assert its importance to aesthetics and artistic innovation. These poetics capacitate the novels to theorize their own interventions and enable Arab Americans to emerge as visible transcultural citizens within transnational and transpoetic frameworks.[8]

The critical attention that Arab American literature receives, while increasing, has yet to deal explicitly with the literature's artistic interventions. Scholarship on Arab American literature has of course paid some attention to form and aesthetics—the complex forms and cross-cultural poetics of these works of art demand consideration—but much of the criticism remains less

---

8. The novels' transpoeticism includes painting/vignettes; counterpoint in the style of Bach; lingual improvisation and blue notes as influenced by black jazz expression; creative overlaps between Christianity and Islam; anagrammatic play; and oral storytelling and framing in the style of *A Thousand and One Nights.*

invested in the artistic valences of Arab American literary production. I am by no means undervaluing timely and important work on the sociological and political aspects of Arab American literature—the exigencies of cultural backlash against Muslims, Arabs, Arab Americans, or anyone perceived as Arab post-9/11 have demanded sociological, political, and activist responses. Rather, my book aims to gauge these crucial modes of engagement through an investigation of the poetics of visibility at play in Arab American novels. Without a nuanced understanding and appreciation of their political aesthetics, multigenre forms, and interart combinations, we miss the transcultural exchanges and challenges to pernicious stereotypes as effectuated by artistic form and expression. These novels' complex and multiple genres and forms mediate the ineluctable political content both to uncover the hypocrisy of anti-Arab racism in the US and to present polyphonic possibilities for Arab Americans as transcultural citizens. This book, then, sets out to expand, complicate, and unfix dominant notions of "Arabs" in the US through an investigation of what I call the "poetics of visibility" in Arab American novels. One of the project's principal goals is to demonstrate how Arabic, Arabs, and Islam are in continual dialogue and negotiation with their adopted country and its myriad cultural inheritances despite Arab Americans' ostensible linguistic, cultural, and religious opacity and otherness. Transcultural and transpoetic forms of visibility challenge the confinements of racial/racist organization in the US, offering a poetic justice, a justice of poetics, in the process.

Pre-9/11 calls for more, and more careful, attention to Arab American cultural production are implicitly premised on the idea that some types of representation, or ways of achieving visibility, have value in that they both validate the communities from which they emerge and hold the potential to shift how these communities are viewed by others. Tahseen Shams argues that "the observed's visibility is not always only repressive. Rather, it can be used strategically to resist imposed categories, to some extent" (75). These strategies include managing visibility socially or visually (e.g., the interplay between wearing and not wearing traditional Muslim clothing, changing one's name, and/or accepting an Americanized nickname) to avoid dangerous situations or to confront prejudice. A key strategy that Arab American novelists employ to resist stereotypes and racializations is a poetics of visibility. But what exactly does the term "poetics" in relation to visibility mean? Mark Axelrod states, "What constitutes one critic's notion of poetics from another's is as variable as one's notion of the cosmos [. . .] There is a kind of enigma to the notion of 'poetics'" (xviii, xix). Certainly, poetics can mean many things, and it can have divergent meanings in different contexts. The term's enigmatic quality is not a weakness, however. Its nebulousness is replete with possibility.

In defining poetics of visibility, I am more concerned with what they do in the Arab American novel than with what they are. Poetics as a term shares the capaciousness of the term "Arab American," which makes it a powerful means by which to propel forms of visibility on Arab American terms. As Tzvetan Todorov observes, "What it [poetics] studies is not poetry or literature but 'poeticity' or 'literariness.' [. . .] Poetics will have to study not the already existing literary forms but, starting from them, a sum of possible forms: what literature *can* be rather than what it *is*" (33). My use of the term follows Todorov's in that I am concerned with poetics as the study of the creative principles at play in Arab American novels, the ways in which they use formal and aesthetic combinations as a means to undermine dominant perceptions of Arab Americans and, crucially, to imagine new transcultural possibilities. Inasmuch as literary, social, cultural, political, and aesthetic constructions manifest symbiotically in much Arab American fiction, this theory of form is more precisely a theory of trans-form that mediates variegated content and identities, a theory both of what is and what is possible in and across formal, poetic, interart, and multigenre formations.

Poetics of visibility is thus a method by which to explore Arab American transcultural, polyphonic, and transpoetic combinations. As people travel, combine, and overlap, so do cultural and aesthetic forms. In their introduction to the *MELUS* issue on Arab American literature, Salah Hassan and Marcy Jane Knopf-Newman contend that "with more experimental aesthetic choices represented in the literature, Arab American writers [. . .] are not merely constructing an identity but remaking identities" (8). Charged with transcultural and prodigal tendencies, these experimental aesthetic choices set to work in driving neoteric Arab American identities and political causes. As such, transcultural poetics provide the occasion and space to imagine new lived realities. These poetics do not clearly belong to their cultural origins or to their new locations; in other words, the poetics of visibility are a poetics of possibility.

In the case of Arab Americans, the term "transcultural" is critical on more than one level. While "transcultural" and "cross-cultural" appear to overlap in meaning (and both may describe people and things as well as many different aspects of literature), I use "cross-cultural" to suggest more clearly delimited or identified actions or practices of moving between cultures. For example, Salwa Haddad, a character in Laila Halaby's *Once in a Promised Land,* is born in the US to Jordanian parents of Palestinian descent, grows up in Jordan, and reimmigrates as an adult to the US as a US citizen. While Salwa is able to negotiate the cultures that constitute her identity, she largely relinquishes her Palestinian and Jordanian roots in favor of a consumerist US citizenship.

Matussem Ramoud, a Jordanian American character in Abu-Jaber's novel *Arabian Jazz*, drums to the music of John Coltrane while fusing the beats of a vagrant drummer in his childhood village in Jordan. Matussem's combining of two musical expressions is an example of transculturality. Novels that explore "transnational connections and the blurring of cultural boundaries" have the capacity to "negotiate the fuzzy edges of 'ethnic' or 'national' cultures, and participate in the creation of transnational public spheres as well as transcultural imaginations and memories" (Schulze-Engler ix–x). In this formulation, Matussem's blurring of musical boundaries is not an act of appropriation; rather, it is an act of participation, an acknowledgment of the transformative power of African American cultural expression. The African American experience is long and arduous, and it provides myriad models for cultural and creative resistance to racism and silencing. Matussem's compound rhythms attest to that and place Arab and African American drumming traditions in dialogue. The poetics of sound and rhythm call forth transcultural visibility out of the reductive silences of invisibility.

Silencing and invisibility are closely related. For many disenfranchised and vilified groups in the US, cultural apartheid is a lived reality. The continuing intimidation and silencing of Arabs and Muslims in the US closely relate to the denigration of Arab American cultures. Arabs and Muslims (who are often conflated) are perceived as an un-American, violent group whose backward culture has nothing of worth to contribute to the US. And this perception facilitates cultural silencing and cultural apartheid. If these are the ravages of Arab American hyper-in-visibility, the lived transcultural experiences of Arab Americans speak otherwise. Said states that "partly because of empire, all cultures are involved in one another; none is single and pure, all are hybrid, heterogenous, extraordinarily differentiated, and unmonolithic. This, I believe, is as true of the contemporary United States as it is of the modern Arab world" (*Culture* xxv). Arabs are a heterogeneous and mixed people, and they carry a long transcultural memory that derives from their trade with Asia, North Africa, and Europe. Europe and the US's interactions with the Middle East and North Africa are filtered largely through the machinations of imperial, colonial, and interventionist ambitions. From the Crusades to the US's multiple interventions in their region, Arabs continue to add to their already rich cultural topography by virtue of exposure to the cultures of occupiers.

When they immigrate to the US, Arabs enter a negotiation with the multiple cultural inheritances of the US population, both adding to and acquiring cultural capital in the process. Theirs, like any other group's, is a specific mode of transculturality, an Arab American–oriented transculturality, which, while productive, is not immune to the coercive influences of power within their communities and in relation to the dominant culture. Nonetheless, Arab American–oriented transculturality, which operates on both individual and collective levels, is valuable in that it dialogically interweaves Arab America into the sociocultural and artistic fabrics of the US. Furthermore, transcultural citizenship counterpoints transnational forms of the same, but it further deemphasizes the nation as a point of reference. The Sikes-Picot Agreement (1916), which divided the Ottoman-held areas of Syria, Iraq, Lebanon, and Palestine between the French and British, ultimately created "national" spaces of European making. Add to that anti-Arab racism and Islamophobia in the US, which represent Arab Americans as un-American, and the utility of transculturality as a designation becomes clear. The multiplex poetics of visibility in the novels I explore underscore transcultural modes of being in their combinations and forms. They do so, as Jacques Rancière contends in *The Politics of Aesthetics,* more "in terms of horizontal distributions, combinations between systems of possibilities, not in terms of surface and substratum. Where one searches for the hidden beneath the apparent, a position of mastery is established" (49). Poetics of visibility—a poetics that disrupts the racialization of Muslims and Arab Americans—allows us to revisualize Arab and American cultures horizontally, as they create dialogic connections that are more equal and transcend, in the space of poetics, the inequalities of power relationships.

Poetics of visibility might seem somewhat paradoxical: To challenge racialized visibility (a fallacious formulation that renders Arabs and Muslims identifiable by sight) is to undermine visibility as a lens of identification; and yet this very visibility enables possibilities of countervisibility. These, however, combine non-ocular social, political, cultural, and/or, importantly, poetic forms of visibility in Arab American novels. In this sense, poetics of visibility provides a counterpoint, which in turn reinforces the political. As Crispin Sartwell identifies it,

> the political function of the arts—including various crafts and design practices—is not merely a matter of manipulation and affect: the aesthetic expressions of a regime or of the resistance to a regime are central also to the cognitive content and concrete effects of political systems [. . .] The aesthetic embodiments of political positions are material transformations and interventions, with concrete effects. (1–2)

If Islamophobic and anti-Arab constructions are capable of creating diversionary fear and loathing, in which scapegoated groups become the receptacles of all socioeconomic and cultural ills, the aesthetic expressions countering them must be effectively transformative and interventional even though they lack the public-relations arsenal available to the dominant culture. This is no small feat, and Arab American writers alongside many other disenfranchised groups have had to take on this difficult responsibility.

Arab American writing frequently conveys an awareness of the role that art plays in giving voice to Arab American truths and lived realities. In this respect, "literature and painting and music have something strongly in common: a positive sense of the absence that prevailed before [their] presence" (Albright 7). And the presence of painting, photography, and music in the novels I analyze is further amplified by the combinations into which they enter. These include combinations of literary and art forms, identities, languages, and/or names. For instance, the character Matussem's accented English combines with the poetics of jazz improvisation. The resulting musical-lingual overlap creates what Deleuze and Guattari describe as an

> atypical expression that produces the placing-in-variation of the correct forms, uprooting them from their state as constants. The atypical expression constitutes a cutting edge of deterritorialization of language, it plays the role of *tensor*; in other words, it causes language to tend toward the limit of its elements, forms, or notions, toward a near side or a beyond of language. (99)

Matussem's accented jazz improvisations deterritorialize American English and produce lingual-musical expressions that are neither simply lingual nor musical but an improvisatory combination of both. Such poetic combinations have a direct relationship to the identities of the characters who produce them, demonstrating that the "self can be a combinatory reality both in space and time, and what provides its transitive form is the capacity for navigation" (Clingman 22). In other words, the transitive/improvisatory aspect of poetic combinations sets the framework for further combinations on the levels of aesthetics and identity. No combination is ever complete or final.

Furthermore, acts of combination navigate seemingly disparate cultures and experiences, using contiguity to suggest equivalence. In this way, they participate in what Sirène Harb terms "associative remembering": "The importance of such juxtapositions lies in the fact that they bring together spaces of trauma traditionally understood as separate and unable to meet, since they belong to countries that are economically and politically unequal in terms of power and influence" (29). For instance, Alameddine's *Koolaids* juxtaposes the war on AIDS—and the war on gay men—in 1980s and '90s San Francisco with the Lebanese Civil War in intersecting vignettes/fragments told by multiple narrators. The novel's fragmentary form, consisting of 244 vignettes capable of entering into seemingly inexhaustible combinations, exposes the cruelty and hypocrisy of representations of the AIDS epidemic and the Lebanese Civil War in the mass media and religious discourse. Readers of *Koolaids* struggle to find their way through the vignettes, which mimic aesthetically the vertiginous and painful experiences of AIDS and civil war.

The associations and combinations do not end there, however. The characters' Arabic names travel to the US and appear in English-letter transliterations. As markers of difference and/or of Islam, names also reflect inequalities of power. The narrator of Ameen Rihani's 1911 novel *The Book of Khalid*, which is considered to be the first Arab American novel written in English, asks, "For after all, what's in a name?" (17). The question is undoubtedly rhetorical (and likely ironic), as names carry cultural meanings that tend to become invisible as they travel to non-Arab locations. Despite the names' reappearance in transliteration, allowing non-Arabic speakers to approximate their sounds, their meanings do not readily translate. Yet names carry much significance to the characters attached to them. Furthermore, the narrator's question is itself a quotation from Shakespeare's *Romeo and Juliet*: "What's in a name? That which we call a rose / By any other name would smell as sweet" (2.1.85–6). In the context of Shakespeare's play, Juliet uncouples Romeo's name from its association with the house of Montague. As such, Romeo's name becomes Juliet's enemy, not Romeo himself. Needless to say, such uncoupling is not available to Arab and Muslim Americans. Quite the contrary, their names render their owners guilty by cultural association. This consideration extends beyond Arab America and Arab American fiction. For example, "Moor" (Moraes) Zogoiby, the narrator of Salman Rushdie's *The Moor's Last Sigh*, also asks "What's in a name?" (84) in his investigations of his family's history. The novels I analyze in *Poetics of Visibility* pay close attention to characters' names, and the novels' poetics attempt to recover their meanings and cultural resonances from forms of invisibility, including curtailment and Americanization.

Framing is another important aspect of formal and associative play in my archive of Arab American novels. The influence of *A Thousand and One Nights*' frame-narrative is palpable in *Once in a Promised Land* and *Crescent*. Both novels offer a storyteller and a narrator, who share the overall narrative. *Once in a Promised Land* uses the classic framing device—offering two storytelling sections "Before" and "After" the central narrative—to challenge and reframe dominant stereotypes of Arab Americans. *Crescent* offers a storyteller and a narrator who must share the space of every chapter, most of which begin with Sirine's uncle's storytelling before moving into the realist narrative. The uncle's storytelling metaphorizes and recultures Sirine's experiences, and the novel tasks readers with reconciling the storytelling and realist sections, and, consequently, the largely manufactured rift between Arabs and Americans. This is no easy task, however, as "the number of frames available for any text are far greater than the number of narrators and [. . .] the juxtaposition of those frames will generate new meanings and/or conflicting responses that any reader must resolve" (Berlatsky 183). In other words, transculturality is not easily attained, and those seeking it must engage framing in its multiple and complex valences. Todorov reminds us that "the object of poetics will be constituted by literary 'devices'—which is to say, by concepts which describe the functioning of literary discourse" (236). The novels in this study make their political and cultural interventions as much through literary devices as through content. It is the novels' heterogeneous and combinatory poetics that bring forth complex forms of visibility from invisibility and, in so doing, constitute a poetics of visibility that makes visible Arab American transpoetics. This is no mere tautology, however, but a mutually constitutive association: poetics of visibility, visible poetics.

Bringing together Arab American writers of varying origins, *Poetics of Visibility* covers four countries (Syria, Jordan, Lebanon, and the US). Its historical trajectory includes flashpoints of the Arab American experience from the 1990s through the first decade of the twenty-first century. The book's theoretical and thematic unity derives from a constellation of novels that—aesthetically, formally, and politically—reshape, reframe, and challenge dominant prescriptions of Arab and Arab American immigrants and migrants. These texts from diverse times and places all participate in a poetics of visibility that, while accounting for representational inequalities, seeks to alter dominant Arab and American cultural and poetic formations. I have chosen these novels from a growing Arab American literary repertoire specifically because they offer variegated combinations in their poetics of visibility, which reflect the richness and heterogeneity of Arab American experiences. This heterogeneity does not, however, preclude nuanced connections between Arab Americans themselves and the cultures they straddle. These novels answer the "rising need among Arab-Americans for a transformative project of communal and individual self-representation, one that captures the complexity and heterogeneity of their communities" (Fadda-Conrey, *Contemporary* 2). These novels are not meant to be comprehensive or absolute emblems of poetics of visibility in the contemporary Arab American novel or literature. Rather, my selection is designed to emphasize artistic diversity, complexity, and overlap in Arab American novelistic production, which necessitates a more intricate consideration of the artistic combinations in each novel that most powerfully exemplify poetics of visibility and transcultural citizenship individually and communally.

CHAPTER 1

The Disease as Queer Cure

Rabih Alameddine's *Koolaids: The Art of War*

What do the AIDS epidemic and the Lebanese Civil War have in common? It turns out that these seemingly disparate trials share much if one considers the religio-cultural representations and the mass media coverage of both. In his first novel, *Koolaids: The Art of War*, Lebanese American author and painter Rabih Alameddine draws attention to the Lebanese and Lebanese American gay communities and to the suffering of the Lebanese during Lebanon's Civil War. *Koolaids* juxtaposes the war on AIDS—and the war on gay men—in 1980s and early 1990s San Francisco with the Lebanese Civil War (1975–90) in 244 intersecting vignettes (including newspaper clippings, philosophical and religious quotes, hallucinations, and playlike dialogues) apparently told by multiple narrators (some identified and some anonymous), including one that I like to call a war storyteller. In this chapter, I investigate the novel's decentering form and poetics, which expose the poverty of monolithic representations of the AIDS epidemic and the Lebanese Civil War. I argue that *Koolaids* employs a poetics of AIDS dementia and a poetics of repetition (on inter- and intravignette levels) both to undercut facile and stereotypical religious and multimedia representations of gay men, the AIDS epidemic, Arabs, Muslims, and the Lebanese Civil War; and to offer nonnormalizing counternarratives and the perpetual combinational possibilities of its vignettes. "Vignette" is a rich term with multiple meanings, but it readily lends itself to denote a photograph or portrait with shaded edges or a short prose episode. I opt for the term to describe the form of *Koolaids* for two reasons. The term holds narrative, visual, and musical possibilities, and *Koolaids* itself utilizes the term to theorize its formal and thematic interventions.

In terms of the vignettes' interart potentialities, likely and unlikely combinations of vignettes expose and correlate religious, moral, cultural, and political hypocrisies in Lebanon and the US. If one vignette focuses on its episodic centrality in the softening or shading away of its borders (as in a vignetted portrait), the possible combinations of vignettes decenter and complicate that episodic centrality by highlighting the shades and counterpoints among vignettes, allowing for mutually constitutive (even if unstable) forms of visibility and representation to emerge. In vignette 41—a playlike dialogue between Arjuna, Krsna, Eleanor Roosevelt, Krishnamurti, Julio Cortázar, and Tom Cruise[1]—Arjuna questions his charioteer, Krsna, about the purpose of life just before they go into battle: "Are you suggesting life has no purpose? No unity, nothing to pull all these illogical vignettes into a coherent collage? If that is the case, then how do biographers do what they do?" (37). In the context of war, Arjuna is frustrated by Krsna's "peripatetic dialectics" (37), which do little to relieve his anxiety. Arjuna's questions resonate across the form and themes of *Koolaids*. Confronted by the seemingly "illogical vignettes," readers of *Koolaids* find themselves in an impossible position, between yielding to the ill-logic of AIDS and the Lebanese Civil War (also a form of illness) and attempting to reform the vignettes into a "coherent collage." Furthermore, this unstable collage of illogical vignettes constructs an equally slippery biographical account. Nor does Krsna's answer provide any relief to Arjuna or to the readers: "What if I told you that life has no unity? It is a series of nonlinear vignettes leading nowhere, a tale, told by an idiot, full of sound and fury, signifying nothing. It makes no sense, enjoy it" (38).

Apart from Krsna's emphasis on the experience (rather than the purpose) of life, his repetition with variation of Macbeth's words in William Shakespeare's *Macbeth* and his allusion to William Faulkner's *The Sound and the Fury* forestall any singular or definite interpretation of his words.[2] If Krsna's quoting

---

1. Arjuna is a main character who plays an important role alongside Krishna (a major deity in Hinduism) in the *Bhagavad Gita* (Sanskrit scripture); Eleanor Roosevelt (1884–1962) was the First Lady of the United States during her husband President Franklin D. Roosevelt's terms in office and a political figure and activist in her own right; Jiddu Krishnamurti (1895–1986) was an Indian philosopher; Julio Cortázar (1914–84) was an Argentine novelist and essayist; and Tom Cruise (1962–) is an American actor and producer.

2. In act 5, Macbeth reacts to the news of Lady Macbeth's death: "Out, out, brief candle. / Life's but a walking shadow, a poor player / That struts and frets his hour upon the stage, / And then is heard no more. It is a tale / Told by an idiot, full of sound and fury, / Signifying nothing" (5.5.22–27).

(with variation) of Shakespeare is not uncanny enough, his allusion to Benjy Compson, the intellectually disabled character whose perspective permeates Faulkner's novel, places Arjuna and the readers of *Koolaids* in the positions of idiots and fools, who perpetually err in their analyses. Krsna's repetition and allusion, in effect, speak to what I call a poetics of AIDS dementia, which mimics the condition's symptoms of disorientation, memory loss, and confusion ("AIDS Dementia Complex"). In *Koolaids,* we can locate AIDS dementia in the perspective of a central character, Mohammad. Mohammad, who suffers from late-stage AIDS dementia, narrates many of the vignettes that are "full of sound and fury." The other characters' narratives all relate—directly or indirectly—to Mohammad's experiences in Lebanon and San Francisco.

Koolaids functions on one important level as a combination of Mohammad's autobiography and biography. On another level, however, *Koolaids* resists such classifications in that the "nonlinear vignettes" lead nowhere conclusively. Krsna's demand that Arjuna (and the readers) enjoy life, as represented by the dizzying vignettes, brings us to the art of repetition in *Koolaids.* Repetition is an "essential unifying element in nearly all poetry and much prose" (Cuddon, "Repetition" 742). Interart repetitions in and across vignettes provide aesthetic imperatives for complex enjoyment, but also suggest combinations by establishing cross-vignette and multigenre patterns. Art is critical, both as critique and as lifeline, to our experience of *Koolaids,* and repetition—as a perceptible art pattern—counterpoints the chaos of the vignettes. That is, repetition on the formal level produces possible connections in and between vignettes, while repetition at the content level (as in Krsna's repetition of Macbeth's words) forestalls and satirizes singular interpretations. This relationship becomes clearer as Mohammad repeats phrases and words—because AIDS dementia prevents him from completing his thoughts—that become cross-vignette leitmotifs. In some of the civil war vignettes, repetition also serves as a coping mechanism (a mantra) with which to make sense of the madness and chaos of war. This chapter, then, engages the poetics of AIDS dementia and the art of repetition as they travel between the US and war-torn Lebanon, between the character Mohammad and his cohort, between Christianity and Islam, and within and among vignettes, all the while complicating the perception that Lebanese and Lebanese gay immigrants find in the US a safe harbor away from their exceptionally homophobic and violent country of origin.

To do so, I must first account for *Koolaids*'s pastiche form—the medley of vignettes from various sources and genres—and its influence on the novel's complex content. Steven Salaita argues that the publication of *Koolaids* "represented a milestone in the modern Arab American literary tradition, not merely because of its artistic quality [. . .] but because of all the new directions and possibilities it represented" (*Arab American* 73). Of course, *Koolaids*'s artistic quality, its form and poetics, allows for "seemingly endless analytical possibilities" (72). The "intensely fragmented narrative consisting mainly of a dizzying patchwork of journal entries, first-person narrations, and excerpts from emails and letters" (Fadda-Conrey, "Alameddine, Rabih" 122) is matched by equally fragmented and dizzying themes. Alameddine, states Susan Muaddi Darraj, "tackles two very difficult subjects [the Lebanese Civil War and the US AIDS epidemic] in a novel whose form is experimental and new for Arab American literature, especially in its adoption of homosexuality as a major theme" ("Arab American Novel" 181). In other words, *Koolaids*'s formal, poetic, and thematic possibilities are manifold. As I show earlier, *Koolaids* itself, through Krsna's words, theorizes the difficulty of interpreting its vignette form.

Lest we overlook this message, Mame Dennis—in vignette 168, another iteration of scripted dialogue—restates Krsna's earlier advice to Arjuna: "Just live, darling. Stop trying to make sense of the book of life. It is a series of nonlinear vignettes leading nowhere, a tale, told by an idiot, full of sound and fury, signifying nothing. It makes no sense, enjoy it" (168). Not only does Mame Dennis reemphasize Krsna's prescription, but the reiteration of Krsna's words (themselves double repetitions) highlights repetition's function in Alameddine's work. While Mame Dennis's repetition establishes a pattern that connects these two vignettes (along with scripted dialogue), it produces neither sense nor direction between the two. The recognition of repetition patterns does not produce thematic intelligibility; rather, repetition reinforces the nonsense of the vignettes, which destabilizes and disrupts interpretative agency. As Sebastian Duda notes, repetition in experimental writing "is regarded to be very problematic since [it] opposes two main principles that the reader expects of a text: linearity and intelligibility" (5). This is precisely the point in *Koolaids*: The novel allows for its 244 vignettes to enter into myriad combinations, as it resists any stable or stabilizing interpretation of its form, poetics, and thematics. Susan Stewart makes the related point that "nonsense, with its embracing of play and paradox, is a critical activity [. . . that offers] a critique not only of the texts of common sense, but of the influence of common sense upon other forms of discourse such as proverb [and] myth" (50). *Koolaids*'s mode of play—its nonsense—critiques forms of religious and cultural common sense without prescribing alternative senses—only possibilities and paradoxes in varying combinations. Even so, *Koolaids* establishes patterns of repetition across different registers as a counterpoint to the vertiginous array of vignettes.

This interplay between repetition (a semblance of order) and the combinational possibilities of vignettes (chaos) is in effect a political aesthetic. I would like to return here to Crispin Sartwell's contention, which I engage in the introduction, that "the political function of the arts—including various crafts and design practices—is not merely a matter of manipulation and affect [. . .] The aesthetic embodiments of political positions are material transformations and interventions, with concrete effects" (1–2). *Koolaids* compels its readers and critics to engage the fragmented form of vignettes as it mediates complex and troubling content. On the one hand, the vignettes, like "the fictional and the nonfictional narratives of the [Lebanese Civil] war[,] are laid out in confusing and incoherent—schizophrenic—disorder" (Makdisi 102). The form of *Koolaids* necessitates that readers experience some of the incoherence, disorder, and even violence of the Lebanese Civil War, and that they endeavor—like the war-beaten Lebanese—to make sense of a war (as mediated by the war-form of vignettes) that generates "its own rules and orders, over which no one seem[s] to have any control" (Makdisi 101). Readers find that they must improvise around the novel's seemingly imperceptible rules in order to survive the 244 vignette bombs. On the other hand, *Koolaids* also seeks to queer its readers, to trouble and "dis-ease" (Taylor 528) them with the poetics of AIDS dementia so that they can see queerly the fallacies and follies of religious and sectarian fundamentalisms in the US and Lebanon. As Mark C. Taylor observes, "In this case dis-ease need not be destructive and can actually be productive" (528). The disease is the unjust and sparse representations of the Lebanese Civil War and the AIDS epidemic in the US, but the dis-ease is a queer cure that—in lieu of a traditional cure's finality—induces an ongoing state of unease without the possibility of ease. Combining the effects of war with those of illness, the poetics of AIDS dementia—of confusion, disorientation, and memory loss—permeates the body of *Koolaids* as both queer cure and aesthetic insurgency. It is in this spirit of incompleteness that I offer my intervention, through a provisional combination of vignettes along the lines of AIDS dementia and repetition.

AIDS dementia as a consciousness sets in motion a novelwide poetics structured by an aesthetics of repetition, and Mohammad is the main progenitor of this dis-ease. On some levels Mohammad overlaps with or doubles as Alameddine.[3] Like Alameddine, Mohammad is a painter and writer who leaves Lebanon and ends up in the US. Furthermore, Mohammad exhibits the traits of "an errant non-conformist" (viii), as Alameddine describes himself in the acknowledgments section of *Koolaids*. At some level, *Koolaids* participates in the genre of the *faux mémoire*. Syrine Hout describes *faux mémoire*

---

3. Syrine Hout also observes that "Alameddine's main character, Mohammad, comes closest to representing the author himself" ("Of Fathers" 287).

(in relation to the post-1995 Lebanese exilic novel) as a genre that "features a male protagonist—a fictional extension of the author—who tells his story, which constitutes either all or most of the text, as recalled from the vantage point of the present being lived in exile" ("Of Fathers" 286). If Mohammad is in fact telling his and—in part—Alameddine's story, it is fragmented and non-unitary, given voice by multiple narrators. The present, which frames the story, can be found in five vignettes that make strategic appearances through *Koolaids*. They provide "the sole chronology in this mosaic text" (Hout, *Post-War* 34) in which Mohammad is hospitalized, struggling five times with the four horsemen (of the apocalypse) before his death at the novel's end. Hout's analysis opens the possibility that Mohammad's late-stage AIDS dementia and his impending death propel his consciousness across time and space to gather the fragments of his life, even those obliquely related to him, into a slanting autobiographical/biographical account.

The novel offers a multitude of unnamed first-person narrators. Some are identifiable (as they are recurring characters) and some are not, at least not readily. In combination, they constitute a heterogeneous collective, not unlike the Lebanese themselves, who are a composite of multiple ethnicities and cultures. Some are dark and some are fair, and their cultural, religious, and political affiliations vary widely. Mohammad, his friend Samir tells us in vignette 107, "was what we would call cursed. He was dark, looked like an Arab. In Lebanon, that's a curse" (101). Many Lebanese, including those who would like to think of themselves as European or at the very least as non-Arab, believe that dark skin is a curse. The fact that Alameddine chooses the dark-skinned Mohammad as a site for diasporic Lebanese fusion is significant. Mohammad is a complex, erudite, and sophisticated artist and thinker; he is a transcultural citizen who draws on and combines multiple cultures (as exemplified by the vignettes of *Koolaids*). The curse is not, in fact, Mohammad's dark skin but the fetishizing of white skin in Lebanon. The curse travels with Mohammad to the US, which continues to obsess over racial categories. This multifaceted fusion/confusion seems to ironize the US's motto, *e pluribus unum*, as the one out of many could be Mohammad, a gay, dark-skinned immigrant with Muslim roots.

But the fusion or confusion does not end there. The front and back jacket art and the title page of *Koolaids* feature paintings by Alameddine, titled *Hélas #251, Hélas #119,* and *Hélas #185. Hélas* is French for "alas," an exclamation of grief, pity, or concern. *Hélas #251* is a close-up of Alameddine's face, his expression sorrowful against the gray canvas/paper, his eyes looming at the top of the painting. Etchings seem to cover his face. Are they war scars and/or Kaposi's sarcoma lesions? On looking more closely at *Hélas #251*, one discovers that the etchings are, in fact, ethereal sketches of Alameddine. Some are close-ups of his face, some contain his head and torso, and some represent his face and shoulders. It is as if the looming eyes witness the sketches of Alameddine in varying degrees of erasure. These sketches, like the confusion of the first-person pronoun "I" in the novel, represent facets of the larger close-up of Alameddine's face even while they seem to deface it. *Hélas #119*, which begins below *Hélas #251* on the front jacket and continues on the back jacket (where it meets the top part of *Hélas #251*, placed under it on the back jacket), is more difficult to decipher. The background is yellow-orange with shadings of gray, and the middle appears to be a close-up of Alameddine's face set ablaze by a blood-red color. Is this infected blood that consumes the face, and/or the fire of war, and/or the hellfire to which fundamentalists condemn gay men? Both *Hélas #251* and *Hélas #119*, in their contiguous and circular placement on the front and back of the jacket, speak to the ravages of the Lebanese Civil War and the AIDS epidemic, and an exile's present suffering against counterpoints of past selves. *Hélas #185*, the title-page painting, consists of nine squares, each containing a close-up of Alameddine's face in different mutations of grief, pity, or concern. The nine squares construct one large square in which the different close-ups of Alameddine's face can be examined against each other horizontally, vertically, and diagonally. That is, the squares can enter into multiple combinations without offering a stable or complete portrait of Alameddine's face. Alas, the large square does not reveal a unitary composite of Alameddine's face, but nine distinct close-ups placed next to and around each other. Here, the whole is less than the sum of its parts. If we get one square out of many, the reverse is also true: out of one, many squares. This is no simple tautology, however. *Hélas #185* allows for many combinations of Alameddine's face in lieu of a whole, and it offers each of the square close-ups its own distinctness.

Neither unrelated square-fragments nor a viable whole, *Hélas #185* exemplifies the state of in-betweenness in the chiasmus that makes up vignette 43: "In America, I fit, but I do not belong. / In Lebanon, I belong, but I do not fit" (40). The exchange of places between "fit" and "belong" offers neither solution nor resolution, but rather a counterpointing of possibility and loss. These exchanges and combinations are not unlike the vignette form of *Koolaids* and Mohammad's AIDS-dementia consciousness, which permeate the entire novel, and certainly not unlike the diasporic experiences of the Lebanese. *Koolaids* theorizes its polyphonic form and poetics in vignettes 107 and 197 in relation to Mohammad's paintings. Both vignettes are narrated by Samir, also a gay Lebanese character, who recounts attending Mohammad's exhibit with his lover Mark. In vignette 107, Samir has a conversation in which an art dealer called Jack refers to Mohammad's paintings as abstract, while Mark remarks that they "are all just paintings with irregular rectangles" (101). Samir, however, sees the paintings as the stones of the houses in Lebanese villages: "They were of every village, Druze, Christian, or Muslim. [Mohammad] had captured Lebanon" (101). Yet the Lebanon they capture is fragmented by sectarianism, a colonially constructed geopolitical space with a confessional system that makes for a perpetually unstable state.

Like Alameddine's paintings, Mohammad's paintings are at once fragmentary and combinational. Out of many, one and out of one, many. At another exhibit, Samir offers an alternative interpretation of Mohammad's jackass painting, which he describes as "a simple image, an upside-down jackass, or donkey, floating in water, submerged, with only the legs showing" (188). Whereas American reviewers see mythological symbolism and a commentary on homosexuality in the painting—"*Upside-down* and *invert* were once derogatory terms for homosexuals" (189)—Samir perceives the jackass as representing the Lebanese. At the end of vignette 197, Samir comes to the realization that it is "possible everyone was right. The painting could comment about homosexuality [. . .] and, at the same time, mourn the death of a country" (190). In combining seemingly variegated interpretations of Mohammad's painting, Samir counterpoints the struggles of gay men and those of the Lebanese, rendering their overlap polyphonic. Samir's interpretative intervention, like those of Krsna and Mame Dennis, theorizes the form and poetics of *Koolaids*, pointing to both possibility and loss in the interplay between the AIDS epidemic and the Lebanese Civil War, rendering their visibility mutually constitutive. How, then, do the poetics of AIDS dementia—as theory and praxis, as political aesthetics, and as a poetry of form and multigenre—intervene against pernicious stereotypes of the Lebanese, Muslims, and gay men suffering from AIDS?

THE FOUR HORSEMEN VIGNETTES: REPETITION WITH VARIATION AND HETEROPHONIC/POLYPHONIC INTERPLAY

Koolaids's first vignette opens with a statement on death: "Death comes in many shapes and sizes, but it always comes. No one escapes the little tag on the big toe" (1). Death, the great equalizer, comes to all, including gay men suffering from AIDS and Lebanese Civil War victims. But this statement is not merely a truism; it also serves as the incipit of the book that Mohammad had wished to write: "I have had many ideas which could not translate well into painting. I wanted to write them down. I never really did. I just did not have a good command of the written word" (18). Mohammad alludes to the movement between painting and writing, a key feature of the interart poetics in *Koolaids*. Remarkable, however, is Mohammad's claim in vignette 19 that he never wrote down his ideas: "I never went beyond the incipit [. . .] I wanted to make sure death and sex were associated. Look at the words *shapes, sizes,* and *it always comes.* Sexual allusions galore" (18). *Koolaids*'s opening sentence is in fact a stealth repetition of Mohammad's sexually loaded incipit that conjoins death and sex (note that Mohammad provides a critical lens through which to read the novel). What comes after the first sentence in the first vignette, however, is a repetition of an absence, of a fictional work that could have been. Not only does this phantom repetition attempt to capture the possible and/or forgotten production of lives lost to civil war and AIDS; it also alludes to Alameddine's painting, *Hélas #251,* in which the looming eyes seem to document Alameddine in varying stages of erasure. I will return to this imaginative intervention—what I term a "poetics of documented erasure"—later in the chapter.

In addition to documenting erasure, the phantom repetition in the first vignette combines with a hallucination: an approach of the biblical four horsemen of the apocalypse. The first three riders—on the red, black, and pale horses, respectively—recommend in turn "this good and faithful servant" (1), who is the vignette's narrator, to the rider on the white horse. The rider on the red horse says that the narrator knows war; the rider on the black horse says that the narrator knows plague; and the rider on the pale horse says that the narrator knows death. In effect, the first vignette combines (the Lebanese Civil) war, (the AIDS) plague, and death (as a result of both) and begins the process of interweaving the three in the subsequent vignettes. The rider on the white horse (who likely represents Jesus)[4] responds angrily, however: "Fuck this good and faithful servant. He is a non-Christian homosexual, for God's sake. You brought me all the way out here for a fucking fag, a heathen" (1). The fourth horseman's diatribe serves as a reminder that while many dying patients find solace in Christianity, this consolation is denied to non-Christians and homosexuals alike. The fourth rider's shutting out of the gay narrator is matched by the f-sound alliteration in "for a fucking fag" (my emphasis), which makes him sound like a pressurized container about to explode. The mere presence of a non-Christian gay man seems to disrupt the entire Chris-

---

4. Apart from the fact that the three horsemen in the novel appeal on Mohammad's behalf to the rider of the white horse, establishing him as an authority figure, "scholars sometimes interpret [the horseman who rides a white horse] to symbolize Christ" ("Four Horsemen of the Apocalypse"). In the four horsemen vignettes' treatment of this rider, it becomes more or less clear that he represents a Jesus figure.

tian belief system regarding the afterlife, especially because the narrator, who we learn later is the character Mohammad, places his death and salvation within a Christian framework in his hallucinatory state. The triple offense of being non-Christian, gay, and a religious trespasser triggers the wrath of the fourth horseman. The Jesus figure punishes this perpetrator by denying him death, which would end his worldly suffering.

After the rider on the white horse leads the others away, the narrator discloses that the "hospital bed hurts my back" (1). This final sentence in the first vignette reveals that the narration is in fact a first-person account, after seven paragraphs of a seemingly third-person narration. The shift in point of view, taken with the revelation that Mohammad is in a hospital bed, suggests that he was experiencing a near-death hallucination or dream, in which Jesus denies him the peace of death. This denial is certainly not accidental. Apart from the allusion to Christian-Muslim tensions, the vignette invites questions about the wellbeing of gay men with Muslim backgrounds in the US. Mohammad experiences four more hallucinations of the four horsemen (vignettes 59, 105, 165, and 244) and a dream of Jesus opening the seventh seal (vignette 147) before he is able to die. Therí Pickens explains that we can interpret the AIDS-related complications in these related vignettes in two ways: "First, this could depict AIDS dementia where the intermingling of Mohammad's fantasy life and his bodily sensations indicate a gradual movement toward death. Second, this could be Mohammad's vacillation between dreams and reality—unrelated to AIDS dementia—wherein he tries to make sense of his own dying" (*New Body* 80). In combining Pickens's two interpretations, I proffer AIDS dementia as poetics that begins in the human body—related to the sensations of AIDS dementia—and that permeates the body of the novel as a lens through which Mohammad can make sense of his and his friends' dying in the civil war or from AIDS complications. What I would like to register (before I engage the next four related vignettes) is that the narrative point-of-view shift, Mohammad's AIDS-dementia hallucinations, the phantom repetition of the incipit of Mohammad's unwritten book, and the Muslim-Christian dynamics of power in the first vignette are imperative elements, which begin the process of undermining stable or fixed narratives dealing with Lebanese Americans, Muslim Americans, gay communities, the AIDS epidemic, and the Lebanese Civil War.

The first repetition (second iteration) of the four horsemen encounter takes place in vignette 59, which begins as a verbatim repetition of vignette 1 but varies in the Jesus figure's rejection of Mohammad. The new reason that the rider gives for his rejection is that "this good and faithful servant killed his best friend. Let him suffer" (53). The Jesus figure is referring to Scott, Mohammad's best friend and roommate. In vignette 219, Mohammad informs us that Scott "told me to kill him. He had said if it ever got rough, he didn't want to go on. If at any time, he couldn't think clearly, or read his books, I was to put an end to his life" (209). Mohammad obliges his friend, although he suffers pain and guilt before and after helping Scott die. It is interesting that Mohammad does for Scott what the Jesus figure refuses to do for Mohammad: end his suffering. Instead, the Jesus figure opts to extend Mohammad's suffering as punishment for assisting Scott's suicide, even though Mohammad's undertaking was an act of mercy. *Koolaids* provides us with examples of Christian-fundamentalist versions of mercy as a contrast to Mohammad's action of mercy. One important version takes place in vignette 74, whose narrator informs us that Tim's parents, who were "born-again Christians, refused to have the doctors pull the plug [on Tim]. The machines kept forcing themselves on him. It was rape. Five months later his lungs actually exploded" (67). Vignette 74 raises the question, Why is forcing life on the dying—allowing machines to rape a dying son for five months before causing his lungs to explode—in the name of Christian love and mercy not condemnable, while assisted suicide is denounced as an act of murder? The narrator's choice of "rape" to describe the machines' invasion is striking, as it relates to the issue of rape in the story of Sodom and Gomorrah, which I investigate later in the chapter.

Vignette 105, like vignette 59, begins as a verbatim repetition of the first horsemen vignette. Vignette 105 varies, however, when the first three horsemen begin chanting together. Surprisingly, they are chanting verses one through fourteen from Surat At-Takwir (The Darkening, or The Overthrowing) in A. J. Arberry's translation of the Qur'an (*Archive.org*). Surat At-Takwir, in keeping with the apocalyptic theme of the four horsemen vignettes, deals with the signs that precede the Day of Judgment. The chanting infuriates the Jesus figure:

> "What the hell is this?" the rider on the white horse asks. "Those are not my words. I never said that. You guys are reading from the wrong fucking book, you idiots. That's the Qur'an. You're not allowed to read from that when you're with me. The Bible is my book. What the fuck am I supposed to do with you guys? Pregnant camels? Pregnant camels? We're in America now. Who cares about stupid camels anyway?" (99)

The slippage from a biblical to a Qur'anic setting reveals the overlap between the two religions, in which one can substitute for the other in certain instances. Unless readers are conversant with the Bible, the verses from Surat At-Takwir might very well pass for biblical verses. It is the possibility of passing (religious, cultural, and racial) that enrages the Jesus figure, who sounds like a foreman yelling at his immigrant and migrant workers. In racialized terms, passing as Christian is passing as white; the Jesus figure reminds us that we are in America now and camels are not part of the equation. The Jesus figure would have us believe that Christianity originated in the US, not in the Middle East.

The Jesus figure makes a point of deriding the Qur'an, which he renders as an inferior version of the Bible. Such derision is commonplace in Islamophobic discourse; Moustafa Bayoumi asserts that in some narratives "it is as if 'Islam' must follow the same world historical script as Christianity. Under such a weight, Islam will always fail, for the simple fact that Islam is not Christianity" (*This Muslim* 113). The three horsemen's error, however, produces a slippage that allows Islam to queer Christianity (not merely to follow its world historical script), in order to create an-other for it, a doppelgänger of sorts. I do not use the term "queer" lightly here. The word *takwir* itself translates from the Arabic as "conglobation, conglomeration, agglomeration" (*Al-Mawrid* 362). That is, *takwir* means to form something into a globe, to group different things or parts into a whole with the parts retaining their distinctness, and/or to collect or form parts into a mass or group. The relationship of *takwir*'s meanings to the techniques of Alameddine's *Hélas #251* and *Hélas #185* to the cross-cultural interpretative possibilities in Mohammad's paintings, and to the vignette form and poetics of *Koolaids,* becomes clear here. The correlations and combinations of biblical and Qur'anic passages are important aesthetically and politically in the novel: They relate both to the homophobia of fundamentalist Christianity and Islam and to their explosive combination during the Lebanese Civil War. In terms of conglomeration, one can perceive a homophonic "queer" in the word *ta-kwir*: queer/kwir. The homophonic combination allows for polyphony to occur. With a rounding (conglobation) of the sound of *ta* to "to," the word *takwir* can become an-other for "to queer," to read—as Dervla Shannahan puts it—"along different lines; between the lines, under the lines and through the lines [. . .] in short, reading across queer lines" (131). The sound-rounding of *ta* and the homophone *queer/kwir* are not unlike the accent improvisations and combinations in the words *Fil'Imm, Hal-Awud,* and *Dar'Aktr* in Diana Abu-Jaber's *Crescent* that allow the words to resonate both in Arabic and in English and to harmonize as Arablish (see chapter 5 for more on Arablish). This "sound and fury" (38)—sound-rounding and the homophone—allows the Qur'anic surah to queer the lines of Christian passing, in which Mohammad is once again denied the mercy of death by the Jesus figure. The chanting of Surat At-Takwir seems to remind the Jesus figure of Mohammad's Muslim status, so he leads the horsemen away.

Before moving to the next four horsemen repetition, I would like to address the terms "Counterpoint" and "Polyphony" (*New Harvard Dictionary of Music* 205–8; 645–46). Many critics identify Mohammad's exilic consciousness and *Koolaids*'s vignette form as contrapuntal and/or polyphonic (Hout, *Post-War* 26, 33; Pickens, *New Body* 66; Rogers 156; and Salaita, *Arab American* 72). Both Hout and Pickens attribute the term "contrapuntal consciousness" to Edward Said's "Reflections on Exile," in which he contends that "most people are principally aware of one culture, one setting, one home; exiles are aware of at least two, and this plurality of vision gives rise to an awareness of simultaneous dimensions, an awareness that—to borrow a phrase from music—is *contrapuntal*" (186). The contrapuntal (thus polyphonic) relationship between biblical and Qur'anic passages in Mohammad's consciousness notwithstanding, the debt to music is worth considering in terms of *Koolaids*'s vignette form. Counterpoint "is a property of *polyphony, [although] its nature is indissolubly linked to the nature of melody [. . .] Melodies relate to each other in counterpoint, with the result that a perceptual balance is struck between the individualities of the lines and their combination" ("Counterpoint," *New Harvard Dictionary* 205). Like the melodies in counterpoint, the multigenre vignettes of *Koolaids* combine in ways that strike a balance between individuality and combination. In addition to the narrative and visual poetics of the vignette form, polyphonic possibilities also play a consequential role in the novel.

The repetitions in vignettes 1, 59, and 105 can be read contrapuntally as well. Such analysis is not arbitrary, as Mohammad often paints to the music of Bach—I explore this interart relationship later in the chapter. Up until vignette 165, the four horsemen hallucinations have a dual function of being at once similar and different. As repetitions with variations, they each contain unique aspects even as they overlap in multiple iterations ending in the near-death of Mohammad. Appearing in different registers throughout the novel, the five vignettes are indeed contrapuntal. The first three horsemen vignettes establish a pattern that is fugal and heterophonic, as one can combine these repetitions vertically, horizontally, or diagonally (vertically and horizontally together). These possibilities coincide with those of Alameddine's *Hélas #185*, the title-page painting, in which the nine-square close-ups of Alameddine's face can be examined against each other horizontally, vertically, and diagonally. As the only vignettes to narrate events that clearly occur in chronological order, repeating with variations in different registers, the four horsemen hallucinations enter a fugal relationship. A "Fugue" is the "most fully developed procedure of imitative counterpoint, in which the theme is stated successively in all voices of the polyphonic texture, tonally established, continuously expanded, opposed, and reestablished" (*New Harvard Dictionary* 327). As will become fully evident, the four horsemen vignettes are chronologically established, expanded, opposed, and reestablished fugally.

If polyphony "represents one, if not *the* constant in western music since the [3rd century]" (Mahnkopf 38), heterophony is more readily aligned with non-Western cultures. As a vertical manifestation, "Heterophony" is the "simultaneous statement [. . .] of two or more different versions of what is essentially the same melody [. . .] The technique is widely found in musics outside the tradition of Western art music, especially in [among others . . .] the Near and Middle East" (*New Harvard Dictionary* 377). As a poetics, disorientation of time and place—a symptom of AIDS dementia—allows us to disrupt and combine iterations temporally and spatially. Taken together heterophonically/vertically, the first three horsemen vignettes are different versions of essentially the same hallucination. This is similar to the oral storytelling tradition in the Middle East in which the same story repeats across time and space with variations: Essentially, the slippages in the storytellers' variations render the story oblique. The four horsemen vignettes, then, operate both polyphonically (contrapuntally and fugally) in the Western tradition, and heterophonically in the Middle Eastern tradition, allowing for cross-cultural interpretations similar to those of Mohammad's paintings and experiences. Describing Claude Debussy's *La Mer* under the definition of "Counterpoint," the *New Harvard Dictionary of Music* reveals that "his orchestral works sometimes demonstrate a *heterophony in which myriad figurational and instrumental details are synthesized into a complex overall texture, a kind of 'counterpoint of colors' (*La mer*), which can be compared with the brush techniques of the impressionist painters" (208). If we think of heterophony as texture, as a "counterpoint of colors," two combinational possibilities emerge. First, this texture reveals an overlap between heterophony and counterpoint (which is a property of polyphony). Second, it combines the techniques of music and painting, which brings us to the next horsemen hallucination: vignette 165.

In vignette 165, the repetitive element is curtailed. After the four horsemen approach, the rider on the pale horse speaks instead of the rider on the red horse. In the three prior episodes, which establish the order of speakers, the rider on the red horse speaks first, followed by the rider on the black horse, and then the rider on the pale horse. All repeat in order the sentence, "This good and faithful servant is ready." In this iteration, however, the rider on the pale horse asks, "Hey, Diego, do you think this one is worthy?" (166). The rider on the black horse turns out to be Diego Velázquez, the seventeenth-century Spanish painter, one of the most important painters of the Spanish Golden Age. Velázquez answers, "This good and faithful servant deserted his country" (166). This is a pronounced departure from the previous three vignettes, in which the three horsemen appeal in turn to the Jesus figure to grant Mohammad eternal rest. Vignette 165 functions fugally as a countersubject, which opposes the fugue's theme prior to its being reestablished. In a nationalistic twist, Velázquez cites Mohammad's so-called desertion of his country as proof of his unworthiness. The problem with Velázquez's condemnation is that the Lebanese themselves cannot agree on a definition, or a common history, of Lebanon. The narrator of vignette 66 (most probably Mohammad) notes that "rewriting history is a passion for most Lebanese. Lebanon is a mixture of races from all over Europe and the Middle East, yet everyone tries to lay claim to being the true descendants of the Phoenicians" (59). If Mohammad does indeed desert Lebanon, one would be hard-pressed to identify which Lebanon constitutes the site of desertion. Is it Muslim/Arab Lebanon, Christian/Phoenician Lebanon, pan-Arab Lebanon, secular Lebanon, heteronormative Lebanon, postcolonial Lebanon, war-torn Lebanon, and/or geographic Lebanon? Salah Hassan reminds us that "the governing bodies of Lebanon are void of the essential content of sovereignty, which is constitutive of a state, and its citizenry is fractured along sectarian lines. The Lebanese state can neither defend its territory nor govern its citizens. It has been unstated" (1622). The state of Lebanon as nonstate, as noncountry, makes Velázquez's claim largely untenable. Furthermore, civilians who flee war zones are refugees, not deserters.

Mohammad reacts to the rider on the pale horse and Velázquez's departure from their expected lines:

"Whoa," I interrupt heatedly. "You guys are diverging from the script."
  Mondrian, on the red horse, says, "No. You diverged from the script. You used green in your paintings." (166)

When Mohammad confronts the horsemen, Mondrian (who turns out to be the painter Piet Mondrian, a founder of the Dutch modern movement De Stijl) counters that Mohammad has diverged from the script by painting with the color green. But why is green a divergence from the script? In his later paintings, Mondrian avoided using green. His artistic choice becomes religious doctrine here, one to which Mohammad must adhere if he is to attain salvation. If we think of the colors of the horses—pale, black, red, and white—in relation to the biblical four horsemen of the apocalypse, green qualifies as a divergence, a countersubject. Green, moreover, holds relevance in Islam. First, the Qur'an in several surahs associates green with the Muslim version of paradise, mentioning lush green gardens, green cushions on which to recline, and rich green garments.⁵ Furthermore, al-Khidr, whose name translates from the Arabic as "The Green One," is an important figure in Islam. Al-Khidr "is widely known as the spiritual guide of Moses and Alexander the Great, a *wali* (saint), a prophet, and one of four immortals along with Enoch (Idris), Jesus, and Elijah" ("Al-Khidr, The Green Man"). As such, Mondrian's objection to the color green relates to its connection with Islam, which makes it an unacceptable counterpoint to the biblical context. Once again, the Jesus figure leads the horsemen away without granting Mohammad death.

The final iteration of the four horsemen hallucinations is also the last vignette in *Koolaids*: vignette 244. This vignette resolves the momentary departure in vignette 165 from the heterophonic and fugal aspects (in which the three horsemen make their plea to the Jesus figure, and he offers varying justifications for denying Mohammad death). Fugally, this vignette reestablishes the fugue's theme or subject. Vignette 244 offers an unexpected modulation, however. Instead of rejecting the horsemen's pleas, the Jesus figure accepts Mohammad in this final vignette, bringing his life and the book to a close:

The rider on the white horse says, "I love you, Mohammad."
The propitious rider on the white horse leads us away.
I die. (245)

Ironically, the last variation manifests in the Jesus figure's conformation to the script of love and mercy that we normally associate with him. In this sense, the Jesus figure's discordances in the earlier related vignettes become a series of dissonant suspensions that resolve harmonically in the final vignette. The script of love and mercy, however, overlaps with Scott's dying words to Mohammad in vignette 12: "His last words before he took his last breath were 'I love you, Mohammad.' An impeccable pronunciation" (13). This instance demonstrates Scott's love for Mohammad and the effort that he puts into impeccably pronouncing Mohammad's name. In vignette 12, Mohammad reminds readers that Americans often mispronounce Arabic names, although they face no repercussions for doing so, in contrast to Arabs who mispronounce European names.

---

5. In the Yusuf Ali translation of verses 62 and 64 of Surah 55: Most Gracious (Al-Rahmaan) in the Qur'an, the verses reveal "And besides these two, there are two other Gardens,—[. . .] Dark-green in colour (from plentiful watering)" (*QuranBrowser.org*). Verse 76 of the same surah relates that the believers would find companions in paradise "reclining on green Cushions and rich Carpets of beauty." In the Yusuf Ali translation of verse 21 of Surah 76: The Human (Al-Insaan), the Qur'an mentions "green Garments of fine silk and heavy brocade" (*QuranBrowser.org*).

Vignette 119, which one of the characters dubs "The Waltons Do AIDS" (114), takes up this issue humorously. Here, Mohammad and his HIV-positive friends take turns repeating the phrase "I love you" to each other in a manner that mimics the Walton family's goodnight ritual. The first iteration is "I love you, Mohammad" (113), which coincides with the Jesus figure and Scott's dying declaration of love for Mohammad. As the other friends relay their love to Mohammad, his name undergoes variations based on common mispronunciations of his name: "I love you, Mo [. . .] I love you, Mr. Momad [. . . and] I love you, Mahomet" (113). These mispronunciations reflect not merely the American characters' difficulty with Mohammad's name but also their ambivalence about Mohammad's presence in the US. These repetitions with variations of Mohammad's name place him in a heterophonic and fugal relationship with himself, as he is made to renegotiate his identity with every new iteration of his name. Furthermore, nicknames save his friends the trouble of learning to pronounce Arabic names correctly. In vignette 45, Mohammad states, "Of all the nicknames I have been called, Mo is the one name I completely abhorred" (41). The multiple, curtailed variations of Mohammad's name, which diminish it religiously and culturally, resolve in the final vignette in which the Jesus figure repeats Scott's declaration of love for Mohammad with an impeccable pronunciation of his name.[6]

If vignette 105 queers the biblical version of the apocalypse by having the horsemen chant verses from Surat At-Takwir, vignette 244 queers the figure of Jesus by imbricating him with Scott. Here, Christian notions of love and mercy extend to include assisted suicide. Scott's final words convey not just love but also gratitude to Mohammad for ending his life. In accepting this act of mercy by repeating Scott's words, the Jesus figure grants Mohammad the mercy of death. In the four earlier horsemen vignettes, Mohammad describes the Jesus figure as "irascible" (1), "testy" (53), "cantankerous" (99), and "crotchety" (166). In vignette 244, however, the Jesus figure is "propitious" (245). Instead of leading the three horsemen away from Mohammad, the favorably inclined Jesus figure leads Mohammad, and all that he represents, away with the other horsemen. Mohammad declares, "I die" (245).

It is worth asking here why Alameddine chooses five iterations of the four horsemen hallucinations instead of, say, three manifestations, which would be more commensurate with the biblical context. One plausible answer is that the five repetitions are a nod toward the five pillars of Islam, which constitute the framework for Muslim life and are important bases for attaining

---

6. Chapter 2 offers a close analysis of the Arabic names (as blue notes) and accentual rhythms in Diana Abu-Jaber's *Arabian Jazz* as they travel across cultures and improvise on American English and cultural formations.

heaven. While Mohammad's trials in the five four-horsemen vignettes do not readily conform to the five pillars (declarations of faith, daily prayers, charity, fasting during Ramadan, and pilgrimage to Mecca), they both counterpoint and queer the notion of earthly trials or duties as the conditions for attaining heaven (or the peace of death) in Islam and Christianity. That is, the five fugal/heterophonic iterations of the four horsemen vignettes across time and space allow Mohammad to cross the religious borders of Christianity and Islam, correlating and queering them in the process. Furthermore, the AIDS dementia-induced hallucinations of the horsemen allow the five strategically placed vignettes to permeate the body of *Koolaids* and to address—in the combinations of the poetics of narrative, music, and painting—Christian/Muslim religio-cultural issues related to the US AIDS epidemic and the Lebanese Civil War alike. Repetition with variation, the heterophonic/polyphonic interplay between familiarity and strangeness, is a critical aesthetic in *Koolaids*. Familiar-strange recapitulations transfigure the unthinking repetitions of traditional cultural prescriptions, rendering them precarious. This modulation takes place in the reiterations of the four horsemen vignettes as well as in phrases and words within and across vignettes.

STRAIGHTNESS LEITMOTIFS: AESTHETICS OF UNCERTAINTY AND OF DOCUMENTED ERASURE

In the second vignette of *Koolaids,* a first-person narrator (who we learn later is Mohammad) states,

> I can't think straight anymore. I should not have said that. I try never saying the word *straight.* Let's say I can't concentrate [. . .]. I can't speak English anymore either. Really. I can't think in English. It's back to my roots. I now think and dream only in Arabic. I haven't done that for the longest time. (1)

Mohammad corrects himself for using the word "straight," thereby drawing attention to its heteronormative imperative. Thinking straight means not deviating from conventional notions of morality. The dominant religio-cultural connotation of straightness preempts and vilifies any complications or counterrepresentations of this construct. In this formulation of straight thinking, AIDS becomes a consequence of homosexuality, a punishment for immoral and unlawful—nonstraight—behavior. Vignette 28's narrator reminds us that, after all, the "acronym [for AIDS] at the time was GRID, Gay Related Immune

Deficiency" (27). In addition to the biblical and moral underpinnings of constructions of straightness, the word "straight" gestures to Qur'anic foundations as well. Verse 6 of Surat Al-Fatiha (The Opening) in the Abdullah Yusuf Ali translation asks God to "show us the straight way" (*QuranBrowser.org*), "straight" being the operative word. On issues of gender and homosexuality, fundamentalist and literalist interpretations of the Bible and the Qur'an have much in common. And the intervention of not thinking straight, ironically, facilitates a cross-religious reading of the many overlaps between two seemingly dissimilar or conflicting religions and their political and material maintenance of doctrine. This intervention also applies to the Lebanese Civil War, which played out on one perilous level as a Christian-Muslim conflict and contributed to the promotion of homophobia by many practitioners of both religions in Lebanon and the US. I will address this overlap in relation to the cross-religious poetics of Mohammad's retelling of the Sodom and Gomorrah story later in the chapter.

The narrator's difficulty in concentrating prevents him from thinking and speaking in English, or so he tells us—in English. His English, however, manifests in short staccato sentences. While the sentences' fragmentary nature points to the narrator's struggle to make himself understood, it also gestures to the overall pastiche structure of *Koolaids*. Readers are confronted with an aesthetics of uncertainty on the novel's first page (Mohammad's hallucination of the four horsemen of the apocalypse and the narrator's inability to think straight), an uncertainty that they must negotiate for themselves as they traverse the work's multigenre vignettes. To aestheticize uncertainty, however, is to activate a lifeline poetics with which to survive uncertainty. In *Koolaids,* the phrase "I can't think straight anymore" and the word "straight" become alternating leitmotifs that repeat explicitly in at least four seminal vignettes: 2, 52, 70, and 118. These leitmotifs work to articulate these vignettes under the auspices of the poetics of AIDS dementia with its attendant aesthetics. If late-stage AIDS prevents the narrator of vignette 2 from accessing any language except the Arabic of his childhood, then it is surprising that he narrates this fact in English and speaks English when his friend James comes to visit him. Furthermore, when James looks confused by something Mohammad says, Mohammad states,

> I must have said it in French and he doesn't speak French. Most Americans speak nothing other than English. Hold on a second. I am an American and I speak French, so that statement does not describe my predicament accurately. Actually, French has been completely forgotten and that describes my predicament more accurately. (2)

In two separate cases, the narrator speaks languages—English and French—that he claims he can no longer speak. This paradox would be troublesome unless we perceive the aesthetics at work and their political ends.

I call this an aesthetics of documented erasure; it echoes *Hélas #251*'s technique, in which Alameddine's looming eyes seem to witness the erasure of past selves and *Koolaids*'s phantom repetition of what Mohammad could have written. The aesthetics of documented erasure points to the fact that while most Lebanese and Lebanese Americans are trilingual, they nonetheless must conform to the dominant singularity of English in the US at the expense of disremembering their other tongues and the cultures attached to them. It at once theorizes this condition of dominant monolingualism and documents the seemingly involuntary, AIDS-dementia-related reversion to (disavowed) trilingualism. In effect, Mohammad performs a trilingual cultural translation—its own trinity resisting lingual and cultural oneness—and balks at speaking English. Furthermore, Mohammad has to correct himself after framing this predicament in terms of racialized citizenship, in which "Americans"—meaning white Americans—are the only authentic citizens and nonwhite citizens are second-class or would-be Americans. Countering this internalized formulation by asserting "I am an American," Mohammad reminds himself that he, a dark-skinned gay Lebanese American painter suffering from AIDS, has as much a claim to Americanness as any member of the dominant culture. The narrator's commingling of nationalistic monolingualism with his AIDS-induced illness suggests that both are in need of a radical cure.

The narrator's inability to concentrate is symptomatic of AIDS dementia complex, which causes cognitive issues, including losing track of actions, "a frank disorientation to time and place," slower speaking and thinking, and a "background of confusion" ("AIDS Dementia Complex"). These clearly manifest in the narrator's style, which activates aesthetics of uncertainty, disorientation, and documented erasure. *Koolaids* refers explicitly to AIDS dementia in at least two vignettes: 29 and 87. In vignette 29, Scott—Mohammad's roommate and closest friend—tells his doctor that he is getting better. The doctor responds that Scott "probably had AIDS dementia, which is why he imagined he was getting better" (28). This response enrages Mohammad, who then "storm[s] into the congenital idiot's office looking for trouble" (28). In vignette 87, which hybridizes biblical and Qur'anic passages on the figure of Jesus, the first-person narrator (most probably Mohammad) exclaims to the sons of Pandu in the Mahabharata that he is "not the Christ but [he is] sent ahead of him" (77). To this the sons of Pandu reply, "We do not believe you. You have AIDS dementia" (77).

In vignette 29, the imaginative aspect of AIDS dementia helps Scott to feel better, until his doctor's clinical detachment and dismissal invalidate his experience. In vignette 87, AIDS dementia allows the narrator to understand himself as a seer or a prophet, answering a question put to Sanjaya in the words of John the Baptist. Notwithstanding the ambiguity of the narrator's identity in this vignette (and in many of the vignettes), one cannot help noticing the punning on Mohammad as a character and as a (would-be) prophet. While AIDS dementia is perilous psychologically and physiologically, it stealthily becomes a metaphoric antidote to thinking straight. It is imaginative—thus departing from the straight and narrow path—and prophetic in its reordering of normative reality. The cure, as Pickens observes, "must come in the form of delusion, discomfort, dystopia, or death" ("Feeling Embodied" 68). *Koolaids*'s poetics and form dispossess readers of absolute representations and prescriptions—be they political, religious, and/or medical—by exposing their contradictions and hypocrisy and by offering counterrepresentations. These poetics refuse, however, to prescribe fixed or stable interpretations, only experiential and creative possibilities.

In *Koolaids*, the conventional, coercive discourses of the Lebanese Civil War and the AIDS epidemic, with their attendant religious, homophobic, and Arabophobic/Islamophobic representations, are fragmented into vignettes capable of multifarious recombinations. Andreas Pflitsch posits, "Only the attempt to reverse the perspective and grasp the normal and normalized as the exception, and conversely deal with deviation as the rule, can enable us to take cultural hybridity and syncretic creativity seriously, understanding them in terms of their own premises" (328). Readers are tasked primarily with synthesizing the 244 vignettes in accordance with their variegated subject positions, yet the possibility of endless combinations forestalls any stable or normalizing teleology. As such, readers confront to some degree the chaos of war and epidemic and strive with the characters to find some semblance of order in a collapsing and uncertain world.

Koolaids's epigraph, which repeats in vignette 189, acts as a threshold and, later, as a reminder of the novel's poetics. In a three-line poem, the speaker ruminates:

I wonder if being sane means
disregarding the chaos that is life,
pretending only an infinitesimal segment of it is reality.

The end-stopped lines highlight the words "means," "life," and "reality," which constitute much of the characters' existential negotiations. The end-words of each line invite us to ponder their import. What does sanity mean? Is sanity a means? If so, to what end? What is life? What is reality? Of course, the contexts for these concepts encompass civil war and AIDS, and the epigraph's question concerning meaning, life, and reality is therefore not solely philosophical. As the speaker asks his question, the lines themselves grow from eight to ten to twenty-one syllables, the third line having more syllables than the previous two combined. It is as if the expanding lines are more than the sum of their parts, outstripping any effort to well-temper their thematic elements. If being sane means normalizing the chaos that is life, so that life is necessarily reduced to a fragment of reality, then what might insanity's kaleidoscopic fragmentations (in the form of AIDS dementia) offer us? Significantly, the repetition of the epigraph in vignette 189 manifests in prose form as one continuous sentence: "I wonder if being sane means disregarding the chaos that is life, pretending only an infinitesimal segment of it is reality" (184). Here, the words previously emphasized by the end-stopped lines of poetry are repositioned in the contiguous form of prose. Previously individuated by poetic form, these words now combine in prose; the genre shift allows for a shift of perspective, a trans-formation. The epigraph and its repetition serve as an interpretative key for *Koolaids*. As in the four horsemen vignettes, repetition is rarely sameness, and difference is sometimes a manifestation of similarity. That is, "the reference of a repetition is a dynamic play between two poles, difference and sameness" (Duda 31). Different perspectives and forms—in combination—encourage polyphonic (horizontal, vertical, and diagonal) interpretations, and they take fundamentalist, literalist, and homophobic interpretations of Christianity and Islam to task.

QUEERING SODOM AND GOMORRAH: POETICS, CROSS-RELIGIOUS OVERLAP, AND TRANSLATION

Koolaids draws attention to the overlap of homophobia in uncritical interpretations of Christianity and Islam and the issue of religio-cultural translation by highlighting the story of Sodom and Gomorrah first in the Bible and later in the Qur'an. The narrator of vignette 70 offers us a quote from the story of Sodom and Gomorrah in which Lot says, "Behold, I have two daughters who have not known man" (63). The line comes from Genesis 19:8 in the Revised Standard Version Catholic Edition (RSVCE) of the Bible (*BibleGateway.com*). The narrator is fascinated with the RSVCE not simply because it shows a father "pimping his two virgin daughters," which it shares with other translations, but because there "is something poetic about it [. . .] It has a ring to it"

(63). The line's poetics impresses the narrator so much so that he repeats it two more times in vignette 70 by interweaving it with his interventions on poetics and biblical translations. The repetition of the line creates another trinity (echoing Mohammad's earlier trilingual cultural translation) with which to resist a monotonic interpretation of the Bible. The narrator is decidedly invested in how the line's poetics mediates its content. Apart from the two disyllabic words "Behold" and "daughters," which underscore the presence of the virgin daughters, the rest of the line consists of monosyllabic words. Furthermore, the h-alliteration and o-assonance in the line, "Be_h_old, I _h_ave two daughters w_h_o _h_ave n_o_t kn_o_wn man" (my emphasis), produce a panting h-sound and a moaning o-sound that accompany the sexually charged line. In addition, the rhyming "two" and "who" flanking the word "daughters," and the repetition of the verb "have" serve to highlight the availability of the daughters to the mob of men. The poetics fall on the mob's deaf ears, unfortunately, but the line's poetics—its "ring"—captures the narrator of vignette 70. The repetition of Lot's line allows us to appreciate its poetics and to think more carefully about the seductions of poetic language.

In addition to the repetition of the RSVCE translation of the line, the narrator counterpoints Lot's words with two different translations of the same line, creating yet another trinity. Shannahan contends that in Alameddine's "very attention to the nuances of translation, the possibility of belief is flirted with, and the way that Scripture is rendered meaningful through the act of translation, the way that it is grafted into something not only meaningful but believable, is hinted at" (135). Taken together, the copious translations of the Bible, in their interpretive nuances across time and space, have added to and reinforced meaning and believability in the ancient text, allowing it an enduring afterlife. Yet this translational project, which repeats and retransplants the Bible with every new translation, also exposes the dynamics of the process at work. Attention to translational nuance is what allows the narrator of vignette 70 to challenge the compounded meaning and the enterprise of believability. He states, "I like this [RSVCE] translation better than 'Look, I have two daughters who have never slept with a man,' or 'Lo, I pray you, I have two daughters, who have not known anyone.' Translation is so important" (63). The first translation of Lot's words comes from the New International Version (NIV), and the second from Young's Literal Translation (YLT) (*BibleGateway. com*). If the repetition of the same line from the RSVCE allows us to better appreciate the line's poetics as it sensually enhances content, then the counterpointing of different translations of Lot's words reveals the mutability of the Bible as it travels across time and space from one translation to the next. Both translational repetitions highlight that repetition does not produce sameness and that interpretation and translation-as-interpretation create heterophonies and polyphonies of meanings that cannot be reduced to a singular or literal interpretation of scripture. In this case, "have not known man," "have never slept with a man," and "have not known anyone" all carry divergent meanings. The RSVCE offers more nuance, as "have not known man," biblical context notwithstanding, is suggestive yet inconclusive. The NIV is blunter in "never slept with a man," and YLT is ambiguous for all its literality, as "have not known anyone" is open to multiple interpretations.

The narrator then provides a more pointed critique: "The new American translations of the Bible sound like a Judith Krantz novel [. . .] The Bible readers today prefer simple fare" (63). Returning to the US context, the narrator criticizes the literal and sensational aspects of the new American translations that pander to a readership that "prefer[s] simple fare." His simile brings American translations of the Bible in line with the writing of Judith Krantz, a "Jackie Collins-style [. . .] author of racey [sic] fictions" (Smith). These simplistic and sensational versions leave little to the imagination (sexual or interpretative). The narrator observes, "I would never believe the men of Sodom called to Lot, 'Where are the men who came to you tonight? Bring them out to us so that we can have sex with them'" (63). In the NIV translation of Genesis 19:5, the men of Sodom are quite forward, and such a crass demand for sex is unlikely to bring to fruition the outcome they desire. Apart from rendering the men of Sodom as flat, stereotypical characters, the NIV leaves no room for alternative interpretations of the men's motivations.

Having revealed the influence of poetics on content, the mutability of the Bible across translations, and the poverty of simplistic translations, the narrator proceeds to (re)tell the story of Sodom and Gomorrah on his own terms, garnishing his version with quotations of pertinent biblical passages. He begins by stating that the "story of Sodom and Gomorrah is a simple story" (63). Perhaps it is, but the narrator's mode of storytelling is not simple; rather, it participates in "the Arab oral tradition of retelling the same story from another point of view [. . . Such] rewriting forces the reader to re-evaluate preconceptions of difference" (Rogers 158). By assuming the didactic role of the storyteller, the narrator-as-storyteller is able to intervene both to entertain and to guide the reader-as-listener.[7] Both Diana Abu-Jaber and Laila Halaby include a storyteller in their novels *Crescent* and *Once in a Promised Land*,

---

7. In Alameddine's 2008 novel, *The Hakawati*, which literally translates as "The Storyteller," the narrator forcefully assumes the position of storyteller: "Listen. Allow me to be your god. Let me take you on a journey beyond imagining. Let me tell you a story" (5).

respectively, to a similar effect.[8] By moving (repeating) himself and the readers into the conjoined yet distinct positions of storyteller and listeners, the narrator of vignette 70 seeks to transpose readers' preconceptions of sexual difference. The narrator-as-storyteller jumps in at strategic moments—timing is everything—to offer his commentary on the very story that he is telling. At the point when the men appear at Lot's door asking to get better acquainted with the angels, the narrator-as-storyteller chimes in with "Those were the days, huh?" (63). Here as elsewhere, the storyteller/narrator's humor and irreverence play an important role in destabilizing gendered and heteronormative prescriptions in, and readings of, the story of Sodom and Gomorrah.

From humor, our storyteller moves into a satirical position:

> So Lot, chivalrous host that he is, says, "I beg you, my brothers, do not act so wickedly. Behold, I have two daughters who have not known man; let me bring them out to you, and do to them as you please; only do nothing to these men, for they have come under the shelter of my roof." Isn't that precious? (63–64)

By using the adjective "chivalrous" ironically, the narrator exposes Lot's gendered double standard. In order to protect his angel guests, who come in the form of men, Lot offers his two daughters to the mob. The lesson here is that girls, even daughters, are disposable if honor between men is at stake. Male chivalry dictates the protection of male guests no matter the cost to the female members of the household. Lot's treatment of his daughters impels the narrator-as-storyteller to interject, "Isn't this precious?" The ironic question flanks the RSVCE passage, which in turn allows for a reframing of the content along queer lines. This practice of "queering religious texts [. . .] has a de-stabilizing effect, through the transgression and de-construction of naturalized and normalized hermeneutics, which reinforces heteronormativity" (Yip 51). In queering the story of Sodom and Gomorrah, the narrator utilizes the storyteller's agency to instruct, but in a particular mode: as a queer theologian.

The queer theologian/storyteller/narrator's "queer commentary exposes the (il)logic of heterosexualism that the narrative is so often assumed to support, and underlines the scriptural allegiance of the Divine with compulsory heterosexuality and gender inequality" (Shannahan 136). By exposing the sexism and heteronormativity in the passage in which Lot offers up his daugh-

---

8. See chapters 4 and 5 for more on the transformative and rehabilitative role of storytelling in the Arab oral tradition.

ters, the narrator's satirical interventions not only queer its "(il)logic"; they also queer the potentially hostile readers' heterosexist and male-supremacist assumptions. Migrating the audiences back and forth between readers and listeners, shaking the very ground beneath their feet, the narrator manages both to decenter potentially hegemonic beliefs and to promote a queer reevaluation of them.

To that end, the narrator continues:

> Let's get this straight, and I do mean straight. God tells us men fucking men is a terrible thing, but a father offering his two daughters, vestal virgins no less, to a horde of horny buggers is heroic. Now that's straight. (64)

The leitmotif of "straight" returns in this passage and appears three times. The "straight" trinity ironizes the word and exposes its underbelly of ethically compromised curvatures. Not thinking straight, under the auspices of the poetics of AIDS dementia, exposes the "(il)logical" process by which religiocultural straightness is constructed. Why is it that homosexuality is a terrible thing, while Lot's offering of his two daughters is an act of heroism? The narrator makes his intervention poetically by repeating the word "straight" and by countering the biblical poetics with his own alliteration and assonance: "Vestal virgins no less, to a horde of horny buggers is heroic" (my emphasis). The h-alliteration and the o-assonance mimic the panting and moaning sounds in the biblical line: "Behold, I have two daughters who have not known man" (my emphasis). In addition, the narrator throws in a v-alliteration in "vestal virgins." The v-alliteration, its sound voluptuous and alluring, pushes against the meaning of "vestal virgins," which positions the two daughters as chaste and devout. Furthermore, this interpretation is itself unstable, as the invocation of Vesta, the ancient Roman goddess of the hearth and household, conjoins pagan and biblical notions of chastity.

"It gets better" (64), the narrator-as-storyteller informs us. God turns Lot's wife into a pillar of salt for disobeying His orders and looking back to witness His wrath. And the vestal virgins contrive to get their father drunk so that they can have sex with him in order to preserve their family line:

> So the pimp gets drunk, his daughter fucks him, and he doesn't remember anything the next day. This is a common pattern among straight men. They always forget what happened the night before while they were drunk. The next night, the pimp gets drunk again and his younger daughter fucks him. All in the family and so on. Vice is nice, but incest is best. (64)

The narrator-as-storyteller continues his retelling sardonically, and intervenes to alert us to a common pattern among straight men: "They always forget what happened the night before while they were drunk." On one level, this statement relates to the fact that Lot's lack of memory coupled with his daughters' ploy serves to absolve Lot from his share of responsibility for the incestuous encounter. The NIV, which the narrator uses for this segment of his retelling, states that with each daughter, "[Lot] was not aware of it when she lay down or when she got up" (Genesis 19:33, 19:35). The biblical formulation, then, suggests that the two daughters are the sexual predators, and Lot is their victim. Yet, unlike their mother, they do not receive a punishment from God. After all, they each produce a son (not a daughter) for their father. On a less obvious level, the narrator's tongue-in-cheek remark on drunk straight men suggests that some straight men feign forgetfulness about having had sex with men while drunk. This intervention leaves us wondering whether Lot was merely serving wine to his angel guests when he was interrupted by the mob of horny men.

The narrator-as-storyteller concludes vignette 70 with:

> So here we have the story of Sodom and Gomorrah. God destroys the faggots with fire and brimstone. He turns a disobedient wife into salt. But he asks us to idolize drunks who sleep with their daughters or offer them to a horny, unruly mob. This is the lesson of Sodom and Gomorrah: Homosexuals are bad. (64)

In the fashion of a *hakawati* (storyteller), the narrator reminds readers of the story he has just finished telling and the lessons found therein. The first lesson: "God destroys the faggots with fire and brimstone." The choice of "faggots" rather than "homosexuals" signals the narrator's bitterly ironic tone in relating this lesson and serves to dissociate faggots from homosexuals. Faggots are what traditional, heteronormative practitioners of Christianity see in homosexuality, and the word reduces complex human beings to mere objects of punishment. The irony of the first lesson also extends to the second lesson: "He turns a disobedient wife into salt." The conjoining of "disobedient" and "wife" highlights, ironically, that, by definition, a wife is obedient (to God and her husband). Disobedience is a mark of un-wifeliness, and disobedient wives deserve to die. The narrator then points out the ugly nature of these lessons: "But he asks us to idolize drunks who sleep with their daughters or offer them to a horny, unruly mob." Lot's serious transgressions—it is hardly a stretch to call incest and the pimping of one's daughters serious offenses—are simply cast aside. Lot's gender and sexual orientation are enough to place him beyond blame; he is not a part of the moral equation.

By intervening in the story of Sodom and Gomorrah, the narrator of vignette 70 participates to some extent in what Andrew K. T. Yip identifies as three strategies for queering religious texts:

1. critique of traditional interpretation of specific passages in the texts;
2. critique of interpretative authority of religious authority structures and figures; and
3. re-casting religious texts. (51)

The narrator, as queer theologian, offers a biting critique of the traditional interpretation of Sodom and Gomorrah. In so doing, he implicitly challenges the often singular and reductive "interpretative authority of religious authority structures." While the narrator-as-storyteller both queers and que(e)ries his tale, he does not offer an alternative story; nor does he recast the lesson of Sodom and Gomorrah so as to ameliorate its homophobic implications. Furthermore, neither his commentary on the original nor his sardonic retelling does away with the biblical story outright. In resisting any stabilizing resolutions to his critique, the narrator leaves behind questions rather than answers. If AIDS dementia dislodges straight and Christian-based representations of reality, it refrains from reconstituting reality as demented, which would recast demented reality as a prescriptive and hegemonic cure. The processes of dementia poetics lead to nonresolutions; they remove us from certainty and render us perpetually curious.

If the narrator of vignette 70 bequeaths questions to readers in the biblical story of Sodom and Gomorrah, nothing is offered on the Qur'anic verses of the same. Vignette 180 combines pertinent verses from Surah 27: Al-Naml (The Ants) and Surah 26: Al-Shu'ara' (The Poets) without any commentary. Readers of *Koolaids* are left to decide for themselves how to transfer the narrator's storytelling, translation, and queer interventions from vignette 70 to vignette 180 from a Christian context to a Muslim one. That is, vignette 180 implicates readers in the process of ironizing, inverting, and subverting religious texts. The narrator's intervention in the story of Sodom and Gomorrah thus serves as a methodology through which readers can engage the Qur'anic version of the story. As "activist art" (Pickens, *New Body* 82), *Koolaids* not only theorizes its own mode of art-political intervention, but it also provides readers with art-critical tools with which to make their own interventions. To participate in this process is to willingly displace and discomfit one's self (as does the narrator of vignette 70), to render one's self a queer theologian who inhabits liminal and marginal spaces, "caught *between* belief and unbelief" (Taylor 519). The process forestalls the production of stable answers and instead encourages readers to traverse "an unstable border along which marginal thinkers wander" (519). Taking this path allows readers to combine likely and unlikely vignettes and to connect the book's manifold repetitions without constructing a stable edifice.

The structural overlap between the stories of Sodom and Gomorrah in the Bible and the Qur'an brings us to the relationship between God and Allah. I use "Allah" and "God" interchangeably in this book because, like Alameddine, I believe that they denote the same referent. Alameddine contends:

Allah means God.
    In Arabic, Muslims, Jews, Christians, and Zoroastrians all pray to Allah. In English, however, Christians and Jews pray to God, and Allah is the Muslim deity. No one would think of using the word "Allah" to talk about any other religion. The two words, "God" and "Allah," do not mean the same thing in English. They should. ("Sacred Semantics")

The parlance of Islamophobia in the US decontextualizes and marginalizes the word "Allah," confining it to Islam. It is worth mentioning here that Islamophobia has existed in the US for a long time; it is not the result of 9/11 or of the Islamic State's acts of terrorism, although these have certainly made matters worse. In fact, "from 1790 until 1952 whiteness was a legal prerequisite for naturalised American citizenship. And Islam was viewed as irreconcilable with whiteness" (Beydoun, "Viewpoint"). In *The Girl in the Tangerine Scarf,* Mohja Kahf takes up the issue of pre-9/11 Islamophobia by telling the story of Khadra Shamy[9] (a Syrian immigrant to the US), who grows up in a tight-knit Muslim community in Indiana during the 1970s. Chapter 3 in *Poetics of Visibility* engages the reductive and overdetermined Islamophobic discourse of the veil and what it means to grow up Muslim in the US. In Islamophobic formulations, which racialize Islam and Muslims, Islam becomes a pariah religion that is denied access to the Judeo-Christian tradition, even when so much of that tradition finds its way into the Qur'an. The repetition (with variation) of the story of Sodom and Gomorrah in the Qur'an is a prime example of this dialogism, and so is the traditional interpretation of Sodom and Gomorrah in Christianity and Islam.

---

    9. Khadra's name, which is the Syrian vernacular for Khadra', means, literally, "green, verdant" (*Al-Mawrid* 513). As in Mohammad's use of the color green in vignette 165, Khadra's name has Islamic connotations.

Alameddine reminds us that we

> never say the French pray to Dieu, or Mexicans pray to Dios. Having Allah be different from God implies that Muslims pray to a special deity. It classifies Muslims as the Other. Separating Allah from God, we only see a vengeful, alarming deity, one responsible for those frightful fatwas and ghastly jihads—rarely the compassionate God. The opening line of every chapter in the Koran is [. . .]: In the name of God, the Gracious, the Merciful. In the name of Allah. One and the same. ("Sacred Semantics")

This brings us back to Alameddine's choice of architect or silent narrator in vignette 180. One might argue that Alameddine avoids any commentary on the Qur'anic version of Sodom and Gomorrah due to the possible threat of some frightful fatwa or of violence. In this case, the architect of vignette 180 would be a silenced narrator. Anyone who has read Alameddine's works, however, knows that he does not shy away from controversial topics. I would argue that the choice of architect in vignette 180 serves to implicate readers as queer theologians while accounting for the fact that as Islam travels to the West and the US, it moves from a hegemonic position to a minoritized, marginalized, and racialized one. Alameddine's poetics of AIDS dementia encourages readers to critique traditional interpretations of the Bible and Qur'an while accounting for the uneven power dynamics at play.

BACH POETICS

The leitmotif "I can't think straight anymore" repeats in vignette 52 in relation to J. S. Bach's aria *Bete Aber Auch Dabei* (But You Should Also Pray). Mohammad says,

> I wake to the most beautiful music in the world. I hear her voice softly singing in the dark. It is always dark now. The violin is playing. Is it two violins? I know this music. I know I know this music. I can't place it. I can't think straight anymore.
> That voice is heavenly. I would stay alive for that voice. I would live for that lovely voice. It is divine. I know this music. I can't understand why my mind is disappearing. I love this music. (45)

Listening to it in the dark, Mohammad cannot place the beautiful aria. He tells us in short rhythmic sentences that he can't think straight anymore. While late AIDS dementia prevents him from naming the song, AIDS dementia as poetics allows Mohammad to capture the sadness and music of the aria in equally sad and sophisticated prose poetry. He faces the music of his impending death with a music of his own. As he wakes up to the most beautiful music in the world, Mohammad states, "I <u>h</u>ear <u>h</u>er voice *s*oftly *s*inging *in* the dark" (my emphasis). The breathy h-sound alliteration in "hear her," the whispering s-sound alliteration in "softly singing," and the humming repetition of "in" in "Singing in" bring to life the vocalist's voice. In repeating the word "dark," Mohammad implies that the aria is a glimmer of light in the darkening of his life. The repetition with variation of "I know this music" as "I know I know this music," places a tripartite emphasis on the phrase "I know" and points to the earlier repetition of "in." These two trinity-like repetitions allude to the religious nature of the aria. This is hardly surprising, as "Bach's counterpoint is associated with a deep, religious expression" (Oldroyd 8). Mohammad knows this music with all his being, but he cannot place it. It is then that he repeats the leitmotif "I can't think straight anymore." As painful as it is, not thinking straight produces a complex prose music.

In the second paragraph of vignette 52, Mohammad states, "That voice is heavenly. I would stay alive for that voice. I would live for that lovely voice." The heavenly voice guides Mohammad to a sensual heaven. Like the earlier sound-repetitions, "voice" appears three times in these three sentences, compounding the trinity-like repetitions. The second and third sentences of the second paragraph, eight syllables each, begin with the anaphora "I would" and end with the epistrophe "voice." The anaphora and epistrophe emphasize the voice's influence on Mohammad's will to live, as he would will himself to live just to hear that voice. He tells us that the voice is divine, possessing the godly power of bestowing life on the dying. Mohammad reiterates the sentence "I know this music," which repeats with variation in the first paragraph. He tells us, "I can't understand why my mind is disappearing." Here, the anaphora of "I can't" relates this sentence to "I can't think straight anymore" in the first paragraph. Both sentences reveal a mind coming to terms with its demise, a mind struggling to document its own erasure. The aesthetics of documented erasure returns us to *Hélas #251*'s technique, in which Alameddine's looming eyes seem to witness and commemorate the erasure of past selves, and to Mohammad's documentation of the erasure of English and French from his mind in vignette 2. All that Mohammad can do in his situation is to register, "I love this music."

In the third paragraph of vignette 52, Mohammad engages the repetition in Bach's aria: "The violin repeats the melody. The second violin repeats after the first. Or is it a viola? It must be Bach. So many times He has saved me" (45). Not only is Mohammad's mind able to recognize repetitions of the melodic sequence as played by a violin and a second violin or viola (in fact a violoncello piccolo), but it is able to compose its own sets of repetitions in response to and recognition of the technique, even if it cannot name or place the song. Apart from the earlier repetitions in this vignette, Mohammad repeats, "It must be Bach," twice after its appearance in the third paragraph, adding yet another trinity of repetition. Mohammad's statement, "So many times He [Bach] has saved me," reveals that the trinity-like repetitions (as a response to the melodic sequence in the aria which alternates between the two obbligato instruments) are Mohammad's prayer-offerings to Bach, whom he deifies by capitalizing the letter "H" in "He." The musical "Sequence" form, which Mohammad imitates in his repetitions, "was basically literary in origin" and in "medieval music, [it was] one of the most important types of addition to the official liturgical chant of the Latin church" (*New Harvard Dictionary* 739). The sequence-like phrase and word repetitions (in addition to polyphony and heterophony) reemphasize the dialogue and cross-fertilization between literature and music in *Koolaids,* with a religious twist relatable to both. As in the chronological (yet nonsequential) repetitions of the four horsemen hallucinations, the sequence-like repetitions of "I know this music" and "It must be Bach" operate contrapuntally in vignette 52.

The counterpoint between sequence-like repetitions does not bring about a resolution to the mystery of the song, however, so Mohammad asks James (who is apparently sitting next to him) to tell him who is singing. James answers, "Kathleen Battle. It's from *The Bach Album* with Itzhak Perlman. You used to have it on all the time while painting" (46).[10] James's reminder brings Mohammad's painting into dialogue with the music of Bach. The techniques of literature, music, and painting all combine in energetic counterpoint in *Koolaids,* and vignette 52 serves as a microcosm of this novelwide polyphony. James's answer jolts Mohammad's memory, and he recognizes the aria as *Bete Aber Auch Dabei.* He tells James that the aria is a prayer. Mohammad recites the English translation of the prayer: "Yet pray, even while / in the midst of keeping watch! / In thy great guilt / beg the Judge for patience, / and He shall free thee from sin / and make thee cleansed" (46). The prayer relates to Mohammad's feelings of guilt for helping Scott end his life, even though he acted in accordance with Scott's wishes. Furthermore, Mohammad also grants Scott's wish of using his ashes in a painting, presumably while listening to *The Bach Album*: "I ground the ashes in linseed oil. I laid down a black ground. I painted a lotus blossom with the ashes in the center, and nothing else on the

---

10. The album to which James refers was released by Deutsche Grammophon in 1992.

painting" (103–4). Mohammad's painting combines art, life, and death as a means of immortalizing Scott. The painting and the aria thus become a polyphonic manifestation of Mohammad's desire for forgiveness, and both become forms of prayer.

Mohammad's feelings of guilt begin before Scott's assisted suicide, however. He tells us in the same Bach vignette (vignette 52) that

> I went to a couple of Catholic churches when I found out I was positive. I wanted confession. The truth was I wanted absolution. I talked to a priest and asked him what the procedure was for confessing. He asked if I was Catholic. I told him I was a Muslim. He looked at me funny. He said I could not get absolution if I were a Muslim. (46)

Mohammad's guilty feelings manifest clearly in the four horsemen AIDS-dementia-induced hallucinations. Like the Jesus figure of the hallucinations, the Catholic priest denies Mohammad absolution because he is a Muslim. The issue at stake here, however, is that of the limits of Christian love and mercy, especially when they pertain to Muslims and to gay men of Muslim origins. A queering of the concepts of Christian love and mercy, so that they can be made to extend to "a non-Christian homosexual" (1), is in order. And AIDS dementia as poetics, as a methodology of not thinking straight, brings about queer and humane possibilities that are, ironically, more in line with Jesus's character and his teachings than with the practices of the Catholic Church as a religio-political body.

LEITMOTIF REGISTERS: RELIGION, PHILOSOPHY, CONFUSION

The "straight" leitmotif repeats next in vignette 118, which begins, "Out of timber so crooked as that from which man is made, nothing entirely straight can be carved" (112). The narrator, presumably Mohammad, informs us that Immanuel Kant is the author of the sentence. The religio-philosophical implication of the line is that no human can ever be entirely free of sin, as we are made from crooked timber or ethically compromised material. The operative word for moral perfection is "straight," and Mohammad cannot help commenting satirically about it: "I wonder if something entirely gay can be carved. That was a bad joke. I apologize" (112). Mohammad places "gay," not "crooked" or "curved," as an antonym for the condition of being "straight," in all of its iterations throughout the novel. Mohammad checks his desire for absolute gayness, apologizing for it as a bad joke. Hilarity aside, the bad joke likely refers to Mohammad's creation of a binary opposite to straightness, an absolute for an absolute. This formulation runs against the nonprescriptive, nonnormalizing poetics of *Koolaids*—hence Mohammad's apology. Toward the end of the vignette, Mohammad relates his inability to ponder, or even recall, Kant's sayings: "I can't think anymore, however. I can't remember" (113). As an echo of "I can't think straight anymore" (1) in vignette 2, the word "straight" is elided from "I can't think anymore" in vignette 118. The narrator's inability to think straight earlier in the novel activates AIDS dementia as a poetics. The progression of AIDS dementia (symbolized by the elision of "straight") as a disease experienced in the body, however, limits Mohammad to documenting the erasure of his thought and memory faculties. Not thinking straight and not being able to think enter into a counterpoint that reminds us that as AIDS dementia progresses as a poetics in the novel, so does it progress in Mohammad's mind.

The leitmotif "I can't think straight anymore" repeats next in vignette 135. In it, Mohammad arrives to the opening of his exhibit, which had been set for months, right after he helps Scott to die. He goes directly to the open bar and drinks himself into a stupor. In this state, he believes that he sees his mother giving him a reproving look from across the gallery, and he screams at her that he has painted her many times. The woman turns out to be Mohammad's sister, Nawal, who tells him in Arabic, "You're making a fool of yourself" (131). Mohammad's thoughts unravel:

> I am so confused. I can't reply. I haven't spoken in Arabic in so long. I want to ask who she is. I know her. I know I know her. I can't place her. I can't think straight anymore [. . .]. I want to say something, but the language fails me. I struggle. The words come out in Arabic.
> "I killed him."

Mohammad's oedipal relationship to his mother is worthy of its own investigation, and I will not engage it here except to say that his mother obeys his father's order to cut all ties with him when they learn he is gay. Mohammad's drunkenness in vignette 135 acts as a counterpoint to his AIDS dementia, and his thoughts in like fashion collapse into short staccato sentences that exhibit his struggles both in recognizing Nawal and in expressing himself linguistically.

Whereas Mohammad declares that "I now think and dream only in Arabic" (1) in the second vignette (which also introduces the leitmotif "I can't think straight anymore"), Mohammad reveals in vignette 135 that he is struggling to express himself in the Arabic language. This seems to point once more to Mohammad's chiastic identity negotiations—"In America, I fit, but I do not belong. / In Lebanon, I belong, but I do not fit" (40)—as they oscillate between the languages of English and Arabic. The intravignette repetition with variation of "I know her. I know I know her," coupled with "I can't place her. I can't think straight anymore" in vignette 135, constitute together a cross-vignette fugal repetition with variation of "I know this music. I know I know this music. I can't place it. I can't think straight anymore" (45) in vignette 52. The intra- and intervignette repetitions with variation of these four sentences, in different registers, remind us that not thinking straight produces a complex interart that combines the paintings of Mohammad's mother as conflated with Nawal and Bach's music. The art of repetition (words and sentences) in and across vignettes and same-genre vignettes (as in the four horsemen hallucinations) produce complex *Hélas*-like paintings and Bach-like counterpoints and fugues that in turn give expression to the poetics of AIDS dementia.

The leitmotif of not thinking straight repeats one more time in vignette 224, in which Mohammad, having lost control over his bodily functions, reveals that he is beyond embarrassment at this point: "Nawal wipes my butt. I must have had an accident. She talks to me constantly. I hear her. I can't seem to think straight. She talks to me of home. I am home. My mind wanders" (212). In this late vignette, which is twenty vignettes away from the end of the novel and the end of Mohammad's life, the short staccato sentences return. Not only do the sentences point to AIDS dementia as both disease and cure; they also act as a microcosm of the short-vignette form of *Koolaids*. Readers (along with Mohammad) struggle to put the sentences together as they struggle to connect the interart and multigenre vignettes. It is clear here that Mohammad does not remember having an accident; he knows only that his sister, Nawal, is cleaning him. This erasure of consciousness carries across to Nawal's ceaseless monologue. He hears her, but he cannot think straight; the sounds of Nawal's words are comforting (much like the sound of Bach's music), but he struggles to recognize their meaning. While some of Mohammad's sentences in vignette 52 enter into a sequence-like repetition that corresponds to the Bach aria, no such repetition occurs in vignette 224. What Mohammad captures from Nawal is her talk of home. Mohammad does not reveal the location of this home, however, only that he is home. Is home Lebanon, San Francisco, Nawal, death, or variegated combinations of possible homes? Mohammad leaves us wondering as his "mind wanders." Not thinking straight, as vertiginous as it is, acts as a cure for straight answers, and home is rendered as a perpetual combination of possibilities. Mohammad's statement, "I am home," is a counterpoint between arrival and departure, between stasis and movement, between life and death. Being home is also a wandering away from a straight concept of home.

MEDIA REPRESENTATIONS AND STORYTELLING

Koolaids connects the AIDS epidemic to the Lebanese Civil War thematically on multiple (often interlocking) levels. It does so primarily in the figure of Mohammad, in the other Lebanese and Lebanese American gay characters, and in their friends and families who have been exposed to AIDS, the civil war, or both. In vignette 7 of *Koolaids*, Mohammad reacts in the exact manner to being sent out of Lebanon in 1975 and to his HIV diagnosis in the US. He repeats the same five sentences in reaction to both trials: "I wanted to scream. Hold on a minute. Hold on. I haven't even begun to live my life. I thought I had more time" (8). The repetition of the five short staccato sentences that are symptomatic of AIDS dementia, and the repetition (within the five-sentence repetition) of "Hold on a minute" and "Hold on," fugally connect the traumatic experiences of AIDS and the Lebanese Civil War early in the work. One chases the other, much as a fugal theme repeats in different registers. To reiterate: *Koolaids*'s poetics of AIDS dementia and repetition are crucial interart and multigenre counterpoints to the cross-trauma experiences of the Lebanese Civil War and AIDS in the vignettes.

Moreover, the poetics of AIDS dementia and repetition provide a lens through which we can see the Lebanese Civil War and its representations (or lack thereof) by the US government and the mass media as forms of disease. An anecdote from James Kinsella's *Covering the Plague* crystallizes the Reagan administration's cavalier attitude toward the AIDS epidemic and the Middle East alike:

> Nothing sums up that attitude better than a joke reportedly told at a meeting of the President and some of his key advisers in 1986 [. . .] The Libyan leader [Muammar Gaddafi] was rumored to be a transvestite, so at the meeting Reagan asked, "Why not invite Gadhafi to San Francisco; he likes to dress up so much." To which Secretary of State George Shultz allegedly replied, "Why don't we give him AIDS?" In the private confines of the Reagan administration, the disease was a laughing matter. In public, the president had uttered the word "AIDS" only once. (3)

Not only is AIDS treated as a laughing matter, but the Reagan administration also seems to have weaponized it rhetorically to deride the enemies of the US. The suffering of AIDS patients and Middle Easterners themselves seems not to matter at all. If Reagan joked about AIDS privately, he rarely mentioned it publicly. The same is true of Reagan's intervention in Lebanon from 1982 to 1984. In vignette 237, the narrator, who I call a war storyteller, states, "America entered the Lebanese Civil War. It paid the price. Two hundred marines were killed by one Shiite. Reagan pulled the troops and avoided discussing Lebanon. Lebanon, like AIDS, was hardly ever mentioned by our president" (234–35). The dominant political attitudes toward AIDS and the Lebanese Civil War in the US demonstrate that *Koolaids*'s intervention is not as unlikely as it might first appear.

In vignette 206, Mohammad reacts to the Oklahoma City bombing, which took place in 1995:

> It looked like Beirut. They still think we're different.
> It turned out an American did it. A true-blue American. No one explained how the wires came up with descriptions of the suspects as two Middle Eastern-looking men. No apologies, no explanations. (196)

Mohammad reminds us that violence replicates itself, whether in Lebanon or in the US, something that escapes the news media outlets. Seeming to take their cue from the irresponsible rhetoric of some US politicians, the US media automatically pointed to "Middle Eastern-looking men" as suspects for the bombing. The issue here is one of forced (and enforced) difference, in which Arabs and Muslims become the receptacles for all social ills and problems in the US. The recklessness of this repetition of difference, however, is exposed by the repetition of "true-blue American" violence. The site of the bombing "looked like Beirut. They still think we're different."

Against the failure of journalistic representations to capture the experience of the Lebanese Civil War on a human level, *Koolaids* offers a storyteller who tells the stories of both its victims and its perpetrators. Those of us who have lived through the Lebanese Civil War understand the importance of such stories, which, despite their discursive and rumor-based character, allowed us to share often lifesaving and life-affirming information. In one such account, which appears in vignette 84, *Koolaids* presents what appear to be three news briefs and then offers a war storyteller, who (re)tells/repeats the story of the third brief in serial but nonconsecutive vignettes. The expansive repetition of the narrative "allows us to examine the diverse discursive spaces and forms within which conflict is mediated, communicated, experienced, imagined and lived" (Matar and Harb 4). Vignette 84, which deals with Lebanese Christian-infighting and vying for power, provides the following in the third paragraph:

"The assassin of the Lebanese Forces, Nick Akra, was found naked, in bed with his paramour, Samia Marchi, legs entwined, lips still joined. Fifty-two bullets riddled their corpses. Coitus interruptus" (75). The dark humor, which proffers assassination as an effective method of coitus interruptus, is the main clue that this paragraph is purely fictive. But the vignette successfully mimics the poverty of news reports in conveying meaningful, human information.

The news brief in question offers reductive and moralistic markers of the identities of the couple, "assassin" and "paramour," for public consumption. It is worth noting here that Samia Marchi's "extramarital affair with Nicola Akra [. . .] is a symbolic crossing from [largely Muslim] West to [predominantly Christian] East Beirut and a union of two religions, cut short by political division and moral corruption" (Hout, *Post-War* 31). That is, apart from the fact that the extramarital affair involves a right-wing Christian-militia thug and a married Muslim woman, the cross-religious aspect of the affair adds a sensationalistic layer to its transgressive nature in the segregated Beirut of the civil war. This act of religious transgression echoes in some ways Mohammad's trespassing into Judeo-Christian territory in the four horsemen vignettes. The pseudo–news brief's detailed attention to "legs entwined, lips still joined," each phrase being trisyllabic, and to the fifty-two bullets implies a religio-moral cause and effect. This is not to say that Akra's (and some of Marchi's) actions are not reprehensible and condemnable on ethical and human levels—they certainly are—but that we must be careful not to forgo the characters' humanity and complexity even as we condemn their actions. In context, the religio-moral cause and effect of the news brief is not so distant from the religio-moral representation of AIDS as God's punishment of gay men. In its spare efficiency, the news brief risks reducing Nick Akra and Samia Marchi to little more than dehumanized tropes in a morality play.

The news brief does not trouble its readers to think beyond the literal, fact-based style of reporting. To be fair, the function of news briefs is not to be conflated with that of investigative or in-depth reporting, but this does not override the fact that news briefs often serve as little more than synecdoches of an invisible whole. As remedy, *Koolaids* offers a war storyteller who repeats the story in an expansive manner that humanizes Nick and Samia, as flawed and criminal as they are, and offers more complex representations of their motivations. That is, the war storyteller allows us to see Nick and Samia as human beings on account of their actions, not in spite of them. The war storyteller's serial but nonconsecutive account spans vignettes 95, 98, 100, 136, 172, 177, 182, 187, 199, and 208. If Nick's and Samia's bodies were riddled with 52 bullets, then *Koolaids* is riddled with 10 strategically placed vignettes that perforate the mass media's reporting of events. I will not go into the intricate story of the lovers' meeting, the problematic seduction phase, the details of the affair, or the repetition of phrases in vignettes 95, 98, and 177. Instead, I will focus on the role of the serial, nonconsecutive vignettes that construct the retelling/repetition of Akra and Marchi's story. Suffice it to say that Samia's husband turns out to be a pedophile who had neglected her for eight years, and Nick's profession as an assassin is complicated by the fact that so many of the Lebanese population were actively killing one another during the civil war. Nick and Samia plan and execute the murder of Samia's husband, and the storyteller leaves us on vignette 208 with Nick and Samia having celebratory postmurder sex that includes the use of Nick's loaded gun. Presumably, this last and scandalous scene returns with us to the news of their murder.

The strategically placed storytelling vignettes both problematize reductive readings of Nick and Samia and allow for a more complex reading of their situation. Pickens reminds us that "in part, it is the text's construction that holds sentimentality at bay" ("Feeling Embodied" 74). The many interruptions, suspensions, and possible combinations of vignettes forestall any sentimental impulses in the text. And the poetics of documented erasure and uncertainty—without which the lives of Nick and Samia would evanesce—also play their part in undercutting sentimentality. Furthermore, the combinational poetics, which open a space for the serial, nonconsecutive vignettes to combine contrapuntally with seemingly unlikely vignettes, gesture toward nuanced interpretations of Nick and Samia's affair. I would like to point to one important combination that results from the serial, nonconsecutive structure of this story.

In vignette 172, which is a part of Nick and Samia's story, we learn that Samia's husband had not slept with her for eight years. This is also the vignette in which Samia and Nick have sex for the first time. The very next vignette offers Qur'anic verses 23 through 27 in Surat Yusuf (Surah of Joseph). In this scene, the wife of the man who takes Yusuf in after his brothers dispose of him—note the similarity to the account of Joseph in the Bible—attempts to seduce him. Verse 24 states, "And (with passion) did she desire him, and he would have desired her, but that he saw the evidence of his Lord" (173). Unlike the case of Samia and Nick, in which Nick seduces married Samia—Yusuf does not give in. In fact, the wife is vilified for trying to seduce Yusuf. The juxtaposition of vignettes 172 and 173, however (in context of earlier unlikely combinations and narrative interventions), promotes a critical reevaluation of the Qur'anic scene and a reexamination of the religio-moral code of the pseudo–news brief's account of Akra's and Marchi's demise. Juxtaposed with Samia—whose husband ignores her so that he can focus on raping boys under the age of seventeen—the man's wife in Surat Yusuf gains a more complex dimension. The war storyteller's (re)telling/repeating of Nick and Samia's story in nonconsecutive vignettes creates a series of suspensions and combinations that compel readers to compare and combine vignettes and their contents critically. This practice raises many questions: Why does the man's wife desire an extramarital affair with Yusuf? How does her husband treat her? Is he also a pedophile who neglects his wife? These considerations do not figure into Surat Yusuf, which renders the man's wife as an adulterous woman. We are asked to accept the wife's wickedness on faith, at least until she attempts to force herself on Yusuf and falsely accuse him of sexual assault. Even then, the combining of vignettes 172 and 173 allows readers to imagine the human motivations behind the wife's actions. The structural intervention of placing these two seemingly disparate vignettes next to each other is what allows us to transfer the critical intervention from one register to another.

CODEX

Koolaids's form and poetics correlate seemingly incommensurable religiocultural and lived experiences: the AIDS epidemic in the US and the Lebanese Civil War, biblical and Qur'anic stories, and violence in Lebanon and the US. If dominant repetitions of difference construct closed borders and homophobic and Islamophobic echo chambers, then *Koolaids* counters with nonnormative and nonnormalizing art-pattern repetitions. That is, *Koolaids*'s multigenre and interart repetitions within and between vignettes mimic and decenter dominant repetitions and representations without (re)prescribing stable counterrepresentations. In addition, *Koolaids* offers a poetics of AIDS dementia as a queer cure for straight and linear narratives. Coupled with the vignette form of Alameddine's work, which provides seemingly inexhaustible combinations, the poetics of AIDS dementia (as an unrelenting process of queering and que(e)rying) destabilizes and decenters both dominant repetitions and any combination of vignettes that readers or critics assemble.

The primary progenitor of AIDS dementia in *Koolaids* is the character Mohammad, who is trying to come to terms with his disabled mind and to document the erasure of his past selves and experiences. Like Mohammad, readers are made to experience (aesthetically at least) the vertiginous effects of AIDS dementia and the chaos of the Lebanese Civil War. Mohammad's experiences also enter into varying combinations with those of his family, friends, and acquaintances. Kim Jensen suggests that "each character represents a different facet of one overall Lebanese [diasporic] personality" (Jensen). If this is the case, then the overall Lebanese diasporic personality is subject to the same decentering process that is effectuated by the polyvocal and mutating vignette form. Mohammad and the vignettes enter multiple heterophonic, contrapuntal, and fugal combinations that allow for vertical, horizontal, and diagonal positionings. These as well are mediated by the techniques and articulations of Alameddine's and Mohammad's paintings, Bach's complex counterpoint, and prose repetitions. The "Fugue," "the most fully developed procedure of imitative counterpoint," has been described as a "conversation, argument, debate, diatribe, or even as a battle among various voices" ("Fugue," *New Harvard Dictionary* 327, 328). *Koolaids*'s polyphonic conversations of voices, vignettes, repetitions, and poetics are certainly fugal in that they imitate and repeat each other across genres and registers. In vignette 188, an unknown narrator describes what appears to be a posthumous exhibition of Mohammad's paintings, titled "Mohammad: The Last Paintings" (184). The narrator states that "Mohammad is an imagist of cultural fugues and choreographies" (184). As such, dark-skinned, gay, and immigrant Mohammad emerges as a complex, transcultural citizen who is not easily stereotyped or racialized. Like the interart poetics of *Koolaids*, Mohammad's paintings are cross-cultural fugues that put Lebanon and the US in dialogue across multiple registers. The complexities of form and poetics confirm Salaita's contention that "*Koolaids* is not a normal novel, so it must be read abnormally" (*Modern* 43). I would add that *Koolaids* is not a straight novel, and we cannot afford to be straitened by a straightforward and uncomplicated reading of it. Otherwise, we "might as well drink [the] Kool-Aid" (Alameddine, *Koolaids* 99).

CHAPTER 2

Blue Notes and Accented Rhythms

Diana Abu-Jaber's *Arabian Jazz*

When Diana Abu-Jaber's *Arabian Jazz* was published in 1993, it "was the first Arab American novel published since Etel Adnan's *Sitt Marie Rose* had appeared more than a decade earlier" (Salaita, *Modern* 96). *Arabian Jazz* (re)generated interest in Arab American fiction, and its critical and commercial success led publishers to seek out Arab American authors, who produced a steady stream of Arab American novels from the 1990s to the present. Its publication also "set much higher stakes for those Arab Americans who would write after it was published" (97). Steven Salaita credits the novel's broader approach to and construction of fictional accounts of Arab Americans and their experiences. Certainly, *Arabian Jazz*'s use of humor and its correlation of Arab American struggles with those of African Americans, the white working class, and Native Americans set higher literary and representational stakes. It also raised the bar for subsequent Arab American authors in terms of its artistic integrity. I argue that *Arabian Jazz*'s employment of African American jazz idioms—improvisation and the blue note—adds a formal and poetic dimension that is crucial to the novel's expansive approach to Arab American identity and visibility. This chapter, then, investigates the role of jazz in complementing the (inter)play of identities and in advancing an improvised (dynamic) and intersectional (dialogic) Arab American identity in *Arabian Jazz*.

The term "jazz" in the title of Abu-Jaber's novel implies a process of improvisation and intertwining that invokes African American musical expression. In experiencing "racial profiling; detention and murder for political organizing or even for the suspicion of political organizing; and [. . .] lynching [. . .] in the South" (Hartman 146), many Arab Americans continue to find common ground with African Americans. It comes as no surprise, therefore, that Abu-Jaber chooses two salient idioms of black jazz to address Arab American invisibility.[1] As an essential characteristic of jazz music, improvisation manifests itself linguistically in *Arabian Jazz*, even as it intertwines with the novel's major themes. Matussem Ramoud, a Jordanian immigrant to the United States and one of the main characters in Abu-Jaber's novel, is a jazz drummer and a devotee of John Coltrane's music, particularly the composition "Naima." Matussem and his daughters, Jemorah and Melvina, are struggling to find their place in the white working-class setting of Upstate New York after Matussem's American-born wife, Nora, dies during a visit to Jordan. The Arab side of the family wants Matussem and his daughters to move back to Jordan permanently, or at the very least to see Jemorah and Melvina marry Arab men. The characters' dilemma of remaining in or leaving the US is exacerbated by the racism they face in Upstate New York. Their straddling of two cultures, two families, two identities, and especially two languages produces a need to improvise and intertwine their individual and collective identities as Arab Americans.

The contrapuntal lines of the characters' negotiations are accompanied by linguistic improvisations in English and in the Arabic words that find their way into the text. These improvisations manifest clearly in Abu-Jaber's rendering of Matussem's and his sister Fatima's accented, "broken" English. These irregularities at first appear to be merely markers of difference or foreignness and of cultural inferiority. The disruptions of accented, broken English, however, challenge the tempo of the dominant language and the temporality of migration as linear progressions. They produce improvisations of the moment that combine different time signatures (compound rhythms) and modalities of expressions that resist normalization and socio-cultural invisibility. In Matussem's and Jemorah's untranslated names and Coltrane's "Naima," the moments

---

1. Black jazz idioms find their way to a vast number of African American literary texts, and this transmusicality has been studied extensively. As jazz interweaves other musical languages into its myriad expressions, *Arabian Jazz* pays tribute to the idioms of black jazz in order to transmit Arab American sounds. Please see Brent Hayes Edwards, *Epistrophies: Jazz and the Literary Imagination*; A. Yemisi Jimoh's *Spiritual, Blues, and Jazz People in African American Fiction: Living in a Paradox*; Carter Mathes's *Imagine the Sound: Experimental African American Literature after Civil Rights*; and David Yaffe's *Fascinating Rhythm: Reading Jazz in American Writing*, for more on African American jazz and literature.

of linguistic, musical, and translational improvisation enter a condition of dialectic density: the blue note. Like the musical blue note, which inflects a musical (usually major) scale of play by reaching for a note from outside the scale, the linguistic blue note forces a dominant language (English) to enter into dialogue with a word imported from another language (Arabic). In combination, the untranslated Arabic names and the musical piece and untranslated name "Naima" create a potent dialectic of both a linguistic and a musical blue note. The interplay of the jazz idioms (of improvisation and the blue note) permeates the composition of *Arabian Jazz*, and provides productive disruptions and unlikely combinations that in turn give voice to complex and anti-essentialist Arab American expressions.

In order to gauge the density of the blue note, it is necessary to explore the improvisational and intertwining elements that provoke its manifestation. Early in *Arabian Jazz*, Melvina asks her sister Jemorah to recall a Bedouin saying: "In the book of life, every page has two sides" (6). The "two sides" are in fact multiple sets of two sides (two cultures, two families, two identities, and two languages) that culminate in the term Arab American. Melvina calls upon the Bedouin saying in response to her aunt Fatima's pressuring Jemorah to marry an Arab man and lead a traditional life. The saying allows Jemorah to better understand the demands of the Arab side of the family and to access her American side to counter those demands. Melvina's recourse to a Bedouin saying might seem paradoxical (she uses it to at once participate in and subvert Arab traditions); however, the nomadic nature of the Bedouin allows for a traveling understanding or cross-translation of Arab and American in the Arab American condition.

For example, when Fatima brings over a potential mother-in-law to inspect Jemorah (including her teeth), Melvina intervenes: "'Back off, lady!' Melvie raised a fist. 'I'm warning you.' 'Allah the merciful and munificent! A demon-*ifrit*' [answered the woman]" (64). This depiction of the potential mother-in-law, as with other representations in the novel, "was viewed as humorous by some readers and as stereotypical and offensive by others" (Darraj, "Abu-Jaber" 10). The debate about the representational responsibilities of Arab American writers is important and worthy of its own investigation. In this chapter, I focus on the jazz poetics in such humorous episodes and the role that improvisation plays in disrupting lingual, racial, cultural, and identitarian norms in the US. Melvina responds to the woman swiftly and forcefully in two phrases that are four syllables (or two feet) each. The uniformity of Melvina's response, which accords with her self-identification as a no-nonsense nurse, stands in contrast to the potential mother-in-law's hilarious outburst of an eleven-syllable phrase followed by a five-syllable exclamation. While Melvina's two phrases create a rhythmic equilibrium akin to a 4/4 time signature, the woman's two-phrase response is uneven rhythmically. Together, these rhythms yield two different sides (steady and varied) of Arab American expression that resist any attempt to essentialize the content of the phrases or Arab American identities. After her appeal to Allah, the potential mother-in-law's tempo itself trips into the two-sided word "demon-*ifrit*," which presents the possible English translation ("demon") alongside the transliteration of the Arabic word, doubly mediated by a hyphen and italics.

Ifrit (or *afreet*) is the accented transliteration of the Arabic word, which refers to a demonlike creature in Muslim mythology. While "demon" and *ifrit* share in denotation, linked as they are by the hyphen, they are also separated in connotation by the same hyphen that connects them. In Western cultural understanding, "demon" begins with the Greeks and later earns a Christian significance. *Ifrit,* on the other hand, is a giant demon in Muslim mythology that makes a marked literary appearance in *A Thousand and One Nights.* As Gregory Rabassa notes, "In such things as 2 = 2, we rarely wake up to the fact that this is impossible, except as a purely theoretical and fanciful concept" (1). In other words, "demon" is not equal to "*ifrit,*" even if one is a possible translation of the other. We are compelled to factor in the sociocultural implications of "demon" on one side and *ifrit* on the other. As such, "demon" ≠ *ifrit*; rather, "demon" ≈ *ifrit*. One approximates the other in a series of possible overlaps of meaning. The manifestation of these two terms side-by-side (suggesting a continuum, even while the terms intertwine and challenge each other) is a contrapuntal improvisation in answer to the struggles of the Arab American characters in *Arabian Jazz.* The variegated rhythms of Arab American idioms find their cadence in the improvisation of "demon-*ifrit*" and the resulting possibilities and anxieties contained in their hyphen-linked cultural meanings. Many words manifest alongside their possible translations in *Arabian Jazz,* but many others, including the characters' names, appear without translation. How, then, do these opaque (because untranslated) Arabic manifestations, these blue notes, yield meaning? Moreover, how do they enter into dialogue with the English language of the novel? Does a jazz reading of accented improvisations and blue notes allow a richer understanding of the novel's linguistic/cultural improvisations and the Arab Americans who produce them? A good place to start is by translating these words and names.

Jemorah's and Melvina's names present two sides in transliteration and translation. In Arabic, Jemorah's name resonates as "Jemrah," which means "live coal" (*Al-Mawrid: A Modern Arabic-English Dictionary* 430). In the Arabic version of her name, Jemorah is close to her father's larger-than-life disposition. Matussem tells Jemorah, "You like me, bambino, [. . .] Your mind all wide open, you hears too much, you hungry for whole big, crazy world" (137).[2] If one were to listen to Matussem's words musically—not merely as representations of an Arab immigrant's weak and accented attempts at English—new possibilities of understanding Matussem's improvisatory mode of expression emerge. As I demonstrate later in the chapter, this exercise is far from arbitrary, as the novel itself theorizes the musical aspects of the characters' utterances. For the moment, let us investigate the musical possibility of Matussem's phrases. Musical expression readily translates as poetry or poetic language in prose. In other words, poetry is how language might impart some of the effects of music to otherwise ordinary phrases. This movement demands a closer listening to the sounds and rhythms of language as it mediates meaning. In this case, Matussem must improvise around linguistic and grammatical gaps to get his message across. This activity relates intrinsically to Matussem's jazz sensibility, and jazz improvisation enables him to create larger-than-life poetry of the moment.

How do we listen to the rhythmic play of Matussem's accented and uneven English as it mediates the content? If we take the punctuation marks (commas in this case) as points of enjambment, the visual representation of the aural emphasis would take shape as follows:

You like me,	(three syllables)
Bambino, [...]	(three syllables)
Your mind all wide open,	(six syllables)
you hears too much,	(four syllables)
you hungry for whole big,	(six syllables)
crazy world.	(three syllables)

The syllabic rhythm or poetic lines, as organized by the punctuation marks, is three, three [. . .] six, four, six, three. All the phrases trot in multiples of three—in triplets—except for "you hears too much." Musically, the "Triplet" constitutes "three notes of equal value to be played in the time normally occupied by two notes of the same value" (*New Harvard Dictionary* 873). The triplet creates a forward motion, a riding of the rhythm, as it fits three notes into the time normally occupied by two notes of the same value. This rhythmic play challenges the measured quality of the dominant rhythmic uniformity, which is exemplified in the fourth line: "you hears too much" evens and contrasts the beats of the triplets in its two sets of two notes (even

---

2. The ellipsis represents the narrator's remark, "Matussem said from his La-Z-Boy whenever Jem fretted over her lack of planning" (137), which does not relate to the music/poetic analysis of Matussem's phrases. Later ellipses in similar passages serve the same purpose.

as "you hears" disrupts the grammar). Furthermore, the "you" anaphora in the first, third, fourth (there is a "you" in "Your"), and fifth phrases/lines, adds to the musical dimension as anaphora "is often used in ballad and song" (Cuddon, "Anaphora" 37). In a way, Matussem is singing his and Jemorah's song about wide open minds and hearing too much. And this is precisely the point. Matussem is inviting readers to see and hear the world as he and Jemorah experience it.

Matussem's rhythms disrupt dominant inscriptions of uniformity (lingual, metrical, and racial), much as jazz idioms challenge the rules of classical music. Reading Matussem's expressions musically/poetically has a direct relationship to how one views him. The shift of audible form from prose to poetry (and as represented visually) marks also a shift from Matussem's sociocultural and racial invisibility to an expression of visibility on his own, even while dialogic, terms. This trans-formation (of audible form and representation) is not unlike the repetition of *Koolaids*'s epigraph in vignette 189 as it shifts from poetry to prose. Listening to the two sides of Matussem's voice, horizontally and vertically, allows for the emergence of a complex and human character. What at first seems to be the arbitrary and stereotypically accented phrases of an Arab immigrant become much more upon closer listening. The instantaneous negotiation of grammatical gaps and the triplets' tripping of the dominant tempo of American English, as improvisations, accentuate the Arab Americanness of the content. These are audibly the words of an Arab American musician, who is negotiating the dominant modality by improvising around lingual and cultural gaps, the markers of his invisibility and exclusion.

Matussem's triplets also correspond to his and his two daughters' trisyllabic names (Ma-tuss-em, Jem-o-rah, and Mel-vi-na) and to their symbolic (and rhythmic) unevenness within dominant constructions of uniformity. The difference between Jemrah and Jemorah is the difference between two and three beats, between being Arab and being Arab American. There is a Jemrah in Jemorah, but Jemorah's added *o* signifies Jemrah's transmutation as it travels from an Arabic context to an English one. Furthermore, one can interpret Jemorah as an accented (Americanized) version of Jemrah. As such, Jemorah highlights the fact that native-born Americans mispronounce Arabic words and names on a regular basis. As in their mispronunciations of Mohammad's name (as Mahomet and Momad) in *Koolaids*, native-born Americans face no consequences for (mis)pronouncing foreign names with their American accents. Accented improvisation, informed by a poetics of jazz, disrupts dominant formulations of error and nonbelonging even while it negotiates with those very formulations. Jemorah's name, as both Jemrah and Jemorah, combines two sides.

If Jemorah's name travels between two languages and two cultures, Melvina's name amplifies the themes of loss, absence, and remaking. Melvina's name seems to be of Irish origin. It derives from "Melvin," which *A Dictionary of First Names* identifies as "a very popular modern name of uncertain origin, probably a variant of the less common MELVILLE" (Hanks and Hodges 234). "Melville" in turn comes from "a place in northern France called *Malleville* 'bad settlement,' i.e. settlement on infertile land" (Hanks and Hodges 234). In these meanings, Melvina's name gestures both to her Arab family's Palestinian origins (their loss of land, their migration to Jordan and to their immigration to the US) and to her Irish American family's origins (that are impacted by Britain's long history of colonization in Ireland). The sisters' names derive from their parents' cultural backgrounds—Arab and Irish American—but the meanings of their names travel and combine across multiple languages and cultures.

While the sisters differ in their perceptions of what it means to be Arab American, they work together to take care of their widowed father. The names' linguistic and cultural differences, which parallel Jemorah's and Melvina's different experiences and perceptions, become indifferent within a familial context in which the two sisters act in concert. As in Jemorah's and Matussem's names, the Arabic words that appear in *Arabian Jazz* do so only in transliteration; that is, they manifest in the recognizable English letter form even while their content remains opaque. Readers are never quite sure about the meanings of these words that improvise on the English linguistic system. The improvisation of "two sides" creates a to-and-fro of meaning-making, one that oscillates rhythmically between English and Arabic. Proper names and musical compositions (Coltrane's "Naima") in English-letter transliterations of Arabic, however, create moments of dialectic density that are at once embedded in and distinguishable from the approximations of the two-sided improvisatory translations. That is, while the imported Arabic proper names and musical compositions share in borrowing English letters in their transliterated manifestation, their content (both Arabic and musical) resists translation. The dense combination of English letter form and Arabic content coupled with what I call a "transliterational suspension" (the suspension of Arabic letters that have no corresponding letters in the English alphabet) propels the dialectic of the blue note.

Arabian Jazz begins with a passage replete with translational, transliterational, and musical timbres: "When Matussem Ramoud opened his eyes each morning, his wife would still not be there. He was amazed by this. By six o'clock, the floors of his house vibrated with drumming and music. 'Naima'" (1). The passage introduces the improvisational/importational technique of *selective lexical fidelity,* or untranslated words. One of the untranslated words in question, "Naima," which is set apart by quotation marks, challenges the novel's linguistic continuum of representation in English and signifies the presence of linguistic and cultural otherness within the novel. The proper name of the character Matussem Ramoud, not afforded any distinguishing markers, also appears untranslated. The authors of *The Empire Writes Back* argue that selective lexical fidelity "leaves some words untranslated in the text [. . . as a] device for conveying the sense of cultural distinctiveness [. . . It is] a clear signifier of the fact that the language which actually informs the novel is an/Other language" (Ashcroft et al. 63). The language of "an/Other" in *Arabian Jazz* is a nomadic language, one that both inhabits and improvises on linguistic and cultural Arabic and English. Untranslated words are the most visible sign of traveling improvisation; however, accentual play and the resulting slippage of meaning are also significantly improvisational. The title of the novel, *Arabian Jazz,* and the close proximity of both untranslated words, "Matussem" and "Naima," to "drumming and music," provoke a jazz/improvisational reading of these words.

In a dream, Jemorah hears "her [dead] mother's voice telling her, as she used to, 'Be bold, be bold. You should learn about yourself by learning the world. See how things come apart and go back together again'" (255–56). These words (those of the dream alongside the untranslated proper names) establish one of the novel's musical keys and the moments of improvisation around that key. This, however, requires one to be "bold," in order to enter the condition of being *a-part*: the untranslated words of multiple import, of importation, exist at once as a part of the text and apart from it; they exist a-part. Nora's words are an invitation to experience "how things come apart and go back together again" musically, linguistically, and culturally. What are the possibilities of meaning at play, then, in the two untranslated names, Naima and Matussem? "Naima" is the female inflected form for the Arabic word "Na'im," which translates as "happiness, bliss, [and] felicity" (*Al-Mawrid* 1181). In the case of Arabic, however, the idea of fidelity in the term *selective lexical fidelity* becomes problematic simply because the Arabic alphabet is dissimilar to the English alphabet. The untranslated word is imported into the text not in its Arabic form but in English letters. This results in the occlusion of the Arabic letter "ain" (ع) in "Naima," which has no corresponding letter in the English alphabet. The ع should appear right before the *i* in "Naima." The transliterational suspension of "ain" undermines the faithfulness or exactness of fidelity and creates a new curtailed word, which does not clearly resonate in Arabic or in English. "Naima" without the crucial ع could be interpreted as "Na'ima," a closely related Arabic word. "Na'ima," the female inflected form for "Na'im," translates as "asleep; sleeping; sleeper" (*Al-Mawrid* 1148). The apostrophe in "Na'im" stands in the stead of the Arabic letter "hamzah" (ء), which also has no corresponding letter in the English alphabet. The act of transliteration in its occlusion of the ع destabilizes the possibility of translating "Naima." As a necessarily improvised transliteration, "Naima" is a syncope away from translation and neologism. I call this a *strategic improvisational importation,* a word that strategically improvises on the English linguistic context, an importation no longer belonging to its origins and continually negotiating its meanings in transliteration rather than translation. How does one then negotiate "Naima"?

"Naima" is a popular Arabic and Muslim female name. As it appears in the novel, the "N" in "Naima" is capitalized and, therefore, lends itself to a reading as a proper name. The name *feminine bliss* adds a transcendent aspect to the linguistic narration in English as a sensual point of climax. Its placement as a fragment in the opening paragraph of the novel (a word inhabiting the space of a sentence) ending a paragraph of three viable sentences heightens its effect. "Naima," as a name between quotation marks, suggests that Matussem is voicing or singing the name: "Na-ع ee-mah!" The quotation marks serve as spatial representations of the temporal and, as such, attempt to free the word from spatial confines. The quotation marks also set "Naima" apart from the sentences before its improvised appearance, but as a part of the paragraph within which it exists; they place "Naima" *a-part*. The word metamorphosed to sound, "Naima," scans qualitatively as an amphibrach (˘ / ˘) with two unstressed syllables surrounding a stressed syllable (two breves surrounding a macron, quantitatively). The sound is percussive and suggestive of a triplet—with a stress on the middle beat. Indeed, the sensual context within which "Naima" exists is that of a house vibrating "with drumming and music." Sixteen pages later, the narrator reveals that "Naima" is, in fact, John Coltrane's famous jazz piece. The quotation marks become reference marks, which also offset "Naima" to the temporal realm of music. "Naima" the sounded name is complemented by "Naima" the jazz piece; one does not occlude the other. Coltrane did after all write the piece for his Muslim wife Naima.[3] As such, "Naima" is not merely a name or a musical piece; "Naima" is a term vibrating with multiple meanings inside and outside the novel. Matussem achieves musical bliss by accompanying Naima on drums, while his deceased wife (Nora) sleeps for eternity. Naima's transliterational poetics, in its slippages of meaning, also accompanies Matussem's experience of Naima. For non-Arab speakers of English, Naima might resonate first as music; for Arabic speakers,

---

3. Moustafa Bayoumi states that Coltrane "himself [was] married to Naima (a Muslim)" ("East of the Sun" 260).

Naima might resonate first as a name; for Muslims, Naima might resonate first as a signifier of Muslim identity, here as Arab and/or African American. In combination, "Naima" enters the condition of density and traveling possibility, the condition of the blue note.

To better gauge "Naima" as a linguistic blue note inside *Arabian Jazz*—one that shifts the linguistic register temporally and unexpectedly, submerges back into context, and resurfaces strategically with another shift—we must also engage the possibilities in the musical blue note outside the novel. Dissonant yet dialogic, the blue note forces the musical key of play to cope with "an/Other" inflection of thirds, fifths, sevenths, and microtonalities of otherwise major scale degrees.[4] In Western tonality, "each pitch of a scale functions in a particular way with respect to the others, scale degrees are both numbered [. . .] and named, as follows: I tonic, II supertonic, III mediant, IV subdominant, V *dominant, VI submediant, VII *leading tone or *subtonic" ("Scale degrees," *New Harvard Dictionary* 729). The blue note strategically lowers the tones of the mediant, dominant, and leading tone of a major scale. The blue note's mode of disruption does not cause the major scale to collapse. It does, however, shake the mediant and leading tones, which mediate the power of the tonic and dominant along the hierarchy of the scale.[5] When the blue note lowers the dominant degree, it forces a negotiational dialogue between the dominant and subdominant degrees of the major scale. For example, the lowered dominant in the key of C major is G-flat. Audibly, G-flat shares the same pitch of the inversely raised subdominant F-sharp. Graphically both G-flat and F-sharp retain their distinct positions, but are inflected by flat and sharp symbols, respectively. The graphical/spatial representation of difference translates to a shared space, musically and temporally.

The Arabic and/or Asian microtone inhabits yet another subspace within this dominant/subdominant dialogic. It seeks dialogue with both the dominant and the subdominant. For instance, a microtonally lowered dominant in a C scale produces a G-half flat, not a G-flat. Inversely, a microtonally raised subdominant produces an F-half sharp, not an F-sharp. Neither the half-flat nor the half-sharp degree is stable, because they can be further divided on the

---

4. *The New Harvard Dictionary of Music* defines "Blue note" as follows: "in Afro-American music, especially in *blues and *jazz, the lowered third, seventh, and sometimes fifth scale degrees of the otherwise major scale. The degree of inflection may vary considerably" (98).

5. The tonic and dominant, in harmonic progression, are essential elements in a tonal work. Stefan Kostka and Dorothy Payne state that the "ultimate harmonic goal of any tonal piece is the tonic triad [. . .] The tonic triad is most often preceded by a V (or V7) chord, and it would be safe to say that V(7) and I together are the most essential elements of a tonal work. It is not difficult to find examples in which the harmony for several measures consists only of I and V chords" (110).

scalar continuum. The Arabic or Asian microtone perpetually approximates its precarious position between the subdominant and dominant degrees. If jazz improvisation is a dominant-challenging manifestation, Arabic/Asian microtonality is a sub-subdominant dialogical sound (the microtone negotiates its presence with both the dominant and the subdominant degrees, thereby inhabiting a sub-subdominant position in approximation) in an American jazz setting; hence Arabian jazz is created.

Accentual improvisations in *Arabian Jazz* are ostensibly more accessible than the rarer untranslated improvisations: The former negotiate the English linguistic dominant as a more recognizable manifestation, and the latter challenge both the accentual and the English linguistic dominant in a manifestation of approximation. Like the Arabic microtonal blue note, opaque untranslated words at once deflect and deconstruct meaning into approximate meanings in contextual negotiation. As such, they are the language of "an/Other," not merely the Other. The linguistic blue notes in *Arabian Jazz* at once draw attention to the precarious conditions of Arab immigrants in the US and improvise on the dominant white culture's and minoritized cultures' varying reactions to Arab presence at the site of struggle and negotiation. One can plausibly argue that, like musical improvisation, the linguistic blue note operates at once inside and outside Western culture, even when its manifestations appear within Western linguistic structures and minority Western linguistic styles. The dominant culture becomes suspicious of the traveling practice of improvisation, since it challenges and negotiates both Western and Eastern musical and linguistic forms.

Consequently, some dominant voices in the Western classical music establishment seek to define improvisation as a primitive, other, and aural (as opposed to notated) manifestation. Bruno Nettl asserts that the traditional music establishment "connects improvisation as a musical practice, but even more as a concept, with a kind of third world of music. Jazz, the music of non-western cultures, folk music, and all music in oral tradition are somehow included here [. . .] In the conception of the art music world, improvisation embodies the absence of precise planning and discipline" (7). The musical establishment seeks to other improvisation as the binary opposite to the disciplined achievements of Western music, which reflect the intellectual and technological advancements of the West. Moreover, the binary also creates a moral judgment against improvisation and "jazz musicians as unreliable, with unconventional dress and sexual mores, [and] excessive use of alcohol and drugs" (7).[6] These stereotypes and racializations make difficult the task

---

6. For more on improvised music and middle-class morality see Bruno Nettl (7–10).

of improvisation as a dialogic entity. However, the audible disruption of the Western scale during a jazz performance is nonetheless able to seduce the listener to its improvisations. After all, the performance usually begins not with improvisation, but with a systematic musical context. The improvisation usually takes place in the body of the musical piece. One cannot dismiss the precomposed aspect of jazz. Improvisation in jazz is at once inside and outside the Western musical system and, therefore, is not plausibly reducible to a space of otherness. Rather, the performative aspect of improvisation creates dialogical spaces of the moment, spaces that are difficult to normalize. The classical music establishment's neglect of improvisation comes precisely from an exaggerated fear of such spaces.

Matussem opens up one such space for himself and the white workers at the local garage cum gas station by inviting them to form a band. Matussem's appeal to Fergyl (one of the workers) is itself musical: "Excuse, Sir, I just happen to notice—as your new neighbor—that you are like me, a big lover of music. I want to says, if you don't mind, that I am thinking that a man of such big feelings as you are being is all wrong in job like these" (59). Matussem's plea creates an improvisatory rhythmic pattern (similar to a drum solo) that both surprises Fergyl and disrupts any potential hostility that he might otherwise have for the dark immigrant with the thick accent. The punctuation marks arrange Matussem's syllabic rhythm: two, one, seven, five, five, seven, four, four, and a roll. Listening closely to Matussem's appeal produces the following poetic representation of the rhythmic play:

Excuse,	(two syllables)
Sir,	(one syllable)
I just happen to notice—	(seven syllables)
as your new neighbor—	(five syllables)
that you are like me,	(five syllables)
a big lover of music.	(seven syllables)
I want to says,	(four syllables)
if you don't mind,	(four syllables)
that I am thinking that a man of such big feelings as you are being is all wrong in job like these.	(roll)

Seemingly random at first, Matussem's words and phrases produce audible rhythmic patterns: two phrases of seven syllables flanking two phrases of five syllables followed by two phrases of four syllables. The two five-syllable phrases ("as your new neighbor" and "that you are like me"), as highlighted by the seven-syllable phrases bordering them, deliver two imperative messages: neighborliness and similarity. That is, Matussem attempts to represent himself as a generous-spirited neighbor and to break down the ethnic differences between him and Fergyl.

Fergyl squints at Matussem and tries "to read his lips because Matussem's voice, lowered and foreign, made it impossible for [him] to get all of what he was saying. He did catch the words 'wrong job'" (59). After his initial confusion, Fergyl recognizes the words "wrong job" that appear in Matussem's multisyllabic roll, in which Matussem also emphasizes Fergyl's big feelings. Fergyl realizes that Matussem—a maintenance worker at the hospital—is a working-class fellow who is also trapped in the wrong job. Accordingly, he says to Matussem, "Hang on. I got some guys I want to hear this" (59), "hear" being the operative word. The capaciousness of jazz as a genre allows Matussem and the workers at Lil' Lulu's Garage to perceive that the "world was musical: cars sluicing down Route 31 through Euclid [. . .] voices—any voices—melodious words tripping in random notes: 'Fill . . . er . . . up . . . please . . . high . . . oc . . . tane.' It all had internal cadence" (58). It becomes clear here that the novel is asking its readers to pay attention to the syllabic play, to the cadences of voices and the sounds of the world. As a result, the "random notes" prove not to be so random after all. Not only do the cadences of Matussem's unusual English impress themselves upon the garage workers, but also the ability to hear the world as music—as musical combinations: cars, voices, and foreign accents—acts as another key of play that informs the jazz poetics of *Arabian Jazz*. Matussem's "music transcends national boundaries. If language is the core of ethnic unity, then Matussem's music allows ethnic particularity to reach beyond its own boundaries" (Salaita, "Sand Niggers" 440) and to combine polyphonically with other modalities of expression.

Matussem himself is certainly aware of his lingual improvisation in relation to music and other cultures. Furthermore, "he knew that his patter tickled [his bandmates] Jesse, Owen, and Fergyl, who, he figured, didn't get all that much fun out of life working at the garage" (148). While drumming with the band during rehearsal, Matussem "chanted on" (148):

Calls me Big Daddy, [. . .] I am Père, Abu, Fader, Señor, Senior. Call me Pappy, Pappa, Padre, PawPaw, Sir! I big Arab coming at you, guy, flying in towel, fifty thousand mile a second. Come down from big daddies of time, of Cozy Cole, Coltrane, and Charlie *Bird* Parker. I honk, I roar, I do shimmy shimmy on kitchen floor! A million big daddies from all time and more right here, starts here in juicy jazz and America the beautiful, the fat, the big eater, peripatetic, so on, so on. You get the picture. (148)

Matussem's chant is replete with complex rhythms and melodious words, which in turn yield transcultural and translingual content. After the opening of the five-syllable "Calls me Big Daddy," which places Matussem at the head of the band whose specialty is "supercharged rhythm" (148), the next sentence evens out rhythmically as Daddy is translated across languages: I am Père (three syllables), Abu (two syllables), Fader (two syllables), Señor (two syllables), Senior (two syllables). The sentence opens with a triplet ending with the French Père, which could mean both father and priest. From there, a series of disyllabic nouns begins with Abu, the Arabic for "father of." Obviously, Matussem is Abu Jemorah and Abu Melvina. As the first translation in the disyllabic series, however, the "of" in "father of" refers to the translations of father to come. Matussem becomes Abu Fader, Abu Señor, and Abu Senior: the father of cross-lingual fathers otherwise known as the Big Daddy of them all. Fader is an accented (probably European) version of father in English. The inclusion of Fader in the list of translations serves to remind us that accents are widespread, even though Western European accents are rarely perceived as evidence of inferiority and otherness. Furthermore, a fader (pronounced *fay-der*) is a device or control for varying the volume of sound, as in a cinematographic film. In this case, Matussem is indeed the father of sound, the controller of rhythmic and accented volume. This series ends with the slant rhyme of Señor and Senior, effectively correlating Spanish and English: Mr. and one holding a high and authoritative position, both offering status and respectability.

If this sentence offers a declaration of identity ("I am") across languages and cultures, the sentence following travels out and makes demands of readers and listeners: Call me Pappy (four syllables), Pappa (two syllables), Padre (two syllables), PawPaw (two syllables), Sir (one syllable)! The imperative mode demands that Arabs and Americans alike acknowledge Matussem as an Arab American Big Daddy, and to do so on his own translingual and transcultural terms. Like the previous sentence, this sentence also offers a series of disyllabic accents and translations of "father." Furthermore, the p-sound alliteration across P̲appy, P̲appa, P̲adre, and P̲awP̲aw (my emphasis) creates rhythmic accents—counterpointing lingual accents—that highlight each syllable of the disyllabic words (with the exception of Padre, in which the "P" stresses only the first syllable). The p-alliteration allows us to identify combinations of rhythms within a disyllabic (one foot) meter or a 2/4 time signature. And the variation does not stop there. Pappy is often a child's word for father; Pappa could be the Swedish version of father; Padre is the Spanish for father; and PawPaw is one of the words for father or grandfather in the American South. By improvising on Big Daddy, Matussem demonstrates that the word "Daddy," as a linguistic blue note, is, in fact, many words that signify both shared and differentiated experiences within the US. This includes Abu, the Arab father who claims a space within the multiethnic composition of the US.

The next sentence, "I big Arab coming at you, guy, flying in towel, fifty thousand mile a second," exemplifies this claim of Americanness in unabashedly "broken" English. From the missing first-person singular present "am" and the determiner "a" in between "I" and "big" to the singular "mile" instead of the plural "miles," Matussem scats his way into sociocultural visibility. Unlike the prior two sentences that even out into disyllabic rhythms, this sentence breaks into fluctuating rhythmic patterns that nonetheless begin and end with eight-syllable phrases: I big Arab coming at you (eight syllables), guy (one syllable), flying in towel (five syllables), fifty thousand mile a second (eight syllables). Matussem begins by claiming Arab bigness, a larger-than-life volume that is not so easily overlooked. He then moves to reclaim and improvise the stereotype of the Arab in a turban, alluding to the pejorative "towelhead" (with all of its orientalist, racist, and exotic resonances). Instead of flying on a magic carpet, Matussem creates an image of himself flying on a towel at the impossible speed of fifty thousand miles per second. Matussem thereby forces the stereotype into absurd and humorous registers and claims Americanness because of the stereotype, not in spite of it. He places himself along with the stereotype on a high-speed collision course with those who would both dismiss and render him invisible.

Upon impact, Matussem declares that he comes down from the big jazz daddies of time: "C̲ozy C̲ole, C̲oltrane, and Charlie *Bird* Parker" (my emphasis). Once again, the alliteration adds a rhythmic overlay: The hard c-alliteration emphasizes the first syllable of "Cozy" and the monosyllable of "Cole," which repeats as "Col" in "Coltrane." Matussem's Arab American jazz (musical and lingual) comes down from the sounds of iconic African American jazz musicians. Matussem's identity, visibility, and musical expression are intersectional and intercultural. The next sentence highlights this musicality: I honk (two syllables), I roar (two syllables), I do shimmy shimmy on kitchen floor (ten syllables)! The "I" anaphora appears in all three phrases that constitute the rhythmic sentence, highlighting Matussem's intersectional expression. He honks, roars, and does the ragtime shimmy on the kitchen floor; "roar" and "floor" rhyme, and "shimmy" repeats to stress the shakes and sways of the ragtime shimmy. From there, Matussem returns to the concept of big daddies: "A million big daddies from all time and more right *here,* starts *here* in juicy jazz and America the beautiful, the fat, the big eater, peripatetic, *so on, so on*. You get the picture" (my emphasis). The repetition of "big daddies" now includes figures from all time, not merely US time. The music and rhythm of Matussem's expressions trip US national time and gesture to compound transnational time. This present complex time is stressed in the repetition of "here," in the j-alliteration of "juicy jazz," in peripatetic existence and possibilities—movement is life—as exemplified by the repetition of "so on."

If accented rhythmic improvisation disrupts dominant discourses of race, class, and nation, the case of Arabic and Asian microtonal improvisation (as it manifests in the names of the Arab American characters), gives rise to a further problematic of foreignness. The improvisation in this case consists of importing elements of another system into the Western system's modes of improvisation. This results in an epistemological negotiation between improvisation and *taqsim*, the closest Arabic word for improvisation. *Taqsim* is a valued musical art form in the Arab world. *Taqsim* means "division, dividing, partition, parting, splitting, separation, section(ing); distribution, apportionment, allotment, portioning, dealing out, sharing out; solo; [and] division of labor" (*Al-Mawrid* 354). What *taqsim* does is divide an instrument from the ensemble, which then shares out a solo before returning to the ensemble; this cycle repeats with another instrument as part of a division of labor between instruments. *Taqsim* is an individuating-collective effort then, with all instruments of the ensemble getting a fair share of participation. One way to better understand *taqsim* in relation to improvisation is to place it alongside the jazz phrase "break it down" or "break." A "Break" is an improvised jazz solo, often without accompaniment, "that serves as an introduction to a more extended [accompanied] solo or that occurs between passages for the ensemble" (*New Harvard Dictionary* 113). The breaking down in *taqsim* and "Break" accentuates the solo and ensemble parts of the performance in the contrasting textures and colors it creates.

The blue note allows the Arabic/Asian microtones into its function, as discussed earlier. Therefore, the blue note is, in fact, many notes. It comes as no surprise that the essays comprising *In the Course of Performance: Studies in the World of Musical Improvisation* emphasize "three areas that have received the greatest amount of attention—jazz, South Asia, and West Asia [which includes the Arab world]" (Nettl 16). The density of the blue note is a fruitful place to engage the identity of the improvisational techniques (untranslated words and accentual slippages) in *Arabian Jazz*. How do we read that which resists translation? Let us look back to the novel's opening with its two untranslated words, "Naima" and "Matussem."

Like his daughter Jemorah's name, Matussem's name is subject to transliterational and accentual slippages that produce diverse meanings. As it stands,

Matussem does not readily resonate in Arabic or English. It is an Americanized (accented) transliteration of "Mu'tassem" that rounds the o-like sound of *u* to *a* and sheds the letter "ain" (ع), which is difficult to pronounce in English (not to mention the fact that "ain" has no corresponding letter in the English alphabet). As it travels from Arabic to English, Mu'tassem transmutes dialogically to Matussem, so that Americans can pronounce it with less difficulty. Mu'tassem is the proper-name version of the verb i'tussema, which translates as "to cling to, adhere to, hold fast to, keep to, hang on to; to maintain, keep (up)" (*Al-Mawrid* 128). The transliteration of the name as Matussem, like the transliteration of "Naima," causes an occlusion of the letter "ain" (ع), which should appear after the *a* in both Matussem and Naima. This transliterational suspension causes yet another crisis of meaning. Matussem without the crucial ع, now as an Americanization of "Muttassem," could also mean "marked by, characterized by, [and] distinguished by" ("ittesema," *Al-Mawrid* 30). Both "Matussem" and "Naima" cause crises of meaning in transliteration and translation, but Matussem produces yet another complication: an absent referent. Whether Matussem translates as one who "cling[s] to" or one "marked by," the referent of the name is absent. Who does Matussem "cling to"? What is he "marked by"?

A probable cultural answer to the former question is Allah. But the concept of God, like the proper name, resists translation. How does one translate abstractions and absent referents? In *The Ear of the Other,* Jacques Derrida discusses the God-like desire in every proper name:

> I would say that this desire is at work in every proper name: translate me, don't translate me. On the one hand, don't translate me, that is, respect me as a proper name, respect my law of the proper name which stands over and above all languages. And, on the other hand, translate me, that is, understand me, preserve me within the universal language, follow my law, and so on. (102)

To translate "Matussem" and "Naima" is to attempt to understand their biographies—to translate their positions within their cultures. Interestingly, one of the definitions of *tarjama* (the Arabic word for "translation") posits biography as the translation of a human's life.[7] The *Muhit-Ul-Muhit Arabic-Arabic Dictionary,* which traces *tarjama* etymologically, states that

---

7. *Al-Mawrid: A Modern Arabic-English Dictionary* offers the following definitions for *tarjama*: "1 translation, interpretation, explanation; 2 biography, memoir; 3 auto-biography, memoirs; 4 introduction, preface, foreword" (307). These definitions warrant their own investigation. For the purposes of this chapter, I focus on the definition of biography as translation.

translation is also the remembering/referencing [often in praise] of a person's life history, his character, and genealogical origin, even if it is limited to the mentioning of a person's name and his ancestors' names including the birth order; this is what rhetoricians call the uniformity of succession.

والترجمة ايضاً ذكر سيرة شخص واخلاقه ونسبه فان اقتُصر فيها على ذكر اسم الشخص واسماء ابآئه على ترتيب الولادة فذلك يُقال له عند البديعيين الاطِّراض

(my translation, 69).[8]

This definition alludes to both the translatability and untranslatability of proper names within an intracultural setting, and to the disruption of their genealogical linearity in the movement between cultures. Memory is hardly reliable, especially when its objective is praise. Consequently, the memory that informs the rhetoric of biography is self-subverting, because it recreates what is not necessarily there. Biography as translation is, then, another version of the original even while it tries to normalize the untranslatable aspects of the original by the act of listing ancestry. The listing of ancestry tries to enlist all genealogical versions into the latest one to accentuate the social standing of the person in question. The narrative of biography creates a uniformity which is simply nonexistent in its subject.

When translated interculturally, biography as translation produces an added slippage of meaning in transliteration, which in turn sheds light on the instability of any linguistic system (whether it purports to be universal or not). Not to translate "Matussem" and "Naima" as a form of respect to the untranslatability of proper names, which should not be diffused into the realm of common nouns, is to occlude the very histories which give the proper names their social, cultural, and economic statuses. Matussem's history is disclosed over the course of the narrative. And yet Matussem's history reveals that his home of origin is Palestine, not Jordan, which he and his family claim as origin (this is referred to obliquely in the meanings and the uncertain origins of Melvina's name). Salwa Essayah Cherif explains that the concept of home in the novel is ironic "considering the family's Palestinian origin on the father's side and their loss of any geographic homeland [. . .] followed by the [immigrants'] illusion of making a home in the United States, echoing their parents' illusion of making a home in Jordan" (210). For the Arab American immigrant, especially the Palestinian immigrant, the idea of home is perpetually elusive. Not entirely here and not entirely there, the immigrant is always negotiating the continually changing spaces between the here and there.

---

8. This is my translation of the Arabic definition of *tarjama* pertaining to biography. *Tarjama* has many definitions, as noted above.

The narrative form, then, aims to evade the dilemma of whether to translate Matussem's name; however, the narrative is disrupted by the loss of the geographical origin. This disruption, like that of the blue note, does not stop the biographical narrative from revealing much about Matussem and his family despite the gaps of untranslatability and biography. Furthermore, *Arabian Jazz* disseminates these gaps "through a multiple set of alignments [that] links the white working class with the figures of the Native American and the Palestinian refugee" (McCullough 804). These gaps combine transnationally and transculturally to highlight the connections between disenfranchised groups, allowing us to better appreciate the plight of the Palestinians both under occupation and in the diaspora. Homelessness, in its many forms, is reconfigured along the lines of solidarity and narrative improvisation. In "Beyond Silence," Lisa Suhair Majaj states, "I began to take solace in the written word. Though much of my childhood is a blur, certain memories emerge unbidden [. . .] clinging to the amazing durability and resilience of language I found there, the evidence that homelessness and fear could be narrated, and through narration transformed" (48). Majaj argues here that gaps and blurs are better than silence. Gaps are relational to presence and, therefore, provoke further inquiry and further translational versions. For Majaj, language, not home, is the opposite of homelessness. Narration is transformative, because it offers refuge in another register, a register of presence. And jazz narratives, in their unpredictability and capaciousness, demand attention and close listening.

"Naima" does not afford us the luxury of biographical translation within the novel. As an extratextual importation, which becomes *a-part* of the novel by virtue of that importation, "Naima" provokes us to seek out its history both inside and outside the novel. In the novel, the third-person omniscient narrator reveals that Matussem accompanies the jazz piece "Naima" on drums as a prayer for his Irish American wife, Nora (16), who died of typhus many years ago on a visit to Jordan with Matussem and their two daughters. Matussem thinks that "Coltrane's music seemed to have been written for her, especially 'Naima,' a song so slow and sweetly agonizing that it didn't sound like there were drums in it at all, but on closer listening they were there, on the edges, moving it along so the song didn't just stop and close on itself like a wound" (16). Matussem's scope of representation of "Naima" is in his drum accompaniment to the piece. Even there, the drumming is almost inaudible. The drumming needs a nuanced "closer listening" for one to appreciate its quiet yet essential presence in "Naima," in order to prevent the piece from just stopping and closing "on itself like a wound." Matussem's drumming invites us to pay attention to the varying nuances in "Naima" so that it does not collapse into the wound of memory; in "moving [the musical piece] along" the rhythm re-places "Naima" and, consequently, Nora, in the present tense. It is worth noting that the room in the club in which Matussem and his jazz band perform is called the "Room of the Absolute Present Tense" (286). Drumming to "Naima" ameliorates the pain of Nora's memory because it transposes Nora to the beats of the present to a presence in improvisation. "Naima" is, for Matussem, a version of Nora; the n-alliteration and the a-assonance of both names produce a certain confluence. This intersection of similarity is also an attestation of difference within the names. Points of confluence can be so only when the entities in question exist *a-part*.

What complicates matters further is that Coltrane's wife, "Naima," was born Juanita Austin (Porter 96). She took the name "Naima" after she converted to Islam. Improvising on and changing names to reflect shifts in identity are common to the characters in the novel and to the Arabic linguistic importations that adopt English letters in their migration.[9] For example, Sally, a white aunt of Jemorah and Melvina's who resides in Jordan, changes her name to Salandria to emphasize her newly acquired Middle Eastern identity: "Sally of Howkville dwindled and faded, while Salandria of Amman emerged" (213). Sally is free to choose, inhabit, and emphasize her identity as Salandria; however, name improvisations and changes are sometimes subject to racism, poverty, and coercion. Jupiter Ellis, Ricky Ellis's alcoholic father (Ricky becomes Jemorah's boyfriend later in the novel), gives a different name each time he is admitted to the hospital because he cannot afford to pay the hospital bills: Hank Bovine, Perry Pensch, and Mandingo Fred (164). Apart from her olive-colored skin, "another source of Jemorah's racial victimization is her name, which distances her from normative Americanness" (El-Hajj and Harb 150). Portia, Jemorah's boss, states cruelly, "Oh, sure, you're tainted, your skin that color [. . .] Now, if you were to change your name, make it Italian maybe, or even Greek, that might help some [. . .] I'm telling you, Jemorah Ramoud, your father and all his kind aren't any better than Negroes" (294). Improvisation inverts to impossibility here.

In an earlier conversation with Melvina, in which the two sisters remark on the fact that people always liken them to their father and not their mother, Jemorah states, "People see color first" (194). Portia is not interested in Jemorah's character or her experiences, only in her darker skin color and Arab-sounding name. In attempting to convince Jemorah to pass as white, Portia seeks to reduce her to an inferior version of one possible original: European American. Ironically, Portia's racially compromised rescue attempt (Jemo-

---

9. Such shifts in names are not uncommon in Arab American novels. For example, in the first chapter (titled "Our Given Names") of Randa Jarrar's *A Map of Home*, the narrator, Nidali, informs us that her father's "name is Waheed [but he] was known during his childhood as Said" (3). Furthermore, Waheed riffs on his wife's latent desire to give recently born Nidali a music name: "'you wanted to call her Mazurka? Or Sonatina? Or Ballade? Or, or . . . Waltz?'" (6).

rah does not need rescuing from her father and his culture) places Jemorah perpetually as a second-class citizen who always misses the mark of whiteness. Mona Fayad has challenged the Western construct of the Arab/Muslim woman as "silent, passive, helpless, in need of rescue by the west. But there's also that other version of her, exotic and seductive, that follows me in the form of the Belly Dancer" (170). By reducing Jemorah to a state of silence and helplessness, that is, by placing her first in a position of inferiority, Portia reinscribes that inferiority in relation to whiteness. Jemorah, however, is more at home in the versions and possibilities of her identity, including the choice of exoticism (the "exotic and seductive" as improvisations that offset the stereotype of silence and passive helplessness). Here, "Jemorah's position in the American racial hierarchy becomes more nuanced; instead of resulting in her exclusion from mainstream society, [her skin color] informs her definition as the ethnic female exotic" (El-Hajj and Harb 150). To Portia, however, Jemorah's traveling name and darker skin tone, as products of interethnic and cultural mixing, can exist only as markers of shame and inferiority.

In other words, Jemorah's visibly darker skin and foreign-sounding name are unacceptable markers of mixing in Portia's formulation. But Arabs are already a mixed people. As Evelyn Shakir observes,

> Arab Americans come in a range of colors. Some are nearly as dark as sub-Saharan Africans, a few are blond and blue-eyed, most—eyes brown, hair dark, skin tending to be olive—occupy the middle ground shared by other Mediterranean people [. . .] The desire to assimilate has foundered on this hard rock, this physical evidence of foreignness with all its irrational implications of moral inferiority. (112)

The term "Arab" is loaded and often used pejoratively in America. Indeed, Arabs find themselves misunderstood and unfairly vilified (not unlike black jazz in its early days).[10] Conversely, the dominant culture represented by Portia uses the term "American" as a marker of superiority and exclusivity. What does one then make of this inferior American, this Arab American who nonetheless qualifies as an American? After all, some Arabs can pass as white and have Western names to match. On the other hand, some Arabs are North African. Are they then Arab-African-Americans? Many Arab countries are part of the Asian continent (southwest Asia): Are immigrants from these countries Arab-Asian-Americans? Once the term "Arab," as constructed by the West, becomes applicable to a person or a group, the nuanced shades or tones of

---

10. For example, see Theodor Adorno's *Essays on Music*, "On Jazz" and "Farewell to Jazz."

complex identities and colors are effaced; only the term "Arab" (with its reductive and derogatory tones) remains.

Furthermore, there are differing tones and shades between the terms Arab and Arab American. Homi K. Bhabha argues that "the identity between stereotypes which, through repetition, also become different; the discriminatory identities constructed across traditional cultural norms and classifications, the Simian Black, the Lying Asiatic—all these are *metonymies* of presence" (90). As in Alameddine's *Koolaids,* repetition works on multiple identitarian and musical levels. Repetition of "discriminatory identities" can create identities of resistance; shame created by discrimination becomes a marker of pride and presence. Repetition of discriminatory identities, however, can also create identification by inferiority to the dominant culture. As Randa A. Kayyali notes, many Arabs

> rallied to avoid the stigma and possible immigration exclusion of being classified as "nonwhite" by arguing that they were Caucasians. These arguments were rebuffed on the basis of what was perceived to be popular opinion, called "common knowledge" by the courts. This opinion took into account various factors such as skin color and stereotypes of attitudes toward democracy, the United States, and Islam. (45)

Some Arabs pass as white and some do not. While the term "Caucasian" can overlap with the term "white," the two are not identical. The designation of "Caucasian," as fallacious as it is, used to allow for different tones of skin and included peoples from Europe, West Asia, North Africa, and some parts of India.[11] These terms are as problematic as Western and US constructions of the term "Arab" because they often fail to account for the divergent lived experiences of the peoples they describe.

Moreover, the repetition of "discriminatory identities" has further highlighted sectarian divisions between Arab Americans. Many Christian Arabs have tended to identify with white Americans, while many Muslim Arabs have tended to identify with African and Asian Americans. This religious divide that seeks to mimic the racial one is unsettling because it undermines the very real interaction between Christian and Muslim Arabs. Nada Elia contends:

---

11. This definition of "Caucasian" is dated, and the term currently refers almost exclusively to white-skinned people of European descent. This further problematizes Arab Americans' incorporation "into the United States' system of racial categorization as white" (Abdulrahim 131). For more on the designation of whiteness in relation to Arab immigrants to the US, please see Sawsan Abdulrahim.

> I [...] make it a point to specify that although my family is Christian, I grew up in West Beirut; that is, that part of the city the media refers to as "mostly Muslim." Why should my narrative be simple? [...] I also identify with Muslim culture [...] I believe Islam to be part of Arab culture, my culture. I am sure the Lebanese Christians will choke on this one. (114)

Arabs seeking whiteness by conflating it with Christianity are better off embracing their varied and continually improvised identities, which would allow them to extend meaningful lines of connection to marginalized groups and people of color in the US and to white Americans (the white working class in particular). To some degree, Jemorah and Melvina's Arab side of the family exemplifies this. In a conversation, Jemorah's cousin Nassir states, "Our family is *mejnoon*, you know? Crazy, nuts. Half Muslim, half Christian, they switch back and forth when the mood possesses them. Or they come to this country and pretend to be Presbyterians. Do you understand any of this?" (339). The Arabic importation *mejnoon* is accompanied by its translation "Crazy, nuts." The two sides of *mejnoon* and "Crazy, nuts" (importation followed by translation) are answered contrapuntally by "Half Muslim, half Christian." Earlier, Nassir tells Jemorah, who is tempted to re-immigrate "home" to Jordan, "You're torn in two. You get two looks at a world. You may never have a perfect fit, but you see far more than most ever do. Why not accept it?" (330). The linguistic, cultural, and transliterational/translational improvisations allow this Arab family continually to scat its identity. According to Nassir, though, craziness is the starting position for improvisatory empowerment. Perhaps so, but the concept of "*mejnoon*" is also that of courage and unpredictability, of improvisation and survival, and of solidarity with other oppressed groups.

A cynical reading would unthinkingly reduce "Naima" and Matussem to Arabic and Muslim stereotypes. "Naima," however, is mediated to us by Matussem in reference to Coltrane's piece. This mediation produces voluntary and involuntary improvisations. Matussem's drumming to "Naima" recalls a history that he does not know. Unbeknownst to him, Juanita surfaces with "Naima." Juanita and/or Naima was crucial in helping Coltrane out of his self-destructive habits of alcohol abuse and heroin addiction (Porter 95). Coltrane's exposure to Arabic and Asian forms of Islam through Naima and Muslim musicians had a tangible influence on his musical language. Like Nettl, who groups together jazz, South Asia, and West Asia, Moustafa Bayoumi tells the musical and spiritual stories of "Blacks, Asians, and Middle Easterners" ("East of the Sun" 251) in an American setting. In American minorities' narratives of struggle, the interconnections between blacks, Asians, and Middle Easterners become increasingly clear. These stories and soundings of profound connections are dispersed by the "dominant chord," by the dominant culture. To "modulate" away is only a "minor" excursion, which leads back to a "major ideology" (251). What Bayoumi seems to be prescribing is a sound of many, one that is able to challenge the "dominant chord" beyond the limitations of "minor" subversions that lead back to the "dominant ideology." The prescription is one in which the voicing is clearly differentiated from the "dominant chord."

This is evident in Matussem's musical language, in which he is "poised over his drums, raveling beats through the air, telling story after story through them, like Shahrazad, giving life" (99). The narrator, who is relating Jemorah's impressions of her father's drumming, creates rhythmic cadences that imitate Matussem's percussive expressions. These fall (as enjambed by the commas) into syllables of five, seven, ten, four, and three. The unpredictability of Matussem's rhythms echoes the function of Shahrazad's fantastic stories, which affirm life and rehabilitate King Shahrayar.[12] Matussem's earlier musical appeal to Fergyl and the garage workers had a rehabilitative and generative effect on them, disrupting the dominant culture's (the dominant chord) desire to separate disenfranchised groups. Indeed, Matussem, Fergyl, Owen, and Jesse become family. This solidarity finds its expression in the dialogic compound rhythms that are "the band's specialty: rhythm, supercharged rhythm springing from the tips of Matussem's sticks, rhythm that conjured up trees and swinging vines, waves, and palpitating wings" (148). The word "rhythm" appears three times in the passage, creating a holy trinity of life-giving beats. Matussem's drumming leads the band into a promised land that acknowledges roots (trees and vines) while offering fluidity and freedom (waves and wings): the compound rhythms of uniformity and improvisation—one is of the other as one needs the other.

This struggle with the dominant culture, the "dominant chord," finds resonance in the interactions of the interethnic family in *Arabian Jazz*. Matussem's pain of losing Nora to typhus is coupled with murder accusations. Nora "had refused to get all of the shots and vaccines the family had advised for the trip to Jordan," dubbing the advice "typical Arab patronizing" (78). Arab and American tensions notwithstanding, Nora's racist parents had attempted to create a rift between Jemorah and Matussem when Jemorah was thirteen years old. While talking to Jemorah on the phone, Nora's parents order Jemorah to ask Matussem to tell her the truth about what really transpired in Jordan:

---

12. After discovering his wife's infidelity, Shahrayar marries a virgin every night and puts her to death in the morning to protect his honor. Shahrazad avoids this fate by telling Shahrayar fantastical stories over a thousand and one nights that both save women's lives and rehabilitate him.

Jem had said good-bye [to her Irish American grandparents], hung up, and asked: "Dad, what *is* the truth?"

Matussem looked down, shrugged, and said, "How could I ever know?" Then he put on a Coltrane record and said, "Listen, here's the gospel according to Saint John." And Jem stood in the living room, thirteen years old, listening. (85)

Jemorah, not understanding her grandparents' insinuations, asks Matussem about the meaning of "truth" in general. Baffled, Matussem says, "How could I ever know?" He answers Jemorah by putting on a Coltrane record and asking her to listen to the "gospel according to Saint John [Coltrane]." Matussem places "truth" in Coltrane's jazz. But what is that "truth"?

Coltrane's liner notes for his album *A Love Supreme* shed light on this truth. Bayoumi investigates the language in the liner notes: "The notes continue in this tenor, and anyone with an ear attuned to Islamic language will hear its echoes. 'NO MATTER WHAT . . . IT IS WITH GOD. HE IS GRACIOUS AND MERCIFUL [. . .] IT IS TRULY—A LOVE SUPREME—.' Al-rahman, al-raheem. The Gracious, the Merciful" ("East of the Sun" 261). Coltrane clearly references Islamic language in "He is Gracious and Merciful" to describe his musical language. In *Arabian Jazz* this is inverted: Jazz, especially Coltrane's music, reveals much about the cultural contexts within the novel by linking them transnationally and transculturally. As a young boy in Jordan, Matussem met a sailor who "played a tape machine [. . .] and Matussem heard Dizzy Gillespie walk over the ocean, part the veil of dust, and speak. It was his first intimation of home" (260). This manifestation of cultural cross-referentiality shows the real connections among minority struggles in the US. For Matussem, these begin even before he immigrates to the US. In the jazz of Dizzy Gillespie, he finds his first intimation of home. In this spirit, Bayoumi imports the Qur'anic phrase "al-rahman, al-raheem," Arabic for "He is gracious and merciful," to reveal the Islamic and musical relevance of "A Love Supreme." The translated Qur'anic phrases also reveal the interconnectedness between Muslim African Americans and Muslim Asian Americans, where African Americans "could become 'Asiatics' and remain Black, could be proud of their African heritage *and* feel a sense of belonging to and participation with Asia" ("East of the Sun" 256). Black jazz's capaciousness as a musical genre allows for transcultural musical expressions, and this includes the West Asian (Arabic) *maqam*.

The first track of *A Love Supreme* is "Acknowledgement," which, constructed around a four-note musical line, seems to participate in an Arabic musical *maqam*. "*Maqam*" is "the main modal unit of Arabic music [. . . and] consists of a diatonic scale (sometimes with 3/4 and 5/4 tones)" (*New Harvard Dictionary* 468). But *maqam* also means position, locality, shrine, sanctuary, context, and key in Arabic (*Al-Mawrid* 1086). Bayoumi clarifies this connection:

> Two-thirds of the way through ["Acknowledgement"], Coltrane meanders around the simple theme in every key, as if to suggest the manner in which God's greatness truly is found everywhere, and then the ways in which the band begins to sing the phrase "A Love Supreme," like a roving band of sufi mendicants singing their *dhikr*. The words could change. As the Love is extolled, the phrase begins to include the sounds of "Allah Supreme," another Arabic expression, Allahu Akbar. ("East of the Sun" 261)

Notice that Bayoumi italicizes "*dhikr*" to insist on meaning in the Arabic word's own terms. "*Dhikr*" is a "Sufi ritual consisting of the repetition of words in praise of God" (*Al-Mawrid* 563). Meanings could change, as he argues, in the repetition of "*dhikr*," which itself describes a ritual of repetition. Bayoumi italicizes "*dhikr*" to individuate it. This individuating, however, reflects a collective contextual practice of both placing physicality in the present and transcending it. Context reveals intercultural/interlinguistic negotiational meanings of "*dhikr*." As such, I believe that Coltrane's *A Love Supreme* provides another layer to Bayoumi's interpretation of "Allah Supreme." "God is Love" is a Christian phrase. The word "Supreme" in relation to the Arabic "*Akbar*" refers to Islam. Coltrane places both renderings of Allah/God next to each other. The resulting epistemological rubbing charges the words and translates into Coltrane's musical language, finding its way into Matussem's sometimes Muslim, sometimes Christian, family. *A Love Supreme*'s language is supremely improvisatory and dialogic.

The sphere of dialogue, however, is embedded in human interaction. As Naima effects change in Coltrane, so does Nora change Matussem's life as an immigrant who barely speaks any English; "she taught him how to speak a new language, how to handle his new country. His American lover. Through the year of their courtship she took his hands and fed him words like bread from her lips" (188). It is as if the musical language of "Naima," which translates Coltrane's indebtedness to Naima, inverts to Matussem's need to resurrect Nora. After all, Nora was Matussem's guide, his lifeline, in his new country of residence. Nora's teaching Matussem "to speak a new language" finds its way to his musical language. In drumming to "Naima," Matussem creates musical improvisations (of the present) on what Nora meant to him.

For Matussem, however, drumming also exists apart from "Naima," just as Juanita/Naima the person also exists apart from "Naima" the piece; both are viable on their own even if they are interconnected. At a very basic level, "drumming was living" (187) for Matussem. It is essential for life, even if

> some musicians believed there was no point to drumming without an overlay of melody [. . .] Matussem knew different [. . .] There had been a drummer in his family village, a vagrant, who pounded at hide-covered drums with his hands at sunup and sundown. He had gone to weddings, funerals and births; the other men would sit with him, overturn pots and kettles and drum with three fingers and the heel of their palms, singing, the women ululating their high voices into the desert. (239–40)

The drumming sounds of the vagrant in Matussem's childhood village in Jordan also haunt his drumming in the present. The vagrant drums alone and at weddings, births, and funerals. He experiences solitude and social occasions where both men and women participate in and accompany his drumming. As Matussem drums to "Naima," he also drums to myriad memories that make up the complex of his identity. His ability to drum in solitude allows him to recognize other forms of drumming as well, such as "when Chief Stormy Weather and other men of the Onondaga Nation spoke of sun dancing and ghost dancing, of their movement together to the weaving of voices and drum" (240). Matussem's fluid and hospitable philosophy on drumming, jazz, and improvisation allows him to extend dialogic and cross-cultural lines. Even the Native American chief changes his name as a result of sharing the language of jazz with Matussem. In "sharing [. . .] Matussem's jazz tapes, [Chief] Dean Martin changed his name to Chief Stormy Weather" (194).

"Naima's" multiple meanings attest to these fluid improvisations and possibilities, especially as Matussem seeks to resurrect his Irish American wife's memory through Coltrane's blue note. Music also creates social bonds that cross racial lines. Matussem has dark skin, and his daughters are a lighter shade representing the color combination of their parents. Differing shades of color make for painful identity negotiations in *Arabian Jazz*. Matussem's boss refers to him as "the dirty sand nigger" (99). Fred, the gas station owner whose poor white workers play jazz with Matussem, calls Matussem the "'damn fool, foreign A-rab' that lives next door" (113). Jemorah's boss Portia recalls that Nora had "to ask for a picture of [. . . Matussem] for her parish priest to show around to prove that he wasn't a Negro. Though he might as well have been, really, who could tell the difference, the one lives about the same as the other" (293–94). Dominant traits of power manifest themselves in the novel's middle-class and, ironically, the working-class and lower-middle-class white Americans. They compensate for their lower economic status by asserting racial superiority to African Americans and "sand niggers." Yet Matussem is able to overcome some of this racism by inviting the gas station workers to form a jazz band with him. It comes as no surprise that Matussem chooses jazz, which allows for myriad styles of music, to extend communicative lines to working-class white-Americans. The *strategic improvisational importation* of "Naima," Matussem, and Jemorah as blue notes, ostensibly singular but fraught with multiple positions, shades, and vibrancies, encourages us not to fall into the trap of stereotypes and essentializations.

As I demonstrate earlier in the chapter, Abu-Jaber's accented (accentual and percussive) improvisations accompany the blue notes in *Arabian Jazz*. The playfulness of Abu-Jaber's humorous representations finds its expression in accentual improvisation. In one such example, Jemorah and Melvina's aunt Fatima rebukes her husband Zaeed for not having affairs with other women:

> "But don't you ever think about it? Aren't you even curious about other women?" This he misunderstood as teasing. Gradually she became more insistent until, some years after they'd immigrated, she began speaking only in English and saying things like: "What wrong with you? Are you man or blob? All the husband of Ladies' Pontifical Committee are having affair. Am I to put up with your big husband demands all by myself? I am a wife or a maid, I want to know!" (55)

Abu-Jaber turns the stereotypes of the womanizing Arab man and the abused Arab woman on their heads. In this passage an outspoken, bullying wife demands that her poor docile husband have an affair. The caricature is full of humor, but it surreptitiously makes a political statement by improvising on linguistic representation. Here, English represents immigrant English as well as a foreign language (Arabic). When the English represents the Arabic, the sentences are grammatically sound ("But don't you ever think about it? Aren't you even curious about other women?"). When the English represents immigrant English, the sentences are grammatically unsound ("What wrong with you? Are you man or blob? All the husband of Ladies' Pontifical Committee are having affair").

Fatima's articulations in English break down rhythmically into four syllables and five syllables and then a nineteen-syllable roll ending with the word "affair." Two almost syllabically equivalent questions yield a roll of syllables as an answer. While Fatima's English is uneven, the rhythms of her sentences produce audible, aesthetically pleasing patterns. Furthermore, the formal representation of Arabic is positive because it is grammatically sound, while the contextual (cultural) representation is preposterous. It is difficult to believe that a Christian-Arab wife would bully her husband into having an affair. The translation of Arabic into proper English and the nontranslation of immigrant English into grammatically unsound English devilishly combine translation and representation to produce a striking caricature. By placing translation and caricature-like representation together, Abu-Jaber exposes the deep biases of the dominant culture manifested in translation as representation.

These biases are intensified by Fatima and Zaeed's religion: they are Christian Arabs, members of a group in the Arab world that rarely gets any representation by the West and the US. In stereotypes "Arab" is usually conflated with "Muslim"; that is, there is no real distinction between an Arab and a Muslim. The passage represents Christian Arabs as the preposterous opposites of Muslim stereotypes: The meek Muslim woman who has to cope with her husband's infidelities becomes the overbearing Christian woman who coerces her husband to find a mistress. Furthermore, Fatima gets the mistress idea from her church group in the US, the "Ladies Pontifical Committee," whose husbands have affairs. This inverse and grotesque misrepresentation implies that Christian/American ethics openly allow for infidelity: Christian women champion their husbands' infidelities to free themselves from their husbands' sexual demands. Thus, the mistresses become the husbands' maids so that the wives can have leisure time. In this inversion, Abu-Jaber's caricature-like play pushes the illogic of Islamophobic discourse to its conclusion, exposing its representational poverty.

The comical play with Christian and Muslim stereotypes reinverts to Matussem and Nora's serious and loving interethnic relationship. The novel ends with Matussem playing drums to "Naima" in what appears to be a full circle:

> He pulled out a battered copy of *Giant Steps* and went to his drums. When "Naima" came on he swirled the brush around his drumhead and gently, sweetly, began tapping. In the swish of the drum, in the high register of the sax's voice, she came to him again, dancing like the original mystery of her language, its jinni's tongue. Her image turned, bent to him, the world in her gesture, the mystery of her love, releasing him. (373–74)

The return to "Naima," like the repetition in the Sufi "*dhikr,*" changes the meaning of "Naima" for Matussem. He calls to his dead wife from his drums, and she appears again—only this time she is there to release him "in the original mystery of her language," which Matussem translated into many versions in his previous drumming. He could not release her then because he did not realize that he could not reconstitute his life with her in his musical translations. The quiet of the musical piece "Naima" softens the pain of Matussem's identity negotiations as an Arab American without his wife Nora, who had mediated America for him. Matussem realizes that "his memories had run too sweet; they needed the bitterness of earth to temper them, and the clarity of the present, of music, to bring out new life" (353). Jazz's modality of the present wins out in the end, even when Matussem's previous drumming sought Nora in the tempos of the past.

This release of music spreads to Jemorah, who dances to her father's drumming with her mixed (white and Native American) boyfriend Ricky. Jemorah and Ricky had always had a connection. As teenagers, they recognized the mixings within each other; as adults, this recognition developed into a love relationship. Unlike Jemorah, Ricky passes as white, but Jemorah had always sensed the layers in him, imagining him as faun (also a mixed being) playing the panpipes: "She stared at him, thinking of the panpipes and the faun, the impossible music, sounds that haunted the forest and enchanted animals" (372). Ricky's is a complex and magical music that is capable of conjuring the impossible. When Matussem senses their closeness, he invites Ricky to join the band as their vocalist, making him a part of the motley family. It is important to note here that Matussem's sensitivity and love for his daughters pose a serious challenge to the stereotype of the controlling and abusive Arab father. Dancing with Ricky to the sounds of Matussem and his band, Jemorah "could hear the sound of the drums through the movement of Ricky's chest, jazz and trills of Arabic music, bright as comet tails, and through this, the pulse of the world" (374). Like Matussem's connection to Nora through Coltrane's "Naima," Jemorah is able to hear "trills of Arabic music" in Ricky's chest.

In a final improvisation at the end of the novel, Matussem says, "Coaltrain [. . .] We're pulling out" (374). Coltrane becomes "Coal-train," pulling the family away from the weight of the past to bring out new life. Jemorah's name, as an accented version of the Arabic Jemrah, as "live coal," combines with the music. Matussem places Jemorah in his improvisation of "Coal-train," and that infuses new life into Matussem's understanding of Coltrane and "Naima." Hence, "We're pulling out." The family is "pulling out" of pain, stereotypes, and fixed spaces into dynamic, traveling negotiations. In this closing gesture of improvisation, the family enters a condition of density as a collective and inclusive blue note, as a traveling compound rhythm, one that is truly Arab American.

The linguistic blue note in this novel, with its musical implications, is in fact many notes. As an importation from another language (Arabic) into English, the linguistic blue note extends a dialogic bridge to the dominant language by adopting the English letter form while insisting on its Arabic content. At some level, the blue note challenges the adequacy of English to represent linguistic, cultural, and political Arabic issues. This dialogic compromise, as we have seen in the names of Matussem, Jemorah, and Naima, comes with a price: Transliterational suspensions in which Arabic letters that do not have corresponding letters in the English alphabet are both occluded and occulted, and are Americanizations that render the names in perpetual improvisation between languages and cultures. Consequently, the curtailed transliterated words find possible resonances and retranslations in Arabic words other than the originals. Origin modulates to myth of origin and yields multiple origins; the Arabic blue note enters a mode of self-reflexivity in its ontological search as it challenges the English linguistic system. The challenge comes from necessity, because the blue note manifests strategically across the novel. Symbolic of Arab underrepresentation in the US, the blue note speaks back, even if opaquely and obliquely, from that same reduced space; and it does so dialogically. It is precisely jazz, and the jazz idiom of linguistic, accented improvisation in the characters' articulations and names, that allow Matussem, Jemorah, and "Naima" to travel and extend lines to African Americans, Asian Americans, Native Americans, Irish Americans, working-class Americans, and white Americans. While the blue note, as many notes of blue, and Matussem's accented rhythms suggest dislocation, pain (they are blue and peripatetic, after all), and continuing negotiation of time and space in terms of improvisation, translation, and transliteration, they are also manifestations of hope in their dialogic capacity. The characters' Arab American names and Matussem's accented lingual rhythms disrupt dominant perceptions of Arab Americans in the US. Translation, transliteration, improvised English, and uneven grammar all create expressions of the moment, propelling Arab Americans to peripatetic and transcultural modes of visibility on Arab American terms.

CHAPTER 3

Sign after Sign

Mohja Kahf's *The Girl in the Tangerine Scarf*

Mohja Kahf's first novel, *The Girl in the Tangerine Scarf* (*Tangerine Scarf* henceforward), appeared in 2006, which places it in the timeframe of post-9/11 anti-Arab and anti-Muslim backlash in the US. Kahf does not tackle the repercussions of 9/11 directly in *Tangerine Scarf*, however. Instead, she takes the rising tide of Islamophobia in the US as an occasion to tell the story of what it meant to live and grow up as a Muslim in the US before 9/11. In other words, Kahf renders visible the challenges of the Shamys, a Muslim Syrian immigrant family in 1970s to early 1990s Indiana, both to humanize them and to demonstrate that anti-Muslim attitudes and violence are not merely reactions to the terrorist attacks of 9/11. Islamophobia has a long history in the US. Unsurprisingly, *Tangerine Scarf* shares many of the themes, as well as the poetics of visibility that manifest in *Koolaids* and *Arabian Jazz*. To challenge Arab American sociocultural and political invisibility, both pre-9/11 novels employ innovative thematics and poetics that promote complex art forms of visibility. *Koolaids* correlates the traumas of the Lebanese Civil War with those of HIV-positive gay men in San Francisco in intersecting vignettes; *Arabian Jazz* uses elements of African American jazz (improvisation and the blue note) to improvise on Arab American identity, extemporizing in the process intersectional Arab American identities that participate in the cultural production and experiences of African Americans, Native Americans, Irish Americans, and the white working class. *Koolaids* and *Arabian Jazz* establish Arab Americans as transcultural citizens who participate in the cultural and political inheritances of fellow disenfranchised and marginalized Americans. Kahf's novel demonstrates that Muslim Arabs and Muslim Americans are also transcultural citizens. What, then, is *Tangerine Scarf*'s poetics of visibility, and how does it complicate dominant perceptions of Islam and Muslim Americans?

Tangerine Scarf became critically and commercially successful precisely because it dealt squarely with Islam as a primary and complex theme (Salaita, *Modern* 32). In a sense, *Tangerine Scarf* acts as an Islam 101 course for non-Muslim Americans and as a critique and a means of self-reflection for Muslim Arab Americans. Because the novel is written in a mostly straightforward and accessible style, critics have tended to write and talk about it sociopolitically. For example, Steven Salaita writes, "Although it is important for literary critics to situate social themes within their aesthetic settings, *The Girl in the Tangerine Scarf* lends itself to a sociopolitical reading because of its obvious activist dimensions" (41). Salaita's point is valid precisely because the novel "often reads like a social document embedded in the genre of fiction" (40). I had a similar reaction to *Tangerine Scarf* when I first read it, and I almost did not include it in my book on that account. This is an issues novel, I thought to myself, and I would be hard-pressed to justify its inclusion among the more aesthetically and formally challenging novels of my project. Not including *Tangerine Scarf* would have been a grave mistake, however. After two subsequent readings of the novel, I realized—its thematic importance notwithstanding—that it offers a nuanced and subtle poetics crucial to its intricate religio-political message. If *Tangerine Scarf* allows for an honest and complex image of Islam and Muslims in the US to materialize, a poetic reading allows the novel to emerge as a work of art.

The first sentence of *Tangerine Scarf* finds the main character, Khadra Shamy, whose name translates literally as "green one of Damascus," calling "the highway sign that claims 'The People of Indiana Welcome You'" (1) a liar. Khadra is on her way to cover a national Islamic conference in Indiana, where she grew up in a religious Muslim community in the 1970s. Immediately afterwards, the third-person narrator reveals that Khadra is olive-skinned and dark-haired, suggesting that these visual markers alone are enough to warrant a denial of welcome. Two pages later, Khadra drives by a burned-out storefront in front of which "burly beardless white men in denim and work shirts sit [. . .] The giant charred store sign, Marsh's, leans against a telephone pole" (3). The narrator personifies Marsh's charred store sign; like the burnt-out white working men who sit in front of Marsh's, the weathered sign itself leans wearily against a telephone pole. Perhaps having no other place to hang out after work or having no work to do, the men claim the storefront as their territory. Khadra "feels [the men] screw their eyes at her as she drives past, her headscarf flapping from the crosscurrent inside the car. She rolls the windows up, tamps her scarf down on her crinkly dark hair, and tries to calm the panic that coming back to Indiana brings to her gut" (3). Neither the Indiana highway sign nor the Marsh's sign seems to offer Khadra any welcome. Instead, she panics when the men screw their eyes at her headscarf. Its flapping in the crosscurrent alludes to the headscarf as a site of cultural contestation, in which one current works to yank the headscarf away from Khadra's head while another current presses it to her head. Khadra's view of veiling is almost certainly at odds with the white men's perception of the hijab-wearing Khadra passing them by. For Khadra, their gaze carries with it the threat of violence. Whether or not this group of white working men in fact wishes her any ill will remains unclear. Khadra's experiences of Islamophobia as a young girl in Indiana—including the rape and murder of Kenyan American Zuhura, who was a member of Khadra's Muslim community—and during her college years, however, tell a story that both the highway sign's blanket welcome and Marsh's white male guardians render invisible.

This chapter argues that *Tangerine Scarf* sets in motion a crisis of signification as effectuated by highway, billboard, and building signs that appear throughout the novel (in the US, Saudi Arabia, and Syria) to highlight the gulf between dominant and marketplace modes of signification and the lived experiences of ethnic and religious minorities. The highway signs and billboards come to parallel the reductive and overdetermined Islamophobic discourse of the veil, in which dominant significations of the veil are at odds with Khadra's complex experiences of veiling and unveiling. I read the epigraphs that begin every chapter in the novel as reliable, intersectional signs that counter sweeping and fallacious signs. The poetics of cross-signification interweaves the epigraph signs with Khadra's lived reality, even as the epigraph signs combine vertically (with the content of the chapters in which they appear), horizontally (with epigraph signs from other chapters), and diagonally (with themes in other chapters before or after the chapters in which they appear).[1] That is, the epigraph signs act as portals to the novel's themes in and across chapters and therefore shrink rather than expand the rift between signification and lived experience. *Tangerine Scarf* offers a constellation of signs—chapter epigraphs, highway signs, billboards, business signs, and even songs (audible signs)—as counterpoint to visible and stereotypical signs of Islam such as veils, beards, turbans, and darker skin tones.

---

1. The epigraph signs' vertical, horizontal, and diagonal combinational possibilities are similar to those of the vignettes in Alameddine's *Koolaids*. They allow for likely and unlikely aesthetic and thematic connections, for shifts in perceptions, and for parallactic modifications.

THE FIRST CHAPTER AS PRODUCTIVE SYNECDOCHE

The first chapter of *Tangerine Scarf* establishes a poetics of cross-signification that permeates the rest of the novel. Acting as a synecdoche for the entire novel, the first chapter offers an epigraph sign, sections separated by gaps, an interplay between the present tense and the past tense (the present tense representing Khadra's present thoughts and actions, and the past tense conveying pertinent episodes in her past), and a range of signs. The first chapter's epigraph sign offers a quote from Sue Monk Kidd's 1996 memoir, *The Dance of the Dissident Daughter*: ". . . my creative life is my deepest prayer. . . ." (1). Kidd's memoir tells the story of a traditionally religious, churchgoing mother who begins to question her role and position as a woman in her cultural milieu, family, and church after she finds herself in the middle a feminist spiritual awakening. That Kahf points to a Christian memoir to begin her novel about Khadra's Muslim spiritual journey is worth considering. This intersectional epigraph begins the process of disrupting the Islamophobic notions that gender inequality is exclusive to Islam and that Syria is exclusively Muslim. Instead, the epigraph invites the novel's readers to associate the gender issues inherent in both Christianity and Islam. In "The Pity Committee and the Careful Reader: How Not to Buy Stereotypes about Muslim Women," Kahf emphasizes that "critiquing oppression in the global Muslim community while simultaneously critiquing oppression committed by and in Western societies, waging a double-fronted battle, pries gender work out of both camps" (121). The poetics of cross-signification's prying of gender work from Christianity and Islam is especially effective in *Tangerine Scarf* because it accounts for the inequalities of power and the racing of Islam in the US. Furthermore, the quote from *The Dance of the Dissident Daughter* combines creativity and prayer, placing Khadra's bildungsroman and religio-cultural negotiations within a poetics of signs (creativity), a poetics which also serves as a novelwide prayer for Muslims and the US.

The first chapter's epigraph sign combines vertically with the content of the chapter. The second page of the novel finds Khadra getting out of her car "at Glen Miller Park to pray *fajr* on the grass near a statue labeled *Madonna of the Trail*." "Fajr" is the first of the five obligatory daily prayers in Islam, and it translates literally as "aurora; dawn; daybreak" (*Almaany.com*). In the context of Islam, however, "fajr" is the prayer that takes place before sunrise. "Fajr" appears in italics as an example of selective lexical fidelity, which "leaves some words untranslated in the text [. . . as a] device for conveying the sense of cultural distinctiveness" (Ashcroft et al. 63).² The cultural distinctiveness is religious here, but it is a dialogic distinctiveness. On the one hand, "fajr" serves as a contrast to the *Madonna of the Trail* statue, next to which Khadra decides to pray. On the other hand, the italics are common to both "fajr" and the statue's label, allowing both to combine visually in the sentence. That is, while both "fajr" and the Madonna statue are distinct religio-culturally, the italics (as common visual markers) refer to possible overlaps between Christianity and Islam. For one, Mary (Maryam in Islam) holds an exalted place in Islam. The Qur'an states: "Behold! The angels said: 'O Mary! God hath chosen thee and purified thee—chosen thee above the women of all nations" ("Surat Al-Imran," Yusuf Ali translation, *QuranBrowser.org* 3:42). Furthermore, Islam upholds the tenet of the virgin birth of Jesus (Isa in Islam). These are facts that Islamophobes willfully overlook, opting instead to obsess over the veil as a symbol of oppression and backwardness. And yet both Khadra and the Madonna's hair is covered modestly (with a headscarf and a bonnet respectively).

The connection does not end there, however. The *Madonna of the Trail* is a recurring public statuary that stands in twelve locations across the US, tracing a historical travel route from the covered-wagon days. The statues all depict a "stony-faced pioneer Mom, in long dress and bonnet, strutting westward clutching a rifle with one hand, an infant with the other, with another little cruncher grasping Mom's skirt" ("Madonnas of the Trail"). Khadra's Muslim missionary parents are pioneers at the Dawah Center, a conservative Muslim community whose mission is to promulgate "true" Islam to the transnational Muslim communities and converts in the US. Like many American pioneers, the Shamys left their country of origin (the secular Syria of Hafez Al-Assad in the Shamys' case) to practice their religion away from persecution. Khadra's "fajr" prayer next to the Madonna statue, seemingly incongruous at first, aligns the missionary hopes of Islam in the US with those of the American missionary pioneers, which are codified into the dominant culture. *Tangerine Scarf* emphasizes that the story of missionary Islam and Muslims in the US is neither alien nor un-American; rather, it follows some of the established routes of the early pioneers in the US. It comes as no surprise that Khadra buys "a postcard of the *Madonna of the Trail: Greetings from Richmond*" (2) to send to her parents.

Eyeing the postcard, Khadra "thinks: sloppy work. I could do better" (2). Khadra is a photographer for *Alternative Americas,* on assignment to cover

---

2. For more on the term "selective lexical fidelity" and its improvisatory role in relation to the English language, please consult chapter 2.

an Islamic national conference taking place at Indiana University's Bloomington campus. How best to represent the Islamic conference, which includes members of the Muslim community in which she grew up, is on her mind. She knows quite well that the stakes of representation are much higher for her assignment than they were for the photographer of the Madonna postcard. The postcard's photographer could afford to be "sloppy," as a careless representation of the *Madonna of the Trail* would not warrant the scrutiny of the dominant culture, at least not in the same way that a sloppy visual representation of Muslims would. Khadra had thought about this before her current assignment. She "wanted her photographs to find the truth of their subject, to see beyond first appearances. To discern. But what truth can a photo get? How do you see something true and real about a person, any person?" (357). Painfully aware of surface messages and interpretations of signs (images, highway signs, billboards, veils, beards, and skin tones), Khadra enters the fray of visual signifiers, conscious that she "could do better," that she must do better aesthetically and representationally. The questions that she raises find resonance in the poetics of cross-signification that permeates the novel.

The first section of the first chapter, which finds Khadra driving to the Islamic conference, begins in the present tense. After the episode in which the white men screw their eyes at Khadra's headscarf, the chapter introduces a gap, which signals the end of one section and the beginning of another. The first chapter consists of two sections in the present tense that frame three consecutive sections in the past tense. This intrachapter movement between tenses and time reflects the "novel's time frame [that] traverses between a present describing Khadra's temporary return to her Muslim community in Indianapolis and a past featuring insightful snapshots of her formative experiences in Indiana as well as in Mecca, Damascus, and Philadelphia" (Fadda-Conrey, *Contemporary* 70). The novel's chapters initially oscillate between the present and past tense, settle into the past tense for the majority of the novel, and then resolve into the present tense toward the end.

Why, one might ask, does *Tangerine Scarf* fall into this pattern? The highway signs, billboards, and business signs that Khadra encounters (as in the lying highway sign and the Marsh's sign) trigger memories of her past. Khadra drives to the Islamic conference in the present, while her mind travels by degrees to the past. Thus, these signs become portals to Khadra's past—which she must reassess critically to actualize her newer self—much as the epigraph signs become cross-cultural and cross-poetic portals that complicate, in combination with the content of the chapters, our understanding of Islam and Muslims. In other words, the novel's form, time play, and poetics of cross-signification all counterpoint and drive Khadra's self-reflections and the subsequent revelations of Islam in the US. Furthermore, her wanderings in the present and past appear in section "snapshots," as Fadda-Conrey identifies them, and these clearly relate to Khadra's aim of taking photographs that see beyond first appearances. The section snapshots, as a poetics of form or a poetic justice of form, realize Khadra's photographic aspirations in that they see beyond Khadra's headscarf and the visual markers of the Muslim community of her childhood.

Before the present-tense section ends with the white working-class men staring at Khadra's headscarf, the section offers a series of signs and a song. As she drives, "Khadra sees a sign for the 'Centerville Christian Church.' Isn't that redundant? she wonders. Like 'Muslim Mosque?'" (2–3). Khadra's questions raise the issue of overdetermined discourse. Although the concept of church can extend to include a non-Christian place of worship, it would be difficult to imagine anyone passing by the Centerville church (in Indiana to boot) and confusing it with a synagogue or mosque, for example. The overdetermined sign signals that Christianity is somehow at risk, that it must be reaffirmed and protected at every turn. The redundancy that Khadra identifies serves as a rallying call in which the dominant religion in the US imagines itself as the victim of encroaching non-Christian religions such as Islam. That is, Christianity is made to appropriate the vulnerabilities and struggles of minority religions in the US, while it continues to dominate the nation's religio-cultural discourse.

The radio in Khadra's car is playing while she thinks about the church sign. The news report covers the ethnic cleansing campaign in the Bosnian War, and the Indy 500. Then, "finally, some music: Sade pouring out 'Bullet Proof Soul'" (3). The radio station's coverage of the Bosnian War serves to demonstrate that Islam, and a raced or ethnicized version of the same, is at risk in multiple areas in the world and that many Muslim communities face discrimination, violence, or genocide. While the US news media outlets covered the Bosnian War, their coverage did not have a measurable effect on the dominant Islamophobic narrative. Anti-Arab and Muslim sentiments rose in the years following the Gulf War (1990–91), which was waged by a coalition of nations led by the US as a response to Iraq's invasion and annexation of Kuwait. The news coverage, along with Khadra's thoughts, acts as a running commentary on the church sign. The news then turns to the Indy 500, which is set to take place around the same time as the Islamic conference. We find out later in the novel that Hanifa (one of Khadra's African American childhood friends) is racing a car in the Indy 500, the first Muslim woman to do so. While this is a Muslim woman's intersectional success story that breaks color, religious, and gender lines, Khadra understands that attending or racing in the Indy 500 is "like following the white man into his lair" (438).

The radio station then plays Sade's song, "Bullet Proof Soul," to Khadra's relief. "Finally, some music," she thinks to herself. Although it is a love song in which Sade pours out her soul in a warm silken voice, the metaphor of love as a gun that shoots slow bullets nonetheless reminds Khadra both of Islamophobic violence and, perhaps, her long-unspoken attraction to Hakim (Hanifa's brother who is now an imam). The inclusion of "Bullet Proof Soul" on page 3 of the novel attests to the ameliorative power of songs. Even while the song reminds Khadra of her painful past, its exquisiteness offers relief from that same past. As Sade's song plays on the radio, Khadra passes by a few more signs: "Mary Lou and Mother, Rabbit Foot Crafts," "Stimpson Grain Drying Corp.," and "100% American" (3). The latter sign "advertises—what, she doesn't know" (3). The sign does not advertise any tangible product, but seems to suggest a state of being that touches upon the commodified lives of all who reside in the US. As such, its statement raises a slew of troubling questions. What does it mean to be 100 percent American? Is such a final and complete state of being possible or even desirable? Who decides what constitutes 100 percent Americanness? If any product or person is less than 100 percent American, are they then not quite American? The questions I raise relate to Khadra and her family, who, although naturalized citizens, are rarely perceived as Americans by members of the dominant culture. The first section of the first chapter, then, clearly places signs at the center of the novel's poetics and themes. And these signs warrant a careful, poetic consideration.

The signs of the first section trigger an early memory in Khadra's mind, and the chapter offers three consecutive snapshots of Khadra's childhood in Indiana, in which she is tormented by the Lott boys. The narrator informs us that the "Lott boys had been the bane of Khadra and her family since day one. The day years ago when the Shamys moved in to number 1492 Tecumseh Drive, Fallen Timbers Townhouse Complex, Indianapolis, Indiana, on the southern city limits where the sprawling city almost met up with the small adjoining town of Simmonsville" (5). The Shamys' place of residence is not accidental. The number 1492 draws a parallel between the contacts of the newly arrived Shamys and their Islamophobic, anti-immigrant neighbors and the European entry into the Americas. When the Lott boys throw beer bottles at the Shamys' doorstep, Wajdy attempts to reason with Vaughn Lott about his sons' behavior. Vaughn yells at Wajdy, "—ACCUSING MY CHILDREN—OFF MY PORCH—BACK WHERE YOU PEOPLE CAME FROM!" (6–7). The Shamys' 1492 address ironizes this moment, as Native Americans should have the final claim to the land, not the Lotts. If the Shamys should go back to where they came from, so should the Lotts. But the allegory of the Shamys' address does not end there. Junaid Rana explains that "Tecumseh also represents a native folk hero who fought against American intrusion into tribal lands and the famous Battle of Fallen Timbers that led to Tecumseh's rebellion" (509). The address, therefore, recalls a long history of settler-colonial violence. It points both to this history's newer iterations in suburban Indianapolis and to the need for resisting Islamophobic and racist attitudes and violence.

What the Lott brothers see when the Shamys move in is "a bunch of foreigners. Dark and wrong. Dressed funny. Their talk was gross sounds, like someone throwing up" (6). The Shamys' (in)visibility hinges on these characteristics, which the narrator delivers in both complete sentences and fragments. The two sentence fragments highlight the Shamys' appearance in trisyllables. The syllabic equality between the two sentence fragments delivers, ironically enough, inequality: "Dark and wrong" and "dressed funny." The racial and sartorial markers of difference, the outward signs, are amplified by the "gross sounds, like someone throwing up" that the Shamys utter. For the Lott boys, the Shamys are not speaking a viable language (Syrian Arabic) but are producing disgusting, nonhuman sounds. The Shamys' visual and audible markers of difference incite the Lott brothers to violence (throwing beer bottles at the Shamys' doorstep). Vaughn Lott's reaction to Wajdy's appeal clearly indicates that this is not a case of two boys misbehaving, but one of systemic racism and xenophobia, which must be resisted. Unsurprisingly, it is the Muslim African American al-Deen family who stands in solidarity with the Shamys. Hanifa and Hakim, young Khadra and her brother Eyad's friends, rush to defend them against the Lott boys.

In one incident, we find Brian Lott gunning for Khadra on his dirt bike, the "back of her head [. . .] still ridged from where he'd knocked her against the brick of the apartment wall last time" (4). Fortunately, her brother Eyad, Hakim, and Hanifa arrive on their bikes before Brian can reach Khadra. Hakim asks Khadra to hop on behind him and they wheel off. Eyad then confronts Brian:

"Brian Lott, whyn't you go pick on someone your own size?" Eyad yelled at the boy on the dirt bike.
"Fuck you, raghead!" Brian shouted back. "We're gonna get all you fuckers!" He wheelied on "fuckers." (5)

Eyad calls Brian out for gendered violence, implying that only a coward would target a young girl. Far from a helpless victim, however, Khadra had "kicked him in the shin [when Brian attacked her on an earlier occasion] and she would do it again, even if it was a fight she must lose" (4). Outnumbered and unwilling to tackle Eyad physically, Brian resorts to Islamophobic name-calling, hurling the epithet "raghead." Next, Brian uses the first-person plural pronoun "we" to remind Eyad that he is not a lone operator, that the threat to the Shamys and their Muslim community is extensive. Since he is alone at the moment, Brian wheelies his bike and flees the scene. Khadra and Eyad learn a lesson in transnational solidarity from Hakim and Hanifa at a young age, and it is Islam, common both to the Syrian immigrants and to their African American neighbors, that solidifies it. Furthermore, this incident draws Hakim and Khadra closer together. After the confrontation with Brian, Eyad asks Khadra to get on his bicycle as their mother, Ebtehaj, might see her riding behind Hakim. Khadra "was getting older now, and her mother said that she shouldn't ride with boys anymore" (5). While Khadra and Hakim's chemistry does not go unnoticed by her family, their attraction to one another does not move beyond that until the very end of the novel. The reasons for this unrealized romance are complex, and they include Muslim-on-Muslim racism. Khadra and Hakim's relationship and the cracks and fissures that it exposes in the Dawah community (including the rift between Islamic teachings and their practice) are worthy of their own investigation. For the purposes of this chapter, I confine my analysis to the poetics of cross-signification in relation to Islamophobia and its gendered praxis.

The final section snapshot of the first chapter, which returns us to the present, finds Khadra passing signs once again on the highway: "'Home of James Whitcomb Riley.' 'Pecans, We Buy and Sell' (hand-lettered on rough boards). 'Merchants and Farmers Bank, your neighbors who care.' 'Indianapolis Motor Speedway, use 465 to 65'" (7). From a poet's home to the motor speedway, sign after sign accosts Khadra. The Merchants and Farmers Bank claims to be a caring neighbor. Like the lying "The People of Indiana Welcome You" sign that Khadra encounters on page 1 of the novel, the bank also offers a misleading slogan. One has to worry when a for-profit financial establishment claims caring neighborliness, as this appropriation redefines neighborliness along transactional and business-interest lines. It is highly doubtful that any bank would help a neighbor who is not a customer or even care about an existing customer outside of transactions that benefit the bank first and foremost. This business appropriation of neighborliness finds its echo later in the novel, when Khadra and her family perform hajj in Saudi Arabia. On the road to Mecca, the Shamys pass "billboards that said, 'Welcome, Guests of the Compassionate One,' 'Seiko,' and 'Panasonic.' 'Give praise to God, the lord of the Worlds,' flashed another highway sign, and beside it, brilliantly lit, a picture of a VCR with a Sony logo" (161). As transnational corporations and mercantilism permeate the globe, they override practices of goodwill or spiritual considerations, rendering them ancillary to profit and market considerations.

It is as if the billboards are asking, "Performing pilgrimage? Why not buy a Seiko watch and a VCR while you are at it?" Advertisements aside, even the signs that give directions to the Indianapolis Motor Speedway are not helpful at this time of year, as there is "no sense getting pulled into Indy 500 traffic" (7). One has to be in the know, to be a local or insider, in order to find better routes than the ones advertised to the general public.

Khadra finds an alternative route, "'New Palestine Jct. 74.' And finally, 'Welcome to Indianapolis—City at the Crossroads'" (7). The substitute route is a shout-out to Palestine. Khadra must pass through New Palestine—a Palestine of the New World—to find her way back to Indianapolis and the suburb in which she grew up. If Indiana is at the crossroads of the US, Khadra finds herself at the crossroads of her past and present. This homecoming of sorts is Khadra's own, parallel right-of-return despite the efforts of white supremacists and Islamophobes who seek to drive Muslims away. She looks "for the exit sign that will lead her back to horrible little Simmonsville. *Back where you came from*" (7). Khadra repeats Vaughn Lott's words to her father when the Shamys were in the process of moving into the Fallen Timbers Townhouse Complex. The exit sign that leads to Simmonsville reminds Khadra of her family's struggles against racism and Islamophobia and allows her to export "*Back where you came from*" to the present. In this iteration, however, Khadra reclaims Simmonsville as the place that she came from. The Muslim community that saw Khadra through her formative years has as much claim on the suburb of Indianapolis as any other group residing there.

This crisis of signification in the signs that Khadra encounters certainly relates to Islamophobic slogans that condemn and race an entire religion while ignoring or repressing any attempts at self-representation from Muslims themselves. *Tangerine Scarf*'s poetics of cross-signification (signs encountered on highways, epigraph signs, veils, beards, and darker skin tones) both cuts across visual markers of difference and opens a dialogic-poetic space that reveals Muslim Americans' humanity, heterogeneity, and complexity. The first chapter acts as a synecdoche for the entire novel in a multiplex mode that should also be afforded to the veil as it, too, continues to (be made to) stand in for Islam. The veil is a complex signifier for Muslims. Khadra's experiences of wearing the veil in different styles and colors, and of unveiling and reveiling, highlight a Muslim Arab American woman's negotiations with the veil on her own terms. Unfortunately, "veiling—to *Western* eyes, the most visible marker of the differentness and inferiority of Islamic societies—became the symbol now of both the oppression of women [. . .] and the backwardness of Islam" (Ahmed, "The Discourse of the Veil" 152). Ironically, it is the Islamophobic appropriation of the veil as a symbol of women's oppression that emboldens white-supremacist males to act violently against veiled women. I am not suggesting that women do not often face oppression in Islam; they do. I am arguing, however, that gendered violence is neither intrinsic nor unique to Islam and that it is prevalent in the US.[3] *Tangerine Scarf* exposes this violence, takes on gender issues in Islam, and points to overlaps between Christianity and Islam. Since the first chapter instantiates the poetics, and raises many of the issues, that permeate the rest of the novel, I will take its interventions as starting points with which to organize my analysis.

HORIZONTAL COMBINATIONS, DIAGONAL INTERVENTIONS

In addition to its vertical religio-cultural connection to the *Madonna of the Trail*, the first chapter's epigraph, "*My creative life is my deepest prayer,*" combines horizontally with those of the following two chapters. The second chapter's epigraph sign offers the fourth verse from Psalm 137 in the King James Version (KJV) of the Bible (*BibleGateway.org*): "*How shall we sing the Lord's song in a strange land?*" This epigraph repurposes the Jewish people's communal lament about their exile after falling into Babylonian captivity to include the Shamys' exile from Hafez al-Assad's Syria. When Khadra and her brother Eyad were young, Wajdy and Ebtehaj left Syria for the US. On a visit to Syria after her divorce, Khadra thinks about her parents' choice: "All it would have taken was accepting a little suffocation, living on a little less air [under the Syrian regime]. Instead, her parents had flown into new air. Home had been left behind, given up. For the utter unknown. What a bitter and marvelous choice" (283). The new air that the family encounters in Indiana proves less than welcoming, however, because "Islam in America has never been simply a religion one chooses. From the gaze of the state and society, Islam was and still is an indelible marker of otherness" (Beydoun, *American Islamophobia* 15). The second chapter's epigraph sign, in combination with the first chapter's epigraph and with the novel's themes, at once historicizes and contemporizes the biblical lament of exile, extending its application to Syrian Muslim immigrants. The poetics of cross-signification in *Tangerine Scarf* offers signs that

---

3. The National Organization for Women (NOW) states that "in 2005 [the year prior to *Tangerine Scarf*'s publication], 1,181 women were murdered by an intimate partner [. . .] in the U.S." NOW adds, according "to the National Center for Injury Prevention and Control, women experience about 4.8 million intimate-partner-related physical assaults and rapes every year." Furthermore, "According to the National Crime Victimization Survey, [. . .] 232,960 women in the U.S. were raped or sexually assaulted in 2006" ("Violence Against Women in the United States: Statistics," *NOW.org*).

cross religious and cultural boundaries, offering protean combinations in the process. In addition to Salaita's insight that "the main point conveyed by the novel is that theology can differ, but the practice of religion can be remarkably similar" (*Modern* 37), *Tangerine Scarf* offers cross-theological overlaps between Islam and Christianity. And these play out in the novel's poetics of cross-signification. The novel's epigraph signs, seemingly singular, refract vertically, horizontally, and diagonally across the novel, allowing for Muslim revisibility in productive intersections and combinations.

The epigraph signs of the first two chapters contain Christian and biblical content that speaks to the struggles of the Muslim Shamys. The third chapter's epigraph, a dialectical product of the first two epigraph signs, offers a translation of verse 41 from Surat At-Tawbah ("The Repentance") in the Qur'an: "*Go forth lightly and heavily and strive with your wealth and your selves in the path of God, that is best for you, if you but knew*" (14). As in the lament of Psalm 137, this Qur'anic verse deals with migration. The verse advises believers to march forth into the world, but in the way of God. Believers should strive for God's mercy by spending their wealth and offering themselves for the promotion of Islam and Muslim virtue. And that is precisely how the Shamys decide to sing the lord's song in the strange land of the US. Here, the second epigraph sign's diagonal relation to the content of the third chapter becomes clear. The third chapter deals with the Shamys' move from the Rocky Mountains, where they initially land after leaving Syria, to a suburb of Indianapolis. Wajdy finds an advertisement for the position of coordinator at the Dawah Center in the classified section of the *Islamic Forerunner* publication. It is worth pointing that the term "dawah" in the Dawah Center literally translates as invitation or

> call. God's way of bringing believers to faith and the means by which prophets call individuals and communities back to God [. . .] In the twentieth [and the twenty-first centuries], dawah has become the foundation for social, economic, political, and cultural activities as well as domestic and foreign policy strategies [. . .] Modern movements focus on universal invitation within faith, rather than conversion of non-Muslims. (*Oxford Islamic Studies Online*)

Ebtehaj's description of the position at the Dawah Center to her children aligns with the social, economic, political, and cultural activities illustrated in the definition above, except that for her it all culminates in a noble jihad.

The position entails (as Ebtehaj explains to her children) going "wherever in the country there were Muslims who wanted to learn Islam better, to teach it to their children, to build mosques, to help suffering Muslims in other countries [. . .] This was a noble jihad" (14). *Tangerine Scarf* does not shy away from using the term "jihad," which has come to signify only Muslim violence (suicide bombings and hijackings) in Islamophobic discourse. The violence perpetrated by some Muslim fundamentalists is unquestionably depraved and monstrous, but this is not how most Muslims practice their faith. While the problematic idea of holy war exists for both Christians and Muslims, jihad is a complex term with many meanings and applications that do not include the use of violence. This is the lesson that Ebtehaj imparts to her children and, by extension, to the novel's readers. The third chapter's epigraph sign relates directly to this practice of jihad. The word "strive" in "*strive with your wealth and your selves in the path of God*" is a translation of the plural verb "جَاهِدُوا" (pronounced *jahidou*), which is derived from the noun "jihad." To strive, then, is a tenable translation of jihad. What constitutes noble jihad, as Ebtehaj identifies it, is *striving* to help other Muslims in the US and the world. This striving includes traveling to aid Muslims, paying alms to the poor, and struggling spiritually against sin. In this light, these values are not so different from Christian values.

The third chapter describes the Shamys' move to Indianapolis as follows: "The little frontier family trekked the Oregon Trail in reverse, with as much wonder in their hearts as the pioneers of an earlier century heading the other way" (16). After Khadra's prayer next to the *Madonna of the Trail* statue in the first chapter, chapter 3 turns once again to the Muslim pioneer allegory. We find the Shamys trekking the Oregon Trail in reverse, seeking fertile spiritual land in Indiana (the pioneers had sought the rich farmlands west of the Rocky Mountains). Like their earlier counterparts, the Shamys have wonder in their hearts as they travel the Oregon Trail. The third chapter, then, underscores that the story of missionary Muslims in the US is an American story through and through, and that Muslims traverse some of the same routes, both literal and figurative, taken by earlier pioneers. At the start of every day of their trek, Ebtehaj recites verses from the Qur'an followed by "her favorite travel prayer: *O Thou My God: I seek refuge in Thee from humiliation or humiliating, from being astray or leading others astray, from wrongdoing or being wronged, from ignorance or having ignorance perpetrated upon me*" (16).

Ebtehaj's recitation of the travel prayer reveals her to be a self-reflective Muslim who is thoughtful about how she inhabits this new world, and how this world perceives her. In effect, the prayer asks God to grant consilient coexistence. In the second and last section snapshot of the third chapter (the first snapshot takes place in the past), Khadra, "returning to this ground that didn't love her, tries to stave the panic in her gut [. . .] She repeats the favorite prayer of her mother aloud [. . .] like someone holding a small lantern and going out to investigate, a little afraid of what she might find" (17). For Khadra, returning to Indianapolis is as perilous as trekking it for the first time. It is as if the very ground is hostile to her presence. Panicking, Khadra takes refuge in her mother's travel prayer. The prayer becomes both a guide and a request, a lantern in the darkness and a wish for safety and coexistence. This is not the first time that Khadra repeats words she had heard in her childhood. We saw her repeat Vaughn Lott's xenophobic phrase (*Back where you came from*) in the first chapter. These repetitions, as occasioned by the signs on the highway, expose patterns of racism and Islamophobia that continue to operate from Khadra's past to her present. As in *Koolaids*, repetition in *Tangerine Scarf* is integral to its poetics of cross-signification and thematics in its interweaving of both into recognizable patterns.

SENSATIONAL HIJABS, INTERSECTIONAL HEADSCARVES

Another important repetition is that of the stares that Ebtehaj's and Khadra's headscarves solicit. Time and again, we encounter people staring at either Khadra's or Ebtehaj's hijab as they go about their business. For example, "at the Kokomo Dairy Queen, Ebtehaj got out of the big clunky station wagon in her tan double-knit polyester jilbab [any long, loose-fitting outer garment worn by some Muslim women] and a beige headcover [. . .] She headed for the restroom, people's stares following her" (103). It seems that a covered Muslim women's walk to the restroom at an ice cream chain is nothing less than a spectacle. Once again, the novel offers a group of people who socially and culturally appropriate a business to the exclusion of visible others. If the white men sitting in front of Marsh's screw their eyes at Khadra's headscarf in the first chapter, the Kokomo Dairy Queen customers' reaction to Ebtehaj's headcover claims eating ice cream as an all-American activity. In this formulation, Ebtehaj cannot possibly be all-American even if she is a naturalized citizen. The "all" in all-American has an uncanny connection to the "100% American" sign in the first chapter, and it does not in fact extend to all Americans. Furthermore, it is worrisome that a Muslim woman's need to use the restroom would solicit such a reaction. Do not Muslim women have bodily functions like all Americans? Or does this reaction betray a racialization of Ebtehaj, who is trespassing into what should be understood as a white space?

While the stares that Ebtehaj receives at the Dairy Queen are hostile, *Tangerine Scarf* offers an episode with a very different reaction to her Muslim garb. On a mission trip to Muslim chapters (similar to the Dawah Center) across the country, the Shamys decide to stop at the Grand Canyon. They stood at the top of a lookout; "Jihad was on his mother's hip. Her sky blue jilbab swept the ground and her white crepe wimple outlined her head against the sky [. . .] Khadra brought [the family] into focus and snapped the picture" (100). If this photographic description of Ebtehaj with baby Jihad on her hip seems familiar, it is because it closely resembles the description of the *Madonna of the Trail* statue. And young Khadra snaps the picture, which captures the family in a heroic, statuesque pose. It comes as no surprise that adult Khadra "addresses the Madonna of the Trail postcard to her parents' home in South Bend. 'Dear Mama & Baba,' she writes [. . .] 'Saw this pioneer lady on the road & thought of you. Love from, Khadra. xxxooo'" (435). Khadra clearly identifies her parents as pioneers toward the end of the novel, which solidifies the pioneer allegory both visually (aesthetically) and culturally. Young Khadra captures her mother's grace and beauty cross-culturally, which accords with her older self's desire to take photographs that "find the truth of their subject, to see beyond first appearances" (357). She does so by attending to "rhythm, color, texture [. . .] Beauty was no frivolity" (293). The composition of the photograph and its highlighting of beauty, much like *Tangerine Scarf*'s poetics, play a critical part in mediating intersectional and cross-cultural content. But the snapshot of Ebtehaj as a heroic pioneer does not end here.

An elderly white-haired man "stopped short before this family scene. '*Santa Maria!*' he murmured. He came up the rest of the stairs without taking his eyes off Khadra's mother. 'Beautiful, beautiful,' he said, to himself—or to her, it wasn't clear. He had some kind of European accent" (100). The elderly man recognizes Ebtehaj as some version of the Virgin Mary with baby Jihad-as-Jesus on her hip. Mary is traditionally portrayed wearing a blue robe and a white veil, much like Ebtehaj's sky-blue jilbab and white crepe wimple. He probably perceives the wimple outlining her head against the sky as a halo. The narrator's choice of "wimple" as opposed to headscarf or veil allows for a rupture in reductive representations of Ebtehaj's Muslim garb. For instance, nuns and women saints also wear wimples. In fact, the narrator uses different terms in addition to headscarf or veil throughout the novel—headcover (103), scarf (25), hijab (25), and wimple (100), for example—to recast the headscarf or "the veil as a multi-layered signifier" (Toossi 641). Furthermore, Katayoun Zarei Toossi reminds us that

> the practice of veiling did not originate with Islam, nor is it a quintessentially Islamic practice. It existed in ancient Greece, the Balkans, Byzantium and pre-Islamic Arabia as an indication of high-class status [. . .] Also, some communities of Jews and Christians adopted the practice. (642)

While *Tangerine Scarf* does not deal explicitly with the veil's history before Islam, the elderly gentleman's perception of hijabed Ebtehaj as the Virgin Mary, in addition to the narrator's multiple designations for the headscarf, points to the veil's cross-religious application. As the veil travels through time and space, the meanings attached to it change and overlap, at times in contradictory ways. This is readily apparent in the movement of the veil from a symbol of high-class status to that of oppression of women and Muslim backwardness in the West and the US. Collapsing this history and the cross-cultural practice of wearing the veil produces erroneous and dangerous designations of veiled women. By giving the headscarf alternative names or designations, the narrator seems to caution us against reducing the veil to a singular meaning.

Later in the day, a policeman waves the Shamys down. Apparently, the "elderly man had climbed out to a ledge and was poised to jump. He kept calling for 'Madonna in the blue robe. Madonna with the angelic child! Madonna of the mountain!' Would Ebtehaj talk to him?" (100). The elderly man calls for the Madonna in a trinity anaphora. Ebtehaj agrees to talk to him, effectively answering his prayer, and things end well. Had the old gentleman not run into Ebtehaj in her jilbab and headscarf and perceived her as Mary, he would probably have committed suicide. He sees what Khadra captures on the camera: a devout holy woman in a courageous and dignified pose holding her angelic child on her hip. Beauty is no frivolity. The fact that Jihad is dubbed angelic is another way in which the novel rehabilitates the term's (as name and as religious practice) reductive meaning in the US. Later, Wajdy asks Ebtehaj about what happened. She tells him that the elderly man had wanted to end his life because the world was too ugly; he had wished to leave this world in order to see God's beauty. Ebtehaj responded to him by saying, "'You can't do that, that's haram [offense, sin, or wrongdoing], of course! In your religion like in ours. If you love Him, you must obey Him.' That was love, she felt" (101). If Ebtehaj doubles as Mary, her answer to the elderly man also crosses religious boundaries. Suicide is a grave sin in both Christianity and Islam. She reminds the elderly gentleman that to love God is to obey Him by doing good in the world, which includes not harming one's body. Ebtehaj asks Wajdy if the prayers of Christians count. He answers, "They're People of the Book; of course their prayers count" (101). In Islam, People of the Book refers to Jews, Christians, and Sabians, people who have received monotheistic scriptures. In the Yusuf Ali translation of Surat Ale-'Imran (The Family of 'Imran), the Qur'an states, "Say: 'O People of the Book! come to common terms as between us and you: That we worship none but God; that we associate no partners with him; that we erect not, from among ourselves, Lords and patrons other than

God'" (*QuranBrowser.org* 3.64). The Qur'an thus calls for a common ground of faith between those who have received monotheistic scriptures. This is precisely why Wajdy answers that the prayers of the People of the Book count, because they too worship the one God. This episode relates clearly to Ebtehaj's favorite travel prayer, which seeks consilient coexistence with the monotheistic faiths practiced in the US.

While the Virgin Mary allegory allows for a positive cross-religious reassessment of the veil, most of the reactions to the headscarf in the novel are negative. Page 424 finds Khadra driving her younger brother Jihad and his bandmates home after a picnic at Uncle Abdulla Awad's, where the band performed a cappella so as not to upset the Dawah folks' conservative Islamic sensibility.[4] It is worth noting here that the band is called the Clash of Civilizations, a rejoinder to Samuel Huntington's book of the same title, and that its members include her brother Jihad, an African American Muslim teen, and two Mormon brothers. The narrator describes the band as "sort of a Muslim John Cougar Mellencamp meets Wes Montgomery, with a Donny Osmond twist" (56). The eclectic makeup of the band and its musical style (which combines heartland rock with African American jazz and Mormon teen idol pop) demonstrates that young Muslims are intercultural citizens who successfully navigate the Muslim cultures of their communities and the diverse cultural production of the US. And *Tangerine Scarf*'s poetics follow suit, combining a musical sign with Khadra's hijab and a highway sign that together allow Khadra to finally grieve for her childhood friend, Zuhura.

On the highway, with the band members asleep in the car, Khadra "switches the radio on—music, some man she doesn't recognize singing *One last cry, before I leave it all behind*—then realizes she is running on empty. She pulls into a gas station off US 31. People stare. She is still in hijab. She pulls that tangerine silk tighter around her head" (424). As Sade's "Bulletproof Soul" operates as an audible sign in the first chapter, so does Brian McKnight's (the man whom Khadra does not recognize) 1992 song "One Last Cry." It is as if the song is prompting Khadra to have one last cry before she leaves behind the weight that she has been carrying. As the song plays, Khadra realizes that she is nearly out of gas. But so is she, psychologically and emotionally—the narra-

---

4. *The Oxford Dictionary of Islam* affirms that "Devotional Music" "can include the call to prayer and recitation of the *Quran*, though strictly speaking, musical accompaniment is always subordinate to the text [...] The place of music in Islamic culture has been disputed for centuries, as has that of women's voices in public." In general (but with exceptions), many Muslims believe that vocal music is allowed (*halal*) and that playing instruments is prohibited (*haram*). Therefore, we find a strong tradition of a cappella devotional singing in Islam. At the same time, some Muslims believe that any instrument is lawful as long as it is used for devotional forms of music.

tor's phrase, "she is running on empty," points both to the car and to Khadra. Once Khadra pulls into the gas station, people stare at her hijab. Two short staccato sentences of three syllables followed by six syllables ("People stare. She is still in hijab") disrupt the flow of sentences in the paragraph to stress this disturbance in Khadra's commonplace task of filling her car with gas. Once again, the headscarf turns an ordinary activity into one that is fraught.

Feeling uneasy, Khadra pulls the scarf more tightly around her head. The "stares only ever make her want to pull it on tighter, not take it off the way [her Pakistani immigrant friend] Seemi keeps suggesting she do after every Middle Eastern crisis dredges up more American hate" (424). Khadra receives these stares less than a year after the Gulf War (1990–91), in which Saddam Hussein was ousted from Kuwait. According to *Human Rights Watch*, the "beginning of the Persian Gulf crisis in August 1990 led to a major wave of hate crimes nationwide against Arabs and Muslims in the United States" ("United States: 'WE ARE NOT THE ENEMY'" 12). Khadra remembers that Seemi's mother's car was keyed in Manhattan after 250 Marines were bombed in Beirut in the early 1980s, and Seemi's mother does not even wear the hijab. What the stares at the gas station underscore is that the threat of violence against visibly Muslim Khadra is very real, that Arabs and Muslims in the US have been on the receiving end of backlash violence for decades. I would like to point out again that *Tangerine Scarf* is a post-9/11 novel that in part historicizes anti-Arab and anti-Muslim violence in the US, taking to task the claim that this violence is merely a reaction to 9/11.

Khadra also remembers how Brent Lott (one of the Lott brothers) and Curtis Stephenson pushed her, tormented her, and ripped her hijab at school during the Iranian hostage crisis (1979–81), when "she was a hostage to the rage the hostage crisis produced in Americans" (123). Although Brent and Curtis do not need much of an excuse to torment Khadra, the "Iran hostage crisis was an important moment in conflating Arab, Muslim, and Middle Eastern identities. Though Iran is not an Arab country, during the hostage crisis Iran came to stand in for Arabs, the Middle East, Islam, and terrorism, all of which terms came to be used interchangeably" (Alsultany 9). In this case, Khadra comes to stand in for the Iranian hostage takers, and as such she becomes a receptacle for white American rage. Khadra drops her books, Theodore Dreiser's *An American Tragedy* and *The Autobiography of Malcolm X*, when the boys push her from behind:

> Curtis grabbed *Malcolm X* off the pukey green floor.
> "Give me that." Khadra glared.
> "Take off your towel first, raghead."

> [. . .] "Why don't we take it off for her?"
> [. . .] A ripping sound. Brent stepped back, waving a piece of scarf. Khadra lunged—tried to grab it—her scarf was torn in two, one strip in Brent's hand, the other wound tightly around her neck. (124)

Khadra's books are important in that they reveal her continued exposure to African American Muslim experiences and her burgeoning questioning of her conservative Muslim-missionary milieu. From Malcolm X's journey through Islam to Dreiser's character Clyde Griffiths, who, like Khadra, is raised by poor and devout missionary parents, these works have a direct relationship to Khadra's identity formation. By causing her to drop her books, Brent and Curtis symbolically impede her intellectual negotiations and invalidate her sense of self. This becomes clear when Curtis demands that Khadra unveil as a condition for his returning the autobiography. It is not accidental that he picks the book off "the pukey green floor," as this relates to the translation of Khadra's name: "green one." Her name derives from the masculine *al-Khidr* (Arabic for "The Green One") who is an important figure in Islam: a spiritual guide, a saint (*wali*), a prophet, and one of the immortals.[5] Khadra's name, with its impressive religio-cultural allusion to which she must live up, is dragged (along with X's autobiography) by Curtis into the mire of a pukey green floor. Curtis tarnishes the green possibility (green is a color associated with new life and verdancy in addition to its importance in Islam) in Khadra's name with a vomit-colored green floor, much as Islamophobia recolors Islam racially and culturally as un-American and anti-Christian.

Interestingly, the possibility of consilient coexistence in Khadra's name becomes clear not in the US but on her visit to Syria as an adult after her divorce from her Kuwaiti husband Juma. On a visit to the Jobar synagogue (*kanees* in Arabic) in Damascus with Téta (Wajdy's aunt who raised him after his mother's early death) and her friend Hayat, Khadra encounters a sign: "an inscription on a tablet in Hebrew, Arabic, and French [that] told why the kanees was built on this spot [. . .] The Arabic inscription called it '*maqam al-Khidr*'" (304). The synagogue was built in commemoration of the biblical prophet Elijah, an important prophet in Judaism, Christianity, and Islam. The Arabic inscription, however, states that the synagogue is also the site of al-Khidr's "Maqam" or "sanctuary; shrine" (*Almaany.com*).[6] Among Muslims and Middle Eastern Christians of the Eastern Church, "St. George and Elijah are considered the same person: 'el-Khidr' [*sic*] a Muslim holy figure mentioned

---

5. In chapter 1, I point to the figure of Al-Khidr in relation to Mohammad's painting with the color green. For more on al-Khidr please consult "Al-Khidr, The Green Man" at *Khidr.org*.

6. Please see chapter 2 for more on *maqam*, including its meaning as a musical mode.

in the Qur'an, whose name means 'The Green One.' The two names are often merged as 'Khidrlas'" (Hill). The inscription on the kanees sign allows Khadra to experience how her name crosses religious and linguistic boundaries, offering hybridization, overlaps, and dialogic possibilities in the process. These, however, do not cross over to the US context in which Khadra finds herself.

After his symbolic miring of Khadra's name, Curtis hurls the epithet "raghead" before he and Brent rip her hijab. This episode is eerily similar to the experiences of Muslim schoolgirls in the days after 9/11: "Many of the reported incidents of harassment or attack took the form of schoolgirls being subject to insults and being spat on and having their hijabs pulled off as they were called 'rag-heads' or told to 'go home!'" (Ahmed, *A Quiet Revolution* 204). Vaughn Lott tells the Shamys to go back where they came from in the first chapter, and Curtis calls Khadra a raghead and tears her headscarf in the twenty-second chapter. With the exception of being spat on, Khadra's experience of violence during the Iranian hostage crisis is almost identical to the post-9/11 anti-Muslim violence against schoolgirls. If Khadra's headscarf is caught in the crosscurrent of Islamophobia and conservative Islamic practice in the first chapter, "her scarf was torn in two, one strip in Brent's hand, the other wound tightly around her neck" in the twenty-second chapter. The aftermath of the attack finds part of the veil in Brent's hand and the other part almost strangling Khadra. *Tangerine Scarf*'s signs (the hijab in this instance) act as portals that historicize Islamophobic violence, exposing in the process the systemic and sociocultural anti-Muslim racism in the US that has little to do with terrorism perpetrated by Muslims. In this episode, history also claims Brent Lott, who becomes "a potential stand-in for well-known conservative politician Trent Lott" (Rana 510). Trent Lott is a former Republican senator from Mississippi, who drew public and political outrage for his remarks suggesting that segregation was acceptable: "At a function honoring outgoing Senator Strom Thurmond, [Lott] says in regards to his state of Mississippi voting for Thurmond in the 1948 presidential election—'We're proud of it. And if the rest of the country had followed our lead, we wouldn't have had all these problems over all these years either'" ("Trent Lott Fast Facts"). The Brent-Trent Lott allegory incorporates the history of racist (political and physical) violence against African Americans into the attack on Khadra during the Iranian hostage crisis.

ISLAMOPHOBIC VIOLENCE

This Muslim African American intersectionality finds its resonance during the snapshot section in which Khadra drives her brother Jihad and his bandmates home after their a cappella performance at Uncle Abdulla Awad's picnic. After Brian McKnight's song "One Last Cry" (an audible sign) and the stares she receives at the gas station, Khadra continues the drive on the rural highway. In a stream of consciousness, Khadra encounters a highway sign:

> *Beanblossom Bridge, one mile.* On a sudden impulse she pulls off at the exit. 'This is where she was found,' Tayiba had told her, driving to Bloomington with her once during college. She parks just before the covered bridge [. . .] *You're not supposed to stop on the way to Bloomington. You're not supposed to stop on these Indiana white people country roads. The friendly back roads of Indiana, full of friendly Hoosier people yeah right. You're not supposed to be here.* (425–26)

While her brother and his bandmates sleep, Khadra's mind recognizes the sign for Beanblossom Bridge. This is where Zuhura was found "Murdered. Raped. Cuts on her hands, her hijab and clothes in shreds" (93). A little earlier, people at the gas station stared at Khadra's hijab. Years earlier, Zuhura was murdered for being black and for wearing the hijab. Five paragraphs earlier, the sentences describing the stares Khadra receives ("People stare. She is still in hijab") trip into short staccato sentences. Three hundred and thirty-two pages earlier, the description of Zuhura's body falls into one-word sentences: "Murdered. Raped." Khadra's and Zuhura's visual difference is accompanied by visibly and rhythmically contrasting sentences. Khadra's stream of consciousness (in italics), markers of the fact that she has not yet mourned for Zuhura (not properly), bridge the past and present. The anaphora, "*You're not supposed to stop,*" recalls past and present warnings against traveling on "*white people country roads.*" Kenyan American Zuhura "may not have had many of the other survival skills developed over generations by American blacks, but everyone in Indiana knew that Martinsville was no place to be unless you were white" (61). Zuhura paid with her life for this transgression; in order to mourn her, Khadra must repeat Zuhura's pioneering incursion into a white-only space.

Zuhura's fiancé, Luqman, also pays a heavy price for her death. Luqman had warned Zuhura against driving late, because Klansmen were returning angry from Skokie, where they were prevented from holding a rally. He had said that "Christian terrorists [were] on the loose" (89). If Luqman's ironic assertion sounds preposterous—since it implies that Christians, not the Klan specifically, are terrorists—the claim that all Muslims are terrorists is equally absurd: The Klan is to Christians what Al-Qaeda and ISIS are to Muslims. It is ridiculous to assert that the KKK speaks for all of Christianity, and it is equally absurd to claim that Al-Qaeda or ISIS speaks for all of Islam. The fact of the matter is that Muslims have much more cause to fear backlash and Islamophobic violence in the US than Americans have to fear Muslim-inspired violence.[7] While the number of Muslims in the US is projected to grow, the "Pew Research Center estimates that there were about 3.45 million Muslims of all ages living in the U.S. in 2017, and that Muslims made up about 1.1% of the total U. S. population" (Mohamed). Being such a small group makes Muslims an easy target for hate. As if the rape and murder of Zuhura were not enough, the police and the media decide to scapegoat her fiancé Luqman. Instead of "looking for the killers, or rounding up any of the APES (American Protectors of the Environs of Simmonsville) for questioning, the police handcuffed Luqman and threw him in the back of a car" (97). The Indianapolis police decide to target Luqman, not the white supremacists (with the ironic acronym of APES), as the guilty party. After Luqman's arrest, the police ask him about his whereabouts on the night of the murder and whether Zuhura was seeing someone else on the side.

The *Indianapolis Star* "reported on [Luqman] being a suspect: *Murder Possible Honor Killing—Middle Eastern Connection,* they said, with a sidebar on 'the oppression of women in Islam'" (97). Luqman, the Muslim/Arab male as oppressor, becomes the receptacle of the sociocultural ills in Indiana. It is much easier to scapegoat Luqman than to deal with racism, Islamophobia, white supremacy, and, crucially, violence against women in Indiana (and the US for that matter). As Moustafa Bayoumi observes, "To focus on 'Islam' [and the veil] is to entertain a distraction that takes us away from attending to the many serious political issues of our time" (*This Muslim* 102). A long history of colonial, orientalist, and anti-Muslim discourses facilitates the construction of false (or at the very least unsubstantiated) claims against Luqman without repercussions. Leila Ahmed reveals that "the Victorian male establishment devised theories to contest the claims of [British] feminism [for laws forbidding child marriage, spousal abuse, etc.]. It captured the language of feminism and redirected it, in the service of colonialism, toward Other men and the cultures of Other men" ("Discourse" 151). In *Tangerine Scarf,* both the Indianapolis police force and the media participate in this long practice of denial and misdirection. They succeed, because "one of the most concerning features

---

7. Anthony H. Cordesman states, "*What* [the] *numbers* [from the 2016 FBI annual summary of the patterns in hate crimes] *do show, however, is that there is no statistical justification for any form of Islamophobia or for singling out all Muslims.* The numbers of terrorist incidents involving any relation to religion are far too small relative to all the other forms of crime and violence driven by religion and race, and more Muslims in the United States suffer from hate crimes than other Americans suffer from terrorism."

of Islamophobia in the United States is the fact that, as Bayoumi explains, most Americans simply don't know a Muslim. 'The number of U.S. citizens who report even knowing a Muslim is quite small,' he explains. 'This allows the media to play a major role in shaping public perception'" (McClennen). The symbiotic relationship between the police and the media in the novel produces the desired result: "No charge of murder was brought against Luqman. He was deported anyway, on a technical visa violation" (97). In short, Luqman pays the price for the rape and murder of Zuhura, while the most likely culprits, the white supremacists, continue their mission of hate unharassed by the police and unreported by the *Indianapolis Star*. In fact, "Zuhura's murderer [is] never caught" (98), the novel informs us.

This injustice should give us pause. It provokes us to "become aware not only of how much we overlook in our daily scans of the newspaper but also of how reading, as much as not reading, can function as an act of erasure: Do we read the news in order to be able to throw it away?" (Beckman 115). While the *Indianapolis Star* and the Indianapolis police are guilty of an Islamophobic praxis that allows them to scapegoat Luqman and then throw him away (deport him), the novel asks us to be aware of our own complicity or apathy as consumers of this discourse and the images it produces. The Zuhura/Luqman episode holds up a mirror to the dominant culture in the US—which misrepresents all Muslim women, particularly veiled Muslim women, as victims of Muslim men—in order to expose the dominant culture's subscription to "some version of the founding paradigm of orientalism and colonialism combined, sometimes crudely put as 'white men saving brown women from brown men'" (Serageldin, "Perils and Pitfalls" 434). The *Indianapolis Star*'s recasting of the murder of a black Muslim woman most likely at the hands of Klansmen as an honor killing with a Middle Eastern connection, revises "white men saving brown women from brown men" to something along the lines of *white men raping and murdering black or brown Muslim women and blaming black or brown Muslim men*. It is incumbent on us to remember that Islamophobic discourse, like that of orientalism and colonialism combined, is not merely discourse: It has a direct, material effect on the lives of Muslims.

The highway sign for Beanblossom Bridge directs Khadra both to the site of Zuhura's rape and murder and to her past, in which she encounters anti-Muslim hate and violence. The sign compels her to take the exit, park the car, and walk to the bridge. Jihad wakes up, leaves the car and his sleeping bandmates, and joins Khadra at the mudbank. He asks her what she is doing out there. Khadra replies that this is where she was killed. Jihad "is about to say, 'She who?' But then he remembers [. . .] that [Zuhura's murder] was a big part of community life growing up, a thing everybody knew. A *sign* for all to consider (428, my emphasis). What kind of sign is Zuhura's murder, and why is it so important to her Muslim community? To begin answering this question, I must point to Zuhura's intersectional positionality: an immigrant from Kenya, a black woman, and a Muslim. To her killers, Zuhura represents a raced and Islamophobic version of Islam (a religion exclusive to people of color), a monolith devoid of nuance and complexity. What the Klansmen seek is not merely to rape and kill black Muslim Zuhura in order to terrorize her community, but also to maintain through violence the dominance of their (paradoxical) views of Islam, black people, and immigrants of color.

The white supremacist view of Islam derives from eighteenth- and nineteenth-century orientalism, which "manufactured a racially narrow understanding of Muslim identity as exclusively Arab or Middle Eastern. Thus an entire religion was remade into a racial identity" (Beydoun, *American Islamophobia* 49). But white supremacists' perception of black people derives from the institution of slavery: "blackness as synonymous with property and slave" (49). Khaled Beydoun reminds us that social scientists estimate that 15 to 20 percent of the enslaved African population (between 600,000 and 1.2 million) were Muslims (56). Because Africans were seen as property, however, eighteenth- and nineteenth-century "American law, institutions and individuals [. . .] prevented the recognition of these *pioneer* Muslims for who they were: bona fide observant Muslims" (48, my emphasis). These fallacious and insidious suppositions and racializations continue to carry over, unfortunately. Islamophobes apply racialized classifications to Khadra and her family, whom Khadra recognizes as pioneers, in order to repress their attempts at self-visibility and self-representation.

Zuhura's intersectional identity, as a black Muslim immigrant woman, is an existential threat to the racial order and classifications that buoy up white supremacy in the US.[8] As Kimberlé Crenshaw states in "Why intersectionality can't wait," "Intersectionality is an analytic sensibility, a way of thinking about identity and its relationship to power [. . .] Intersectionality has given many advocates a way to frame their circumstances and to fight for their *visibility and inclusion*" (my emphasis). Visibility on one's own terms is critical for fair inclusion, whether this inclusion refers to a body politic or to the Dawah Center's version of Islam. While she was alive, Zuhura was invested in "social justice in Islam" (28), in exposing the abuse of zoning laws "that [have] been used as a tool to keep people of other races out" (43), and in becoming a lawyer (44). Zuhura understood these skills to be imperative for the survival of

---

8. For more on the cultural experiences of Muslim women of color, please see Sylvia Chan-Malik's *Being Muslim: A Cultural History of Women of Color in American Islam*.

her Muslim community. They "were not, however, the best skills for getting along as a foreign newcomer in Simmonsville, or as black woman in the social landscape of central Indiana. Zuhura didn't fit into this landscape. She didn't fit what the locals thought they knew about someone who looked like her as they saw her approaching" (44). And herein lies the problem. Zuhura did not fit the role that white Indiana had prescribed for someone who *looked* like her. To be included, Zuhura would have had to play the part corresponding to her appearance as prescribed by white central Indianans, to become visible on their terms, not her intersectional own. Zuhura was raped and murdered not only because she looked different but also because she acted different. Her outer signs of skin color and a hijab enclosed an intersectional identity that resisted reductive definitions and classifications. Zuhura paid with her life for promoting a visibility that showed that there is "simply no coherent way of regarding all American Muslims as a single monolithic community, or of speaking about them as such—not even in terms of broad categories such as race, gender, 'native-born,' and immigrant" (An-Na'im 3). It is not surprising, then, that Zuhura, whose intersectional identity speaks to the complexity and heterogeneity of Muslims, is a sign for all to consider.

It is certainly true that "mere words won't change the way that some people—the *less-visible* members of political constituencies—must continue to wait for leaders, decision-makers and others to *see* their struggles" (Crenshaw; my emphasis); but words are crucial, nonetheless, to our claiming of intersectional positionalities and to our understanding of the power inequalities within which they exist. Visibility is as much a creative pursuit as it is an active one. Creativity surprises, disrupts, and renders visible both the existence of intersectional identities and possible modes of existence—a reality of social justice in the making. In *Tangerine Scarf*, communal and individual remembrances of Zuhura (as a martyr in her own right) and her intersectional identity are pivotal to Khadra's understanding of herself and the interventions that she must make in her personal and professional life. The novel's poetics of cross-signification follow suit, intersecting audibly (McKnight "One Last Cry"), symbolically (Khadra's headscarf), and visually (the highway sign for BeanBlosson Bridge), in order to heighten our experience of Khadra's catharsis at the site of Zuhura's death. The stares that hijabed Khadra receives at the gas station remind her of past taunts and threats, leading her to Zuhura's rape and murder; McKnight's song bids Khadra to have one last cry and unburden her repressed grief for Zuhura; and the highway sign directs Khadra to the site of Zuhura's death, to drive forward in time in order to confront a past that continues to inform the present. This poetic intersectionality is not frivolous. In its heightening of intersectional themes, the poetics of cross-signification appeals to readers' emotions and senses, reminding them of the human and material toll of Islamophobia and racism's long history in the US.

At the site of rape and murder, Khadra falls to her knees and begins to wail:

> She is just this gaping wail, drawing breath drawing drawing then the wail comes again, enormous. And again. Alternating silence and sound, veiling and unveiling, again and again. It has is its own rhythm and its own demand for breath [. . .] The body becomes a reed for the sound to blow through. Hearken, hearken to the body's reed. The throat gives it its tone, and the stomach and the diaphragm and the root give it depth. (428)

Khadra's grieving is so intense that she becomes the gaping wail, her body the instrument through which it sounds. The wail demands its own rhythm and breath, creating its own music. The repetitions and alternations of the words "drawing," "again," and "hearken" construct rhythmic patterns. For example, "drawing breath drawing drawing" creates a rhythm of disyllables in the repetition of "drawing" that is interrupted by the monosyllabic "breath," which acts as a breath in between the repeating "drawing."[9] The resulting rhythm and blues (or, better yet, rhythm and wails) recalls Brian McKnight's song "One Last Cry," to which Khadra was listening a little earlier. If the song, as an audible sign, prompts Khadra to have one last cry before she moves on, her wails act as the song's instrumental solo section, her "body [. . . the] reed for the sound to blow through." The heightening of the language induces us to pay attention to the passage's message while allowing us to experience Khadra's lament emotionally and sensually. The message is itself a series of alternations between "silence and sound, veiling and unveiling." If the former is fundamental to musical expression, the latter is crucial to the progression of Khadra's identity.

ALTERNATION: VEILING AND UNVEILING

Khadra goes through phases of literal veiling and unveiling in the novel, and *Tangerine Scarf* renders this process of alternation both necessary and natural. When Khadra arrives at the Dawah Center after her long car trip early in the novel, we find out that she keeps "an old self-help book with a torn cover

---

9. This is not unlike the rhythmic patterns that Abu-Jaber composes for Matussem's accented English in *Arabian Jazz*.

(*Recovery for Adult Children of Missionaries*)" (47) in her car. On page 378, which takes place in the recent past, we find Khadra reading, "'Anger, Avoidance, Rebuilding,' the self-help book said. It was called *Recovery for Adult Children of Missionaries in 25 Easy Exercises*. It had been dog-eared and scribbled on by others before it passed into Khadra's hands." The fact that the self-help book appears twice in the novel is far from accidental, and the fact that it was "scribbled on by others" relates Khadra's recovery from her religious upbringing to the recoveries of adult children of missionaries from other faiths. If Khadra's parents are missionary pioneers who trekked some of the same paths of early American pioneers, then it is no surprise that Khadra's recovery from their strict religious upbringing follows the recoveries of adult children from different faiths. Furthermore, this process of recovery recalls the first chapter's epigraph sign, which offers a quote from Sue Monk Kidd's memoir, *The Dance of the Dissident Daughter*. Like Kidd, her Christian counterpart, Khadra comes to question her role and position as a woman within her religious community. *Tangerine Scarf* reminds us time and again that Islam and its practitioners are not so different from the other monotheistic faiths in the US and that gender issues cross religious and cultural boundaries.

From Khadra's early adherence to orthodox Islam to her later, more measured approach to Islam and her identity, the veil plays a central role. For instance, when young Khadra was attracted to radical forms of Islam, she "donned black headscarves with a surge of righteous austerity that startled her parents [. . .] She wore a no-nonsense black scarf and a navy-blue jilbab her father had sewn at her request" (149). Despite their surprise at this turn in Khadra (Ebtehaj even asks her sharply on page 149, "Going to a funeral today?"), her parents try—to the best of their ability—to support her religious expression, at least sartorially. It is worth noting here that it is Wajdy (Khadra's father) and not her mother who sews the loose-fitting outer garments (jilbabs) for his daughter. The family's meager means notwithstanding (compelling Wajdy to sew their garments rather than buy them), *Tangerine Scarf* offers an important example in which the family members do not conform to traditional or stereotypical gender roles. Moreover, Khadra's attraction to radical Islam follows Brent Lott and Curtis Stephenson's attack on her during the Iranian hostage crisis (twenty-five pages earlier). Feeling besieged by hate and racism, Khadra attempts to protect herself by exhibiting radical and austere garb. The colors of black and navy blue that she displays fail to deter her tormentors, who perceive little beyond the fact that she is wearing a veil. Even in this phase, however, Khadra thinks that "radical Islam was her James Dean" (152). That is, she combines seemingly incommensurable entities—radical Islam and the iconic cultural figure of James Dean—which nonetheless reflect her cross-cultural identity. Dean, recast as a rebel with a cause, as radical Islam, becomes the symbol of empowerment for Khadra.

Khadra's radical phase does not last too long, however. What precipitates its end is Khadra's friendship with Joy Shelby, an American-born student with Arabic roots. On a visit to the Shelbys, Khadra and her brother Eyad go with the Shelbys to see their friend, Im Litfy, whom Joy's mother was helping with the cooking. At Im Litfy's, Rose (Joy's mother) declares that the food is "for the Arab Pride festival tomorrow [. . .] In the morning, we take the food over to Im Litfy's church, St. George's" (189). Both Khadra and Eyad "do a mental double-take. Church? Im Litfy? Who felt as familiar as their own grandmother, whose kitchen felt like home?" (189). Khadra and Eyad had never been in a Christian Arab American home before, and they assume erroneously that the Shelbys would have only Muslim friends. Their shock comes not from the fact that Im Litfy is Christian, however, but from the warmth and familiarity of her kitchen. Khadra glances

> at their hostess' face, her features so familiarly Syrian, her cadence and voice equally so. What other homes of similar sweetness and joy had they passed by all these years, insisting as they did on their separateness and specialness, then? What a waste. Something started to unravel in Khadra there in the kitchen, bringing her almost to the point of secret tears. (189)

It is Im Litfy's sweetness and kindness, her unmistakably Syrian features and voice, that tear down the wall that Khadra had built to protect herself. She wonders what other missed friendships and commonalities her strict upbringing and its mode of separateness has caused her family. A "little while after returning from the Shelbys, Khadra put on a white scarf with tiny flowers like a village meadow in spring, and a pale blue blouse and soft floral skirt. Her broadcloth navy jilbab and plain black scarves she shoved to the back of her closet" (193). Khadra's experience at the Shelbys' and at Im Litfy's finds its way to Khadra's Muslim clothing, now replete with flowers and soft colors.[10] The passage reflects this newfound sweetness and hope in the simile of "a village meadow in spring," in bl- and f-sound alliteration, and in o-sound assonance: "**bl**ue **bl**ouse and s_o_ft _fl_oral" (my emphasis). Of course, it does not hurt that Khadra returns home with a transient crush on Joy's older brother, Baker. Thus begins Khadra's neoclassical phase in Islam.

---

10. For more on the hijab in Kahf's works, please see Katayoun Zarei Toossi's "The Conundrum of the Veil and Mohja Kahf's Literary Representations of Hijab."

There is a lesson for both Muslim and non-Muslim Americans in this critique of Khadra's upbringing. Coexistence is not enough. Generosity of spirit, social exchange, and intermingling are key to creating goodwill, avoiding misunderstanding, and challenging stereotypes. Kindness and acceptance prompt Khadra to change both her outlook and her appearance. While a floral hijab might not solicit as strong a reaction from non-Muslims as a black headscarf, the discourse of the veil does not allow for nuances in interpretation. For Islamophobes and racists, the veil is a veil in the most reductive sense. But as the novel demonstrates, the veil is in fact many veils, replete with nuance and complexity. Toossi explains, "In order to discover 'the girl' in the tangerine scarf, then, Kahf needs to re-cover her out of all these confining layers of signification" (651). This recovery takes place in considerable part through Khadra's experience of choosing Muslim clothing on her own terms. Khadra's experimentation with headscarves and colors recovers the hijab as "the outer sign of an inner quality [that Khadra] wants to be reminded of, more often than she could manage to remind herself without it" (Kahf, *Tangerine* 425). The symbiotic relationship between Khadra and the headscarf wrenches both out of Islamophobia's web of signification.

Khadra's identity negotiations do not end there. She passes through another phase in which she chooses not to wear the hijab. Khadra's unveiling does not take place in the US, however, where she feels compelled to defend her Muslim identity and her choice to wear the headscarf. Her unveiling happens organically during Khadra's visit to Téta in Syria after her divorce from Juma. In Syria, she spends time with Téta, Téta's friend Hayat, and a "mythical [modernist] poet who is physically dead but spiritually alive" (Salaita, *Modern* 38). Khadra initially meets the mythical poet on Mount Qasyoon, which overlooks Damascus. On the mountain, Khadra has a revelation that photography is her passion and her calling. Looking down on the ancient city of Damascus, she further realizes that one "could not possibly hold that one religion had claim to an exclusive truth" (297). She shifts her camera angle while taking photographs only to find the poet looking at her in her viewfinder. The poet-as-prophet on the mountain, whom Khadra seems to conjure after her epiphany, becomes instrumental in Khadra's shift of angle on the hijab and God. During their many conversations, the poet asks Khadra, "Why do you spend so much time worrying about what God thinks of you? [. . .] It's the other way around, you know. God is what *you* think of God, you know" (301). While Khadra is initially taken aback by the poet's blasphemy, she begins to rethink her previous positions on religion. Furthermore, after the poet teases her, saying, "Your veil is very revealing, you know" (302), Khadra begins to reflect on her reasons for veiling and what, in fact, the veil signifies for her.

Khadra's identity negotiations culminate in an outing at the Ghuta Orchards with the poet, Téta, and Hayat. Taking in the beauty of the orchards, Khadra "was in a position like the first stand of prayer. A yellow butterfly flittered by. The scarf was slipping off. She shrugged" (309). The passage delivers Khadra's unveiling in short, matter-of-fact sentences, as if nothing unusual is taking place. The sentences echo Khadra's acceptance (with a shrug) of the headscarf's organically slipping from her head. Furthermore, the unveiling takes place as Khadra stands as if in the position of the first stand of prayer, and this effectively delinks the headscarf (an outward sign) from Khadra's inner Muslim quality. Prayer and unveiling continue to alternate in the following sentences:

> *Alhamdu, alhamdulilah.* The sunlight on her head was a gift from God. Gratitude filled her. *Sami allahu liman hamadah.* Here was an exposure, her soul an unmarked sheet shadowing into distinct shapes under the fluids. Fresh film. Her self developing. [. . .] How veiling and unveiling are part of the same process, the same cycle, how both are necessary; how both light and dark are connected moments in the development of the soul in its darkroom. (309)

In a stream-of-consciousness fashion, Khadra recites the Muslim expression "*Alhamdu, alhamdulilah,*" which translates as *Praise be, praise be to Allah* as she feels the sunlight on her unveiled head. She continues with "*Sami allahu liman hamadah,*" which means *Allah hears whoever praises Him,* whether they are veiled or unveiled being the implication. This in turn brings forth a metaphor of photographic development in relation to Khadra's soul, which aligns with the section snapshots of Khadra's development that permeate the novel, especially as triggered by highway and building signs. Exposed Khadra is a developing Khadra, who now understands that veiling and unveiling are mutually constitutive.

This realization relates back to Khadra's wails at the site of Zuhura's rape and murder: "Alternating silence and sound, veiling and unveiling, again and again" (428). Alternation reveals intersectionality, the intersection of varying positionalities. It recalls the history of Islam in the US, which has its roots in enslaved Muslim Africans, Zuhura's spiritual (if not actual) ancestors. It also recalls young Khadra's conversation with Aunt Khadija, who tells her, "Imagine being made to stand naked in front of a whole bunch of people [. . .] That's how it was for black women back in slavery times. Up on the auction block. Covering up is a strong thing" (25). In this context, covering up becomes a way for African American women to recover their bodies both spiritually and symbolically from the practices of slavery and to recover Islam as one of the religions practiced by (and stolen from) enslaved Africans. It is perhaps the memory of her conversation with Aunt Khadija that prompts Khadra to reveil on her way back from Syria to the US: "She wanted them to know at Customs, at the reentry checkpoint, she wanted them to know at O'Hare, that she was coming in under one of the many signs of the heritage. And she wanted her heart to remember, in the dappled ruffle and rustle of veiling and unveiling, *How precious is the heritage!*" (313). Khadra chooses to reenter the US as visibly Muslim, "under one of the many *signs* of the heritage" (my emphasis). Although the customs agents would most likely interpret the hijab reductively, Khadra reminds us that her tangerine scarf is only one sign out of many that refer to her Muslim heritage. That is, the hijab is not the determining sign of whether a woman is a Muslim or not. Khadra's phases of veiling and unveiling attest to that, and the slant rhyme of "ruffle and rustle" appeals to our senses of touch and sound, allowing us to feel the headscarf ethereally covering and uncovering her hair. Furthermore, Khadra's statement refers not only to the many other signs and symbols associated with Islam, but also to the intersectional identities within Islam. Both Zuhura and Aunt Khadija provide models of resistance and self-representation for Syrian American Khadra and for many Arab women residing in the US. Islam's complexity and intersectional possibilities are precisely what make it a precious heritage for Khadra.

Khadra's decision to reveil during her return trip to the US finds its echo in Muslim women's affirmations of their identities post-9/11. Shiasta Aziz, "for example, explained [. . .] it was only after 9/11 and 'when the Muslim community around the world [. . . was] under intense scrutiny by the politicians and the media' that she felt 'that I wanted to be a visible Muslim' [. . .] Wearing hijab was for her 'an act of solidarity with Muslim women all around the world'" (qtd. in Ahmed, *A Quiet Revolution* 209). Muslim women's visibility on their own terms is at stake here, and this visibility is possible only in acts of intersectional solidarity in the US and transnationally. Interestingly, Kahf had Khadra take off her headscarf entirely as an adult in an early draft of *Tangerine Scarf*. She changed her mind in later drafts: "People would have read it as 'We won! She is an escaped Muslim woman!' [. . .] People think that all Arab women are dying to uncover" (MacFarquhar). Kahf's choice to reveil Khadra adds a layer of complexity to the hijab. The covering of hair becomes an act of uncovering the fallacies of Islamophobia. In all their struggles, Muslim women remain agents of change and empowerment, offering crucial critiques of the patriarchal practices in their own communities and in the nations to which they migrate.

CROSS-SIGNIFICATION

Tangerine Scarf's poetics of cross-signification yields an interplay between inaccurate signs and sound signs (both audible and reliable). This poetics recovers the human/woman who wears the veil as it accompanies Khadra's journey of wearing the veil in different styles, unveiling for a period of time in Syria, and veiling and unveiling for personal and political reasons in the US. The novel's poetics of cross-signification exposes the poverty of Islamophobic representations of the hijab; historicizes anti-Arab and anti-Muslim racism in the US; reveals the heterogeneity and intersectionality within Muslim communities; and renders visible the women who wear the veil. As cross-temporal portals, epigraph and highway signs reveal that the post–9/11 backlash is a "part of a longer history in which [Americans] have been primed by the media [and the dominant culture] to equate Arabs and Muslims first with [. . .] patriarchy/misogyny and then with terrorism" (Alsultany 9). As cross-cultural portals, epigraph signs put Khadra and her family's experiences in dialogue with cross-religious texts and practices. The epigraph signs allow multiple texts and cultures to travel and combine across time and space with the themes of the novel, and to challenge the mythology that Islam and Muslims are inherently different and un-American. Khadra's name as well as her hijab, signs of her difference from the dominant culture, undergo a series of cross-significations in the past and the present that allow for their revisibility as Khadra experiences them along Arab and Muslim American lines. In witnessing various reactions to Khadra's and Ebtehaj's headscarves, *Tangerine Scarf*'s readers are introduced anew to Muslim clothing. Covered "in various layers of fabric, the multitextured body becomes a visual enactment of the immigrant's multilayered identity and subjectivity" (Sinno 128). Far from a visual enactment of a singular Islam, Khadra and Ebtehaj's Muslim garb is the site of multilayered and intersectional negotiation within Islam and with multiple cultures in the US. Kahf, then, recovers the humanity and complexity of Muslim women through the veil, not in spite of it.[11]

The epigraph sign of the sixty-fifth chapter (the penultimate chapter) offers a quote from Ibn al-Arabi, the Andalusian Muslim scholar, mystic, poet, and philosopher: *"Hence vision is through the veil, and inescapably so"* (434). Here, Ibn al-Arabi comments on the *hadith* (the record of the traditions or

---

11. The issue of the veil comes up again in chapter 5. In *Crescent*, which is in part a reinvention of *Othello*, Abu-Jaber substitutes the handkerchief (which Othello gifts to Desdemona) with a headscarf. The veil has become so ubiquitous as a symbol of Islam and a site of contestation in the US that Arab American and Muslim American women writers have had to respond creatively to the reductive discourse of the veil.

sayings of the Prophet Muhammad) that God possesses seventy veils of light and darkness. As Elliot Wolfson explains, "The veil came to signify the hermeneutic of secrecy basic to the esoteric gnosis of Sufism, envisioning the hidden secret revealed in the concealment of its revelation and concealed in the revelation of its concealment. Accordingly, the task is to discard the veils to reveal the truth, but if the veils were all discarded, there truly would be no truth to see" (129). The symbiotic relationship between veiling and unveiling, and the resulting paradox of envisioning spiritual and material truth through the veil and the disruptions of the veil, find their echo in the visual transpositions of Khadra's veiling and unveiling. Khadra's epiphany and its resultant interplay between veiling and unveiling recovers both her identity and the veil as symbol from the site of reductive contestation, in which the veil is either a sign of oppression and backwardness or a sign of proper moral and religious piety. Signs and countersigns accompany Khadra's identity negotiations and her concomitant acts of veiling and unveiling. As Khadra recovers herself, so do the signs and countersigns resolve in a sign unattached to any chapter that appears at the end of *Tangerine Scarf*. Page 442 (which is unnumbered), offers a stand-alone sign, a stanza from Ahmad Jami's poem "The Idol." Jami was a Persian Sufi, a writer, a mystic, and a poet who lived in the eleventh and twelfth centuries. Jami's stanza is both a resolution and a nonresolution, as it calls into question one's ability to shatter the idol of illusion in order to achieve liberation. It serves as a reminder that perception is flawed even while one requires perception to perceive its flaws. Khadra's (and readers') liberation from the discourse of the veil is both an end and a beginning. Lest we feel too comfortable, the poetic/sign reminds us that our manifestos are also illusory. Perception, negotiation, and epiphany are parts of a continuous process.

CHAPTER 4

Anagrams of Identity

Laila Halaby's *Once in a Promised Land*

In *Once in a Promised Land*, published in 2007, Laila Halaby takes on the backlash against Arabs and Muslims in the immediate aftermath of 9/11. Unlike *The Girl in the Tangerine Scarf*, which responds to 9/11 by alerting its readers to the long history of Islamophobia in the US, *Once in a Promised Land* tackles the post-9/11 backlash against Arabs and Muslims directly. This sociopolitical context, which drives the novel's plot and bears upon the main Arab American characters, has significantly (over)determined the critical responses to the novel. As a result, Steven Salaita cautions, "It is easy to read Halaby only in the context of the political events that frame or appear in her fiction, but there is a great deal happening aesthetically in her novels, so I would like to be careful not to reduce art solely to political commentary" (*Modern* 79). Certainly, the poetics in *Once in a Promised Land* promises more, on the formal and aesthetic levels, than a political account in which the characters' complexities and human experiences are subsumed exclusively under political considerations and abstractions. As I argue throughout *Poetics of Visibility*, art is the vehicle by which the contemporary Arab American novel makes visible the heterogeneity, humanity, and transculturality of Arab Americans, and this chapter's intervention follows suit.

This chapter engages the novel's Shahrazadian mode of storytelling (this is a story of survival and cross-cultural participation after all), which frames its main, realistic section and initiates its anagrammatic play.[1] *Once in a Promised Land* uses the classic framing device—offering two storytelling sections "Before" and "After" the main realistic section—to reframe images of Arabs and Muslims post-9/11. In them, the storyteller anticipates and negotiates the presiding mode of novelistic realism; she uses her influence (even under duress) to forestall and rehabilitate potentially hostile readers. In the Arabic oral tradition (as in many cultures), the figure of the storyteller possesses considerable ethical and political agency, and Halaby draws on this agency to reframe her storyteller's subject position in terms of the novel's realistic section. Furthermore, Halaby arms her protagonist, Jassim, with anagrams in the main narrative. In line with the Greek etymology of the term "anagram," which translates as "writing back or anew" (Cuddon 35), Jassim's anagrammatic play before 9/11 mirrors his hopes of writing his experiences anew in his adopted country. The possibilities within anagrams inverse to impossibilities, however, as Jassim frequently fails to realize perfect anagrams (letters are excluded and the anagrams become reductions, synecdoches, of the original words and phrases) in the aftermath of 9/11.

As in *Arabian Jazz*, *The Girl in the Tangerine Scarf*, and *Crescent*, *Once in a Promised Land* is replete both with Arabic words in transliteration and with translated Qur'anic phrases that challenge the American-English mode of linguistic and cultural representation. This translational/anagrammatic negotiation (in its transposing of letters, an anagram is a form of translation and transliteration) extends to the storyteller, narrator, and characters, and to the novel's combinational—storytelling and realistic—forms. These features work to foreground the dialogic aspects of Arabic and American English in cross-linguistic and cross-cultural negotiations and to acknowledge the failures of translational mediation and agency within a setting of cultural backlash.

"BEFORE" THE FRAME

Once in a Promised Land begins with a section frame titled "Before." This title prompts the question, Before what? Does this section frame exist before 9/11 or before the main narrative? Does "Before" denote a prepositional, conjunctional, or adverbial position in the grammar of the novel? In other words, does the section frame precede or govern the main section, connect to it, and/ or modify or qualify it? "Before" evinces awareness of what comes after inas-

---

1. See footnote 12 in chapter 2 for the basic premise of the frame story in *A Thousand and One Nights*.

much as it frames and influences our interpretations of events yet to unfold. The multilayered and multifaceted gesture in "Before" suspends any ready answers. It opens with a female storyteller relating the poetic phrase "*kan / ya ma kan / fee qadeem az-zaman*" (VII), Arabic for "*They say there was or there wasn't in olden times*" (VII). Here we have the traditional Arabic storytelling mode in transliterated Arabic, followed by an English translation. The Arabic, manifesting in English-letter form (not in Arabic letters), reveals a dialogic and migratory desire, one that actualizes (at least linguistically) in the English translation that follows. Not only does this opening offer two languages (and their cultural baggage) in order to preempt a reductive and singular reading, but the very gesture of "*there was or there wasn't*" resists any normalizing or stabilizing interpretation of what is to come. Furthermore, the phrase "*They say*" aims to deconstruct the appropriation of rumor-based knowledge attributed to an absent and imagined normative authority. Indeed, who are they and why should we take their version of events for granted? Finally, "*olden times*" invert to times to come; past and future collapse into an unstable present in which the desire for a stable past and the fear of an uncertain future collide.

The storyteller then introduces the philosophical, religious, scientific, and poetic aspects of water, relating that

> it was a time when Man's throat was parched and dry [. . .] Many people clutched to the afterlife promise of *gardens beneath which rivers flow* [. . .] More than anything, this is the tale of a man [Jassim] who delighted in the science of water and in word games (reshaping *water* to become *we art*, for example). (VII)

The phrase "*gardens beneath which rivers flow*" is imported from the Qur'an, and refers to the concept of heaven in Islam. The phrase appears multiple times in the Qur'an and promises early believers, who lived predominantly in arid lands, a heaven constructed on water. For example, "The Family of Imran" Surah (translated by Muhammad Habib Shakir) states:

> So their Lord accepted their prayer: That I will not waste the work of a worker among you, whether male or female, the one of you being from the other; they, therefore, who fled and were turned out of their homes and persecuted in My way and who fought and were slain, I will most certainly cover their evil deeds, and I will most certainly make them enter gardens beneath which rivers flow; a reward from Allah, and with Allah is yet better reward. (The Qur'an 3.195)

The storyteller's importation of this phrase as one possible solution to both a philosophical and a material thirst problematizes the concepts of both thirst and heaven. Even as this Qur'anic verse offers a more or less historically progressive view of gender in which "male or female, the one [. . .] being from the other," are equal candidates for heaven, the recompense for persecuted Muslims is deferred to the afterlife. Unfortunately, groups such as al-Qa'eda or ISIS have made this concept of heaven sinister by hijacking and decontextualizing phrases such as "who fought and were slain" and imposing a reductive, cynical, and violent reading that occludes the multiple interpretive possibilities in Qur'anic verses: Would-be suicide bombers seek to attain these gardens (and the promise of the virgins therein) exclusively through acts of violence and terrorism.

Jassim, a nonreligious hydrologist, seeks instead to address thirst scientifically by finding ways to conserve water in Amman and in his city of residence, Tucson; he actively pursues a material solution to the problem of thirst. But the fluid nature of water also inspires in Jassim a translational poetics of possibility that manifests in his anagrams. In a lecture about water conservation at a university in Jordan, where he meets Salwa (his wife to be), Jassim states that water "is the major constituent of living matter. It is the only substance that occurs at ordinary temperatures in all three states of matter: solid, liquid, and vapor" (243). Fluid and anagrammatic in nature, water also comes to serve metaphorically as a major constituent of Jassim's identity negotiations and perceptions of the US. It is not surprising, therefore, that the storyteller reveals that Jassim anagrammatically reshapes "*water* to become *we art*." *Water* as *we art* is a perfect anagram in which a collective and inclusive *we* is present (the archaic *art* standing in for the modern "are"). As such, *We art* is an affirmation of Arab American existence within the fabric of the US. Furthermore, *art* can act as a verbalized noun from *art* as a verbal noun (*Masdar* in Arabic),[2] which is the source for a verb in the Arabic language. As transposed into American English, a verbalized *art* "*arts*" Arab American existence to produce fluid meanings and possibilities irreducible to a singular formulation. In the statement "*we art* our immigrant experiences," for example, *art* can serve both as a second-person singular present of the verb to be and as a verbalized noun. The latter finds Arabs in the US collectively *arting* or creating art out of their experiences as immigrants and migrants. In combination, existence (self-visibility) and art are co-constitutive. Likewise, *water* and *we art* do not occlude each other; rather, they enrich and challenge each

---

2. *Al-Mawrid: A Modern Arabic-English Dictionary* defines "Masdar" as "infinitive, verbal noun, nomen verbi" (1052).

other anagrammatically in a poetics of migration in which meaning travels back and forth in a vehicle of possibility, gardens of plurality.

The storyteller then reveals that "our story takes place in the provincial American town of Tucson, Arizona, a locale with weather and potential (and very little water)" (VII). Although Tucson is technically a city, the storyteller describes it as a provincial town, implying that provincial attitudes run amok there. Yet Tucson offers "potential" to outgrow provinciality. Like Amman, from which Jassim and Salwa move to the US, Tucson has little water. Jassim's plans for water conservation do not merely apply to Tucson's material conditions, however. They also relate to the conservation of fluid (receptive and generous) interactions among Tucson's diverse inhabitants. Moreover, the storyteller explains that Jassim and Salwa are "a couple whose love for each other had parched around the edges, pulled up at the corners" (VII). The two suffer an aridity in their relationship, which clearly needs care and irrigation. Unfortunately, these issues are subsumed under the culture of fear and backlash "after the World Trade Center buildings have been flattened by planes flown by Arabs, by Muslims. Salwa and Jassim are both Arabs. Both Muslims. But of course they have nothing to do with what happened to the World Trade Center. / Nothing and everything" (VIII). In other words, the couple's relationship and the already provincial Tucson recombine in a backlash-induced anagram, which renders Salwa and Jassim's private lives inextricable from the fraught political environment.

The storyteller too enters this condition in the second segment of the "Before" frame. In a seemingly abrupt shift, we encounter the storyteller being interrogated by airport security before she boards a flight. She thus finds herself in the position of flying while Arab.[3] Asked questions such as "*Were you the only person to pack your luggage?*" (VIII), the storyteller interweaves answers directed at readers. She relates that she has placed a tiny wooden box whose lid is inlaid with mother-of-pearl in front of us. She then sets a condition: "Before I tell you this story, I ask that you open the box and place in it any notions and preconceptions, any stereotypes with regard to Arabs and Muslims that you can find [. . .] This box awaits terrorists, veils, oil, and camels. There's room for all of your billionaires, bombers, and belly-dancers" (VIII). In essence, the storyteller places readers in the position of interrogators

---

3. I use this phrase following Akram Fouad Khater's identification of it: "The darkly humorous phrase 'flying while Arab' summarized the waves of main-stream suspicion and hostility that confronted Arab American communities in the wake of the 9/11 attacks. Anecdotes and documented stories of expanded surveillance and curtailment of civil liberties for Arab and Muslim Americans, unfriendly gazes from strangers and sometimes neighbors, and even attacks on individuals and establishments proliferated" (75).

who view Arabs and Muslims with fear and suspicion. Of course, not all readers fit this profile. What this repositioning does, however, is reveal the grotesqueness of racial profiling and the racialization of Arabs and Muslims. As Moustafa Bayoumi explains, "Arabs and Muslims (who, in the real world, are two overlapping categories, but in the world of American perceptions essentially the same thing) have entered the American imagination with full force, but their entry has been racialized" ("The Race Is On"). Under duress, the storyteller finds agency and a poetic voice (notice the b-sound alliteration in "billionaires, bombers, and belly-dancers") with which to address the listening readers.

After the storyteller places her shoes and other apparel in a gray bin and requests that readers place their stereotypes in the wooden box, the security officer states, "*I'm sorry sir/ma'am, you've set off the alarm. Please step over to the side*" (VIII). That the security officer identifies the storyteller as "*sir/ma'am*" speaks to the rote and depersonalized nature of the enhanced screening process. The storyteller is stereotyped and racialized as a member of a monolithic group. Her humanity and individuality matter little in this context, as she comes to stand in for all Arabs-cum-Muslims in the US. In-between questions, she asks her implied listeners/readers to throw into the box excess baggage such as "turbans, burqas, or violent culture [. . .] hateful names as well, ones you might never utter: Sand Nigger, Rag Head, and Camel Jockey [. . .] submissive women [. . .] multiple wives" (VIII–IX). The storyteller counterpoints the security questions with demands of her own, measure for measure. She understands that silence is not an option, that she must push back or lose her humanity.

In effect, the storyteller translates Shahrazad's story from the *Arabian Nights*, in which Shahrazad marries Shahrayar, who had previously married and killed a virgin every night to revenge his first wife's infidelity, to a situation of cultural backlash in which all Arabs and Muslims are punished for the actions of the nineteen terrorists behind 9/11. As such, we can classify the storyteller's frame as a "*Ransom frame* [. . . in which] the telling of stories has a paramount function: it serves to redeem a human life" (Gerhardt 401–2).[4] At stake here are the humanity and complexity of Arab Americans, the invisibility of which encourages discrimination and threats of violence against them. This frame, then, acts as guarantee for the payment of ransom (a nuanced and humanizing story) for Arab American lives, even as it holds for ransom for the

---

4. Mia Gerhardt identifies three frames in the *Nights*: "the entertaining frame, the time-gaining frame, and the ransom frame" (395). For more on the framing strategies in the *Nights*, please consult pp. 395–416 in Gerhardt.

duration of the story the stereotypes and racializations of potentially hostile listeners/readers. In her telling of stories for 1001 nights, Shahrazad reeducates and rehabilitates Shahrayar into a just king. Assuming a Shahrazadian position of survival, the storyteller hopes to transform the listeners/readers by, in the words of Husain Haddawy, telling "tales [that] divert, cure, redeem, and save lives" (xiv). She states at the end of "Before," "I don't need to lock the box, for it has a power of its own and will stay closed for the duration of our story. Do you feel lighter now, relieved of your excess baggage? Trust me; it will make listening to the story easier" (IX). In other words, the storyteller believes that the story itself has the power of keeping stereotypes and prejudices at bay. Without this "excess baggage," readers/listeners are now free to listen to the story from an Arab American perspective.

Although the airport interrogation section of "Before" provides a crucial framing of the novel, it was silently removed from the paperback edition.[5] This surreptitious removal raises larger concerns. In the publishing and marketing of Arab or Arab American novels in English, "political and cultural sensitivities come into play along every step of the way" (Serageldin, "Perils and Pitfalls" 426). Arab and Arab American voices are always under threat of erasure in the US, a fact of which, ironically, the storyteller evinces awareness in the cut segment. Flying while Arab is no less treacherous than writing while Arab or telling stories while Arab. Arab American writers, like "writers of any background have the right—indeed some might say the obligation—to write their reality, regardless of cooptation by external agendas" (441). Certainly, the storyteller's intervention in "Before" is a crucial framing of the narrative that comes after. The novel's frame in both its segments shares the functionality of the *Nights*' frame. In her analysis of framing in the *Nights*, Julie Scott Meisami argues that a "frame may function as an authenticating device [. . .] or as an organizing principle; these functions may or may not be combined" (Dawood et al. 110). In *Once in a Promised Land*, "Before" and "After" authenticate the Arab American characters' experiences and (re)organize the main narrative along the storyteller's Arab American perspective. As will become apparent, both "Before" and "After" (while obviously not anagrams themselves) follow the novel's poetics of the anagram in that they transpose (exchange) potentially Arabophobic and Islamophobic interpretations of the narrative into Arab American ones. That is, the novel's frames make visible an Arab American couple's experience of the post-9/11 backlash on Arab American terms.

---

5. I discovered the removal of this segment when I ordered the paperback edition of the novel for one of my courses on the Arab American novel.

ANAGRAMMATICS IN THE NARRATIVE'S MAIN

Jassim and Salwa are Jordanian immigrants (although Salwa's family is originally Palestinian). Salwa's is not a straightforward case of immigration, however. She was born in the US, but her family returned to Jordan shortly after her birth. Abu Siham (Salwa's father) tells Jassim why they returned: Salwa's mother, Um Siham, "had three small girls, was pregnant with Salwa, and I was constantly working. My father was ill, as was Um Siham's mother. After Salwa was born, we decided that it was not worth losing our souls so we could have nice things" (70). While Salwa's return to the US with Jassim is a homecoming of sorts and an act of reimmigration that continues the story of her parents' curtailed immigration, it is premised on a materialistic fantasy: "The America that pulled at her was not the America of her birth, it was the exported America of Disneyland and hamburgers, Hollywood and the Marlboro man, and therefore impossible to find. Once in America, Salwa still searched and [shopped . . .] in the hope that she would one day wake up in that Promised Land" (49). Jassim receives his master's in hydrology at a university in Arizona and returns home to work at the Ministry of Water Resources. Because he lacks a PhD, his career stalls. Meanwhile, "America was calling him daily, with her Anytime Minutes whispering stainless steel promises of a shiny lab and possibility" (62–63). Jassim returns to the US and earns his PhD. Instead of returning to Jordan again, however, Jassim accepts a job offer from Marcus, a former classmate, at a water consulting firm. The comfort of a predictable, routine life keeps Jassim in the US.

Jassim and Salwa lead a life of upper-middle-class privilege, but their lives remain largely artificial. In the novel's opening, which takes place shortly before 9/11, Salwa is attempting to conceive a child without Jassim's knowledge. Jassim, oblivious, goes through his routine of swimming before work every morning. As the storyteller relates, he delights in "the science of water and in word games" (VII). These word games are predominantly anagrams, and the fluidity of water comes to inform the anagrammatic play in which he attempts to find translational possibilities and to negotiate his position in relation to his adopted city, Tucson. Anagrammatic play allows Jassim to reconstitute his experiences in Tucson on his own terms and to enter a mutually constitutive relationship with the city. Both Jassim and Salwa have striven to make Tucson their own and have met with financial success, but the city that they have come to know mutates suddenly into an unrecognizable and intolerable entity. Jassim and Salwa find themselves renegotiating their altered places of work and leisure. These struggles come to a head as Jassim is suspected of terrorism and Salwa is beaten nearly to death by her lover, Jake. In engaging

Jassim's anagrams as they relate to the novel's fraught sociocultural content, I would like to begin by investigating the possibilities of anagrams as poetics.

Howard Bergerson states, "There exists no book which adequately reviews [the subjects of palindromes and anagrams] against the great background of history" (v). The history of anagrams, at least before the seventeenth century, is obscure, and we currently "tend to regard [. . .] anagrams as mere curiosa" (v). Curiously, the meaning of "curiosa" includes erotic and pornographic books. The historical obscurity of anagrams and the odd, erotic aspects of curiosa are uncannily similar to the perceptions of Arabs in the US. Having inherited Western Europe's orientalist/eroticizing representations of Arabs, the dominant culture in the US perceives Arabs as un-American oddities. As such, it is oddly appropriate that Halaby chooses the anagram as a poetics through which an Arab American character negotiates his experiences in the US before and after 9/11. From Jake's orientalizing of Salwa, to the FBI's investigation of Jassim post-9/11, the anagram in its definition and poetic intervention operates at the crux of *Once in a Promised Land*.

It is worth noting that anagrams do not necessarily form apposite expressions in relation to their source words. Indeed,

> to separate a word [. . .] into the letters of which it is composed is to dissolve it semantically, since the letters are sub-morphemic units. To rearrange the same letters into a new expression related in meaning to the original, thus restoring something like the original content (but without restoring any of the original morphemes), is perhaps the most fascinating of the anagrammatical arts. (41)

What renders anagrammatic play an art form is the successful approximation of the source word's meaning without the restoration of the original letter combinations in the source word. The translational motion of the apposite anagram becomes clear: It is an intralingual translation of the source word's meaning with the added challenge of recombining the letters that constitute the source word. Here as well, we can perceive a connection between the traveling of letters and the migrations of Arab Americans. As immigrants under suspicion, Arab Americans often find their names, identities, and histories recombined along stereotypical lines. As such, Arab Americans are rendered adjuncts to their sociocultural inheritances (source cultures) with little control over the visibility of their transcultural, combinatory identities (anagrams of cross-cultural translation).

The meanings of Jassim's and Salwa's names play important roles in their characterizations and experiences, but their names enter inapposite transpositions as they travel from Amman to Tucson.⁶ When Jassim first meets Salwa, she finds it "odd that his name was Jassim, for if it were not for his face, with the large eyes and very thick eyebrows, he would have looked fragile, breakable" (243). Salwa recognizes that Jassim does not resemble his name. Her previous love interest and would-be fiancé, Hassan Shaheed (whose name translates as "Handsome Martyr/Witness"), thinks that Jassim's "name, implying large stature and strength, seemed inappropriate for such an effete man" (13). Hassan first appears in the third section of the novel's first chapter, which contains three character-based sections: Jassim, Salwa, and Hassan. Salwa's name translates as "distraction," "quail," "honey," and "comfort; consolation; solace" (*Almaany.com*). While her quail-like beauty is a distraction (rendering her a sought-after honey), Salwa embodies neither comfort, nor consolation, nor solace. She certainly is no comfort to Hassan, a Palestinian Jordanian from a poor family, when she quickly accepts Jassim's offer of marriage, in part because she wishes to return to the US, the country of her birth. Both Jassim and Salwa "appear guilty of having dashed the innocent hopes of Hassan [. . .] for a modest future away from the alluring yet destructive riches of America" (Banita 247). Salwa's betrayal repeats in the US when she realizes "she was not happy in her life [. . .] This was the life she had chosen, but it was not the life she wanted" (91). Her affair with Jake suggests that Salwa is ultimately no comfort to Jassim either. Salwa's and Jassim's names are rich in meanings that resonate on the levels of culture, character, and narrative. In the US, however, both Jassim and Salwa's names lose their cultural resonances even as they take on the dialogic English letter form in transliteration.

For instance, one of Salwa's bank clients, a retired marine named Jack Franks, attempts to call Salwa "Sally." Jack, the narrator informs us, is in "his late fifties [. . .] a solid man, too big for his chair" (33). If Jack's description sounds familiar, it is because it aligns with the meaning of "large stature and strength" in Jassim's name. This translational anagram combines Jassim and Jack, who, incidentally, also share the first two letters in their names. Jassim's and Jack's lives will soon become unpleasantly entangled. On meeting Salwa, Jack immediately attempts to rename her:

"Salwa."

"Yes?"

"I was just reading your name. For some reason I always want to say Sally."

---

6. The roles of Arabic names are crucial to the poetics of all the novels I engage in *Poetics of Visibility*. Names come to function as religious markers, blue notes, untranslatable entities, identity synecdoches, mythological referents, foreignizations, and/or cross-cultural hybrids.

"The first part is *el*, like *sell*, with a *wa* at the end, not a *ly*. Salwa." Her name sat in her mouth like a perfect strawberry.

"You make it sound so easy. Salwa." (33)

This passage begins and ends with Jack saying Salwa's name. Presumably, he pronounces it correctly the second time after Salwa instructs him. Interestingly, Salwa dissolves her name into morphemes and puts them back together, which mimics the anagrammatic motion without transposing the letters of her name. Jack, on the other hand, offers an Americanized analogue for Salwa's name: Sally. Even though both names begin with *Sal*, Salwa requires a short *a* pronunciation (as in *sell*) and Sally a long *a* (as in the word *sad*). In essence, Jack wishes to transpose Salwa's name into English so as not to trouble himself with learning the name's correct pronunciation or to acknowledge its cultural source. Were Salwa to accept the name Sally as an American approximation of her own, it would diminish her sense of self both as Arab and as American; it would render part of her identity invisible. This is why she patiently and charmingly teaches Jack how to pronounce her name. The narrator tells us that this pronunciation sits "in her mouth like a perfect strawberry"; the simile sensualizes and exoticizes both her name and her mouth. By attempting to rename Salwa, Jack hopes to make this foreign "honey" palatable on his terms. His response to her—that she makes the pronunciation of her name sound easy—reveals an unspoken assumption: It is not at all easy for Jack to contend with the presence of Arabs in the US. Even when he is confronted with an attractive and intelligent woman such as Salwa, Jack struggles to accept her on her own terms, as an Arab American (the two designations being incommensurable in Jack's mind). He relents, however, as a result of Salwa's "deft demployment of sexual exoticism coupled with a strong dose of American-trained professional charm" (Banita 249). Jack's analogue (Sally) is in effect an antianagram. It reduces the source word (exchanging Salwa's complex identity with a synecdoche) rather than add meaning to it (a metonym that could exist alongside Salwa), as in an apposite anagram.

It comes as no surprise that Jassim's anagrams begin to show signs of stress on the morning he meets Jack, September 11, 2001. Jassim's daily morning ritual—a "ritual as close to prayer as he could allow" (3)—consists of a swim at his gym, Fitness Bar. The third-person narrator, who assumes the narration after the storyteller's initial framing of the novel, states:

After his final lap, Jassim stood in the water and breathed heavily with his arms outstretched. Eyes closed, fingers reaching, palms facing the sky, head left, head right, slight rotation with each arm, and another deep breath to elongate his spine, face, and chest tilted towards the heavens. (5)

Jassim's "palms facing the sky, head left, head right" gesture to the end of a Muslim prayer, except that Muslims turn their heads right and then left in ending their prayers. In the pool, Jassim seems able to hybridize his meditative swimming ritual and his cultural inheritance (although he is not religious). This allows him to "elongate his spine," decompress, and face the heavens. Tucson translates into a garden of sorts constructed around a swimming pool of meditation, rejuvenation, and possibility: a promised land. Furthermore, Jassim's elongating of his spine has a direct relationship to his name, which means (as Hassan defines it) "large stature and strength." In this moment, Jassim is able to actualize and translocate the cultural implications of his name to an American setting and, in his motion, to inhabit his adopted city with a sense of agency.

The two Qur'anic verses in "The Family of Imran" Surah, which follow the verse I quote earlier in the chapter, locate cities as sites of negotiation: "Let it not deceive you that those who disbelieve go to and fro in the cities fearlessly. / A brief enjoyment! then their abode is hell, and evil is the resting-place" (3.196–97). Here as well, the disbelievers are left to their own devices in cities, and their punishment is deferred to the hell of afterlife. But where do we locate Jassim in this formulation? As a secular scientist, does he qualify as a disbeliever to be punished by God? Ironically, Jassim's "brief enjoyment" of Tucson is followed by an abode of earthly hell during the aftermath of 9/11 in which he becomes a terrorism suspect. As such, he falls into what Laila Halaby describes in an interview as "this purgatory stage of 'otherness,' neither here nor there" (Schuman). Not a Muslim fundamentalist, but perceived as one, Jassim enters the condition of double purgatory; it is as if Allah punishes him for being a disbeliever while an altered Tucson suspects him of religious extremism. Neither Islam nor civil society affords Jassim refuge or respite. His life in and experience of Tucson are reduced fundamentally to a singular mode of suspicion, and his anagrammatic play falters as a result. For the moment, Jassim constructs a complete anagram, "*So deep*," from the brand name "Speedo" (4). The apposite anagram derives from the ironic contrast between the ubiquitous commodity and the spiritual, meditative quality of Jassim's swimming ritual. Jassim likes "the way the word [Speedo] broke down symmetrically" (4) in his anagram, completely unaware that his life is about to alter irrevocably.

On his way to the shower, Jassim runs into Jack Franks, who takes a keen interest in him. Although they have just met, Jack asks Jassim intrusive questions about his country of origin. Jassim pushes open the red door whose white letters announced they were entering the men's locker (*rock semen, l* remainder), gestured for Jack Franks to precede him, and hoped that their conversation would end. Jassim liked to start the day with silence, required silence to cement the balance he had achieved by swimming. (6)

Feeling uncomfortable, Jassim produces an imperfect anagram in which "men's locker" reforms as "*rock semen*" with the letter "l" remaining. Interestingly, the narrator leaves out the apostrophe, which also remains behind. The anagram clearly points to a threat to Jassim's sense of masculinity. He responds by hardening a fluid substance (semen). If Jassim's semen is harder than Jack Franks's (an older man), then he may be able to protect himself from Jack's line of questioning. That the letter *l* and the apostrophe remain lost in transposition has considerable implication for the poetics of translation and migration in anagrams. In *A Poetry Handbook,* Mary Oliver refers to an 1860 volume on grammar by Goold Brown in which the alphabet is divided into families of sound. In it, the letter *l* belongs to the family of semivowels, which are "consonant[s] that can be imperfectly sounded without a vowel so that at the end of a syllable its sound may be protracted, as *l, n, z,* in al, an, az" (Oliver 21). The letter *l* then is one of liminality between consonant and vowel; it corresponds to Jassim's position between Arab and American cultures. Furthermore, the fact that semivowels protract vowel sounds elongates the space of liminality and gives it a certain stature (as in Jassim's name). It is as if Jassim occults the letter *l* to protect it from the hardened positionality of "*rock semen.*" The possibilities in the letter *l* do not stop there, however. Oliver continues: "Four of the semivowels—*l, m, n,* and *r*—are termed *liquids,* on account of the fluency of their sounds" (22). The liquid letter *l* remains behind in a space reserved for fluid identity negotiations. Furthermore, the remaining apostrophe relates to Jassim's possessive protection of that fluidity. Ironically, the fluid process of reshaping words anagrammatically produces a hardened content *(rock semen)* and a curtailed possibility in the letter *l* and apostrophe remainders.

Jack asks Jassim if he is "*I-ray-nee-in*" (6) and whether his wife is "veiled" (7), a thinly veiled attempt not only to locate Jassim but also to situate him within a predetermined set of assumptions about Arabs. Jassim answers that he was born in Jordan and that his wife does not wear a veil. Franks then informs Jassim that his daughter eloped with a Jordanian man to Jordan where "she converted. She's an Arab now" (6). Franks seems to conflate his daughter's conversion to Islam with being an Arab. As Nadine Naber demonstrates, such confusion is commonplace: the "meaning of the term 'Arab' is contested [. . .] Although U.S. popular cultural representations often conflate the categories

'Arab' and 'Muslim,' not all Arabs are Muslim [there are many Arab Christians for example] and not all Muslims are Arabs" (Introduction 5). Jack does not stop there. He asks Jassim if his wife is beautiful and then adds,

> "No offense intended. I'm just amazed by the beauty of the women there [. . .] No wonder you fellas cover them up. There's a woman at my bank, First Fidelity, who's from Jordan. Absolutely beautiful. Eyes like magic [. . .] and thick, thick hair [. . .] Never seen anyone like her. Can never remember her name. Starts with an S and sounds like Sally, I think. You know her?" (7)

Although Jassim has just told him that his wife is not veiled, Jack presses on with the assumption that all Arab men force the veil on Arab women. He then describes Salwa in exotic terms, which makes Jassim uncomfortable. Just as Salwa refuses to recognize the name Sally, Jassim lies to Jack about knowing "Sally." After Jack leaves, Jassim thinks to himself that he has "never been *buttonholed* like that" (8).

Jassim runs into Jack again at Fitness Bar after 9/11, and after Jack has learned from Salwa that Jassim is her husband. Before Jack greets him, "Jassim felt invisible as he dressed, deposited his wet Speedo and hand towel into a plastic bag" (111). At this point, Jassim has faced discrimination at the mall and at work, where his coworkers suspect him of being a terrorist. He relishes the respite of invisibility that the gym affords him from the condition of patriotism-induced hypervisibility in which he finds himself. But this short respite ends with the arrival of Jack, who wastes no time reminding Jassim of his lie about not knowing Salwa:

> *What does it matter?* Jassim wanted to say. *I have a right to my private life as much as anyone.* But he didn't say these things [. . .] "How have you been?"
> "Very well, thanks. Tucson is a small town. Salwa Haddad is my banker and your wife."
> *My banker and your wife.* "Nice to see you again, Jack."
> "Likewise." (112)

It is important to note here that the storyteller of the "Before" section derives her agency from a similar line of questioning as she passes through security at an airport. Both the storyteller and Jassim provide stream-of-consciousness answers to intrusive questions, which reveal the precariousness of US citizenship for Arab Americans. Jassim's right to a private life no longer obtains after 9/11. He has already internalized the new reality, so he does not resist Jack's questions and accusations. He tries to move the conversation, or, more aptly, the interrogation, to Jack's well-being, but Jack circles back to Jassim's lie. By calling Tucson a small town, Jack implies that Jassim's movements and connections are always conspicuous. Jack then hurls "Salwa Haddad is my banker and your wife" at Jassim in order to remind him that he has access to his life through his banking relationship with Salwa. After this exchange, Jack begins to investigate Jassim and alerts his FBI friends about him.

Jack does not see (or care to see) Jassim's struggles and his vulnerability after 9/11. Jassim's daily actions are automatic, and his mind repeatedly conjures up the pictures of destruction and suffering. At the office, he feels that "something had been wrong. Had he said something impolite? He couldn't imagine what [. . .] Surely not because of what happened in New York? He had as little connection to those men [the hijackers] as they did" (22). Jassim perceives an altered mood at his office, where the coworkers he has known for years begin to act strangely around him. Later, when Jassim and Salwa go to the mall, a store clerk eyes Jassim suspiciously and then decides to call mall security. After speaking to the security guard, Salwa confronts the clerk, who answers, "He just scared me [. . .] He just stood there and stared for a really long time [. . .] My uncle died in the Twin Towers" (30). Salwa retorts, "I am sorry to hear that. Are you planning to have every Arab arrested now?" (30). Salwa's question identifies the widespread targeting and harassment of "men who had beards, coupled with dark skin," persons "who closely resembled the corporate media's 'Arab/Middle Eastern/Muslim look'" (Naber, "'Look, Mohammed the Terrorist Is Coming'" 296). Not only does this stereotypical formulation render Arabs identifiable by sight, but it also hijacks their humanity and complexity.

As they walk away from this encounter, Jassim tells Salwa:

"It probably wouldn't be so bad if we lived in a bigger city. Salwa, it's okay. She's just a kid. She's doing what she thinks is right."

[Salwa answers] "It's not okay, Jassim. Do you think this is going to get better? For God's sake, she called security on you in the mall, in a teenage clothing store." For all her rage, she could see that Jassim had shut off that part of himself that should be fuming, that he had accepted what had happened and allowed his thoughts to move on. (32)

Jassim's reference to a bigger city has to do with diversity and ethnic enclaves. In a larger city, Jassim and Salwa could live among other Arab Americans, whereas in Tucson they have befriended only one Arab American couple. Furthermore, a larger city would likely have more professionals who look like Jassim, so he would not be as visible as he is in Tucson. Jassim's longing for invisibility, one that affords him translational agency in his anagrammatic play, is akin to the notion of a translator's invisibility: A translator can reshape a work into another language without being visible as the agent of that transposition. In his anagrammatic play, Jassim attempts to control his visibility by privately transposing the words around him into translations of his experiences. It takes Jassim some time to return to his anagrams after he faces multiple forms of backlash that rob him of invisibility and privacy. Furthermore, the upper-middle-class salaries that had previously ameliorated and filtered Jassim's and Salwa's experiences in the city are no longer effective after 9/11. Jassim's justification that the clerk is only a kid, while valid to a certain extent, leads him to a state of denial, whereas Salwa sees things too clearly. Salwa's question, "Do you think this is going to get better?" heralds a sequence of events that make things much worse: Jassim loses his job and accidentally runs over a teenage skateboarder; Jack Franks and the secretaries at Jassim's office both call on the FBI to investigate him; and Salwa has a miscarriage, a bank customer discriminates against her, and her lover Jake beats her nearly to death. The conversation in the mall reveals a growing tension between Jassim and Salwa. Salwa begins to think of returning to Jordan, while Jassim continues to believe that the backlash against Arabs, Arab Americans, and those who are mistaken for Arabs, will subside after some time. Salwa, however, comes to understand that "it was not just her Lie [about not taking the birth control pills] that had brought distance between her and her husband and surrounded them with tension, it was the patriotic breathing of those around them" (184–85).

The chapter after the mall episode finds Jassim sliding

> into the water [. . . ,] the tension of the past two weeks detaching itself in clumps, the wreckage of four planes cluttering the space around him, ash filling his lungs [. . .] Stroke and stroke, smooth and straight, his mind forcing the debris into neighboring lanes as he pulled a picture of his office (of Corey and the secretaries) from between his shoulder blades and tossed it into the water so he could stare at it clearly even as it filled him with disquiet. (39)

Water, the source of Jassim's fluid negotiations, is now muddied, and he has to struggle to repurify it. It is as if the terrorists also destroyed Jassim's secularized version of *"gardens beneath which rivers flow"*: his city beneath which the pool flows. Jassim's secularized version of heaven, his original anagram and the source of its poetics, inverts to a terrorist's heaven, which is more akin to hell. The wreckage of the planes clutters around him and ash fills his lungs. Swimming powerfully, Jassim finally pushes the debris into neighboring lanes but is unable to remove the debris from the water. Moreover, he must deal with a mental picture of his office colleague (Corey) and the secretaries who eye him with fear and suspicion. What the water retains, however, is its ability to make Jassim see clearly the cause of its muddied state even as it fills him with disquiet. Jassim accepts his altered life and city, but the water fails to wash the denial from his shoulder blades, at least not yet. Having internalized this new reality, Jassim is no longer able to produce anagrams (perfect or partial) for the next 125 pages in the novel after his *rock semen* anagram.

As if to make up for lost time, Jassim produces five anagrams for the source *We Deliver,* which he finds on a Thai food menu. Jassim has just returned home after accidentally running over the teenage skateboarder, Evan, who dies as a result of his injuries (the novel offers the possibility that Evan had decided to commit suicide by jumping in front of Jassim's car). Completely distraught, Jassim cannot bring himself to cook food for Salwa, who is on her way home from work after experiencing anti-Arab discrimination at the hands of a bank customer. Jassim studies the flier and finds "his eyes drawn to the words on the bottom: *We Deliver. Live rewed. Devil were. Liver weed. Led review. We reviled*" (131). The first anagram suggests two interpretations. In the first, the word *rewed* is a composite of the preposition *re* and the word *wed*. It warns of or prophesizes a time when Salwa and Jassim live wedded to other people. In the second interpretation, the word *rewed,* the past tense of "rew" in the first anagram, is a "chiefly dialectical variant of RUE" ("Rew," *Merriam-Webster.com*). *Live rewed* can come to mean "live bitterly regretted," possibly reflecting Jassim's and Salwa's unspoken regret for marrying. Here, *rewed* can also serve as a homonym for "rude"; the couple certainly experiences the rudeness of Arabophobes and Islamophobes. Both explanations relate to the couple's marital difficulties, and both foreshadow Salwa's affair with Jake and Jassim's flirtation (which comes close to an affair) with Penny, a waitress he meets at Denny's. The second anagram, *Devil were,* suggests that Tucson now largely perceives the couple as the devil, even while a segment of its population actively bedevils Jassim and Salwa. The third and fourth anagrams, *Liver weed* and *Led Review,* are more difficult to decipher in context of the novel. The fifth anagram, on which Jassim finally settles, *We reviled,* encapsulates the post-9/11 backlash and hate that Jassim and Salwa experience. It is worth noting here that the fifth anagram, which concerns the word *deliver* (*We* is simply a repetition), offers an interesting feature: *reviled* is a palindrome of *deliver*—the complete palindrome of *We deliver* is *reviled ew,* replete with an exclamation of disgust or distaste. It is as if the delivery service delivers revilement, packaged and ready for consumption.

When Salwa arrives home and greets Jassim, he says,

"We reviled."

"What?"

"Have you ever noticed that *we deliver* can be changed into *we reviled?*"

"How about *we relived?*" asked Salwa.

"Oh yes, of course. Good." (131)

Salwa anagrammatizes Jassim's palindrome and transposes *reviled* to *relived*. In so doing, she transforms the abusive *reviled* into the hope of living again. Salwa makes Jassim aware of a possible way out of the hate they experience in the US. For Salwa, reliving is the hope of resettling in Jordan. Much to Salwa's chagrin, however, Jassim remains in denial about the backlash. His version of reliving might include moving to a larger city, where he can regain invisibility and a sense of privacy. Jassim's immediate concern is to tell Salwa that he has run over and accidentally killed a teenage skateboarder. Salwa asks, "'How was your day, habibi?' A question asked from habit but with no interest, but Jassim couldn't see it, was just thankful for the opportunity to answer" (132). Jassim desperately needs Salwa's support. Her positive anagram and her question ending with "habibi," Arabic for "my love," provide him with some encouragement. He answers, "'Not so good, Salwa. Not so good.' / But instead of asking why, Salwa walked out of the room" (132). Perceiving her distance (both physical and emotional), Jassim waits before telling her about the accident. When he does, he gives her the "American version, the one with no crooked neck, no teenage boy with a death wish" (133). The American version is the Hollywood version, "the one that promises a happy ending for everyone if you just believe it hard enough" (119), the version that Jassim wished for after he hit Evan.

Salwa says that she is glad that Jassim is all right. She "sat for another moment looking at him, got up and kissed his forehead, and then walked out of the room" (133). Because she lied to him about not taking the birth control pills and because she concealed her pregnancy and her miscarriage until that morning, a barrier has surfaced between them. As Jassim sits alone, his mind "reached the center of the labyrinth, the key to everything, the memory that just this morning Salwa had told him she had had a miscarriage" (133). He remembers that just before Evan hurled himself in front of his car, his (Jassim's) mind was repeating "*Salwa had a miscarriage.* Jassim's conscious and semiconscious thoughts were colliding, creating a heady, almost blinding panic" (117). If the possibility existed that the couple could relive by having a child, an apposite anagram of their genes and dreams, it has now miscarried. Jassim's recognition that Salwa's miscarriage is at the center of the labyrinth is truer than he realizes.

Salwa miscarries at home that morning and then attempts to erase "what evidence she could of the massacre that was taking place within her" (88). The narrator's choice of diction, "massacre," evokes the mass murders of 9/11. The loss of life finds an echo in Salwa's womb. It is as if the terrorists' act and the subsequent backlash forestall the possibility of new Arab American life. Salwa lies to Jassim, claiming that she is having a "really bad period" (90). After he leaves, Salwa calls her friend Randa, who rushes to her side. The miscarriage over, Randa helps Salwa to bed, where "she drifted. She was floating on an inflatable bed in a pool of diluted blood. From time to time the bed would bump into a buoyed mass, a baby, a wrecked car, her family" (91). In her vision Salwa removes herself to a pool, a location in which Jassim usually finds peace and balance. But Salwa fills the pool with diluted blood. The inflatable bed on which she floats bumps into a shifting mass: her miscarried baby, Jassim's wrecked car, and her family. The vision seems to foretell Jassim's car accident and Salwa's loss of her family as a result of an affair that ends in violence. Blood is common to all the bed touches. Furthermore, in "the redness of her blood she saw the crevice between her and her husband, saw how his life ran right while hers was veering left [. . .] The Lie had come to life, or come to death, and was bloated between them" (91–92). If 9/11 alters the nation, Salwa's miscarriage fractures her marriage.

Drifting in and out of sleep, Salwa remembers her grandmother telling stories "while she and her sisters sat bunched up together, huddled with anticipation entwining them" (93), and she longs for her family and the sense of intimacy that the stories created. Her grandmother would begin each story with "*Kan ya ma kan fee qadeem az-zamaan . . . There was or there wasn't in olden times*" (93), a traditional opening phrase that first appears in the "Before" frame. This repetition reconnects the main narrative to the frame. It reminds readers that oral storytelling counterpoints the realistic narrative and, in its reinterpretation/metaphorizing of the narrative, acts as an apposite anagram. Salwa remembers the story of Nus Nsays, "which in Arabic means *half of a halving*" (93). It begins when Nus Nsays's mother, who could not get pregnant for years, buys a pregnancy apple from a roaming merchant. He promises, "If you eat one apple, you will become pregnant" (93). Instead of eating it right away, however, she places the apple on the counter so that she can finish her chores outside. While she is working outside, her husband comes home, finds the apple, and eats half of it (saving the other half for his wife). Having no other recourse, she eats the second half of the apple down to the seeds and finally gets pregnant. Because she had only eaten half of the apple, however, her son is very tiny. And this is why people call him Nus Nsays.

The diminutive of *Nus* (half) is *Nsays* in Arabic. Ironically, Nsays requires more letters than Nus to actuate the diminutive effect: More letters yield a lesser meaning. Nsays is bad enough alone as a diminutive appellation, as it signifies a reduction of a person's social standing.[7] To halve the diminutive is to further exaggerate its insinuation. Nus Nsays grows up but remains the size of a young boy. As a result, no one takes him seriously. He more than compensates for his size by using his cunning and resourcefulness to save his friend and himself from the clutches of a *ghula* (a female ghoul). Salwa remembers asking her grandmother the meaning behind the story:

> *It is just a story* [her grandmother replies].
> But what is the point of him being so small?
> *To show that with determination and a clever wit, small characters can defeat larger evils. Every Palestinian has a bit of Nus Nsays within him. Or her.*
> [. . .]
> And the ghula? Who is the ghula supposed to be?
> This was one question her grandmother never answered. (98)

Stories are not merely stories. They are meditations on life, on how to live and survive. But Salwa feels dislocated: She cannot travel back in time and the future is uncertain. Salwa struggles to translate her grandmother's storied lessons to her present circumstance. She thinks, "Too bad that forgetting is so easy, especially for fickle girls in fairy tales" (98). By placing herself in the position of a fickle girl, Salwa "becomes the antithesis of the folkloric figure Nus Nsays [. . .] Her privileging of a consumer citizenship [. . .] inevitably leads to the silencing, if not complete demise, of the Nus Nsays within her, the emblem of her political Palestinian identity" (Fadda-Conrey, *Contemporary* 155). Before her miscarriage, Salwa has a revelation: "*We cannot live here anymore*" (54). She realizes that all "those years of schizophrenic reaction to American culture, disdain for the superficial [. . .] she had buried with each new purchase and promotion" (54). Living under backlash opens Salwa's eyes to the lie that has been her existence.

Resting in bed, Salwa thinks that if Jassim is not ready to have a family, "maybe she would turn this into an American story and leave" (92). Struggling to inhabit her grandmother's stories and the hope they provide—she "knew in the marrow of her bones that wishes don't come true for Arabs in America" (184)—Salwa considers switching to an American story, which would facilitate

---

7. In chapter 5, I engage the diminutive appellations for the characters of Othello (*'Utayl* in Arabic) and *Hanif* (Han) in Diana Abu-Jaber's *Crescent*.

her leaving Jassim with little consideration for their families in Jordan. To do so, however, would be to override completely her Palestinian/Jordanian cultural norms, to finish what she has started by her "privileging of a consumer citizenship," as Carol Fadda-Conrey identifies it (*Contemporary*). Salwa does not choose to leave Jassim, at least not yet. Instead, she fantasizes about going home, "back to Jordan, with her family and her language and her predictable world [. . . but] in this fantasy she had not included Jassim, had left him in Tucson" (176). Neither here nor there on multiple registers, Salwa enters into a mode of crisis, which she attempts to sidestep by having an affair with her coworker Jake. In *Once in a Promised Land*, as in many immigrant narratives in the US, "the unraveling of intimate relationships stands in for other representative acts of immigrant struggle in novels and stories [. . .] Adultery, especially, becomes an imaginary space in which authors explore what happens when national and ethnic identity is destabilized" (Friedman 71).[8] Jassim too comes close to having an affair. Although he reaches out to Penny for emotional support (he meets her at Denny's while he is having a panic attack), Jassim's flirtation also derives from a disruption of his identity. After the car accident, Jassim "for the first time [. . .] felt unsettled in his beloved America, vaguely longed for home, where he could nestle in the safe, predictable bosom of other Arabs" (165). His desire for home is similar to Salwa's. The lack of meaningful communication in their marriage blinds them to this fact, however, and pushes them further apart.

Jassim finds himself mostly alone as the FBI begins to investigate him. An FBI agent named Noelle James leaves her card at Jassim's office with a request that he call her. Jassim "dialed the number on the card [. . .] And noted that *FBI* could become *FIB* and *Noelle James* could be *lemon see jail*. No, there was no *i*" (227). Jassim tries to ameliorate the situation by creating two anagrams. The word play exposes the fact that the investigation is a witch hunt. The anagram "*FIB*" signals that it is premised on the lies and unfounded suspicions of Jassim's coworkers and Jack Franks. The second anagram, which transposes the letters of the agent's name to "*lemon see jail*," places Jassim as a lemon (a faulty commodity) that must serve jail time. In his zeal to create this anagram, Jassim introduces the letter "*i*." This addition of a lowercase "*i*" speaks to Jassim's lack of individuality and his diminished position after 9/11. Toward the end of the novel, when Jassim reveals to Salwa that he is under investigation, she says, "They're not looking at who you are as a person, at all the great work

---

8. The issues of betrayal and fidelity are integral to Abu-Jaber's construction of *Crescent*. Like Salwa, *Crescent*'s Sirine betrays her love interest Han (who is an Iraqi exile). While the circumstances for their betrayals differ, the destabilizing of identity informs both characters' actions. I engage the issue of fidelity at length in chapter 5.

you've done. They're looking at the fact that you're an Arab" (301). After Jassim agrees to meet Agent James and her partner at a nearby restaurant, he creates another anagram: "Noelle James. *Jello sea men* [. . .] It couldn't be too serious if she wanted to meet at a restaurant to have lunch" (227). The humorous anagram, "*Jello sea men,*" creates a very short respite for Jassim, as his prediction completely misses the mark. His case coincides with the profiling of Arabs and Muslims in the US. In fact, "more than ninety-six thousand calls to the FBI were made about 'suspicious' Arabs and Muslims [. . .] in the week following the 9/11 attacks alone" (Jamal 115).

At the restaurant, the barrage of questions begins. Agent Fletcher asks Jassim about the accident and whether he was cleared of any wrongdoing at the scene. He asks Jassim if he was aware of Evan's anti-Arab views. He places a photograph of Evan's skateboard in front of Jassim and points to one of the stickers on it, which reads "Terrorist Hunting License" (231). Agent Fletcher continues his questioning:

"When did you first see this sticker?" [. . .]
"This moment."
"Mr. Haddad, are you saying that you never saw this sticker before?"
"Yes, that is what I am saying."
"And you are also saying that it is a coincidence that the boy you killed hated Arabs?" (231)

Jassim is taken aback, but responds truthfully that it was indeed a coincidence that the boy he accidentally killed hated Arabs. The questions continue: "What was your reaction to the events of September 11?"; "How often do you pray in a mosque?" (231). Agent James then asks Jassim to describe his typical day, and he answers that it is not unlike the typical day for the rest of America. Agent Fletcher rejoins, "That may be, but the rest of America does not have access to the entire city's water supply with the means to tamper with it" (232). Although Jassim held back his true thoughts when Jack Franks questioned him at Fitness Bar on the morning of 9/11, he cannot help revealing his frustrations to Agent Fletcher: "Means is one thing, motive is another. I am a scientist. I work to make water safe and available. I am a normal citizen who happens to be an Arab [. . .] Just because I am an Arab, because I was raised a Muslim, you want to believe that I am capable of doing evil. It is sometimes best to look within before casting such a broad net" (232).

Jassim's response emphasizes that he is an American citizen, who is owed the rights and privileges that citizenship confers. These include not facing discrimination based on religion, ethnicity, and/or coincidence in this case.

Ironically, Jassim finds himself under suspicion for Evan's views, not his own. Evan feared and hated Arabs; Jassim, conversely, appreciates the US and is committed to being a good citizen. And yet, "The onus to prove themselves 'innocent' or 'unthreatening,' [. . .] falls on individual Muslims" (Shams 77). He reminds the FBI agents that he has worked for years ensuring that Tucson's water is clean and available. He has no motive to tamper with the city's water supply, and his years of service should attest to his character. He protests the fact that his being an Arab who was raised Muslim is enough to render his personal history in the US irrelevant. Like many Arabs and Muslims after 9/11, Jassim finds that he is perceived as guilty until proven innocent, that he has become a second-class citizen whose rights can be taken away. In fact, Jassim later thinks to himself that "in more than a decade of good citizenship, he had never for a minute imagined that his successes would be crossed out by a government censor's permanent marker [. . .] Things like this aren't supposed to happen in America" (299). But they do, as "U.S. history is rife with examples of immigrants being targeted and denied the benefits of citizenship because of their appearance and cultural backgrounds" (Jamal 116–17). Jassim finds that he must remind the agents of the promise of an America that treats all of its citizens equally. He argues that since he has no motive, the agents should look to their own motives in stereotyping him. Undeterred by his speech, the "agents asked more questions, each more farfetched than the previous one. (*Did you ever meet any of the hijackers personally?*)" (232), trying to establish Jassim's guilt by association. To the agents' surprise, Jassim ends the interview and leaves. In his car, Jassim "willed away the ridiculous wordplay that dwelling on any subject for too long always brought with it" (235). Understanding that he is no longer an agent in his own life, Jassim stops himself from constructing anagrams.

Jassim's and Salwa's pre-9/11 invisibility, which allowed them privileged access to a consumerist citizenship, inverts to hypervisibility post-9/11. But this state of hypervisibility is more a state of pernicious invisibility. Far from revealing Salwa's and Jassim's complexity and individuality, post-9/11 hypervisibility renders them "Arabs," would-be terrorists. As a result, they find themselves under unrelenting suspicion, while their culture of origin is reduced to acts of mindless violence and terrorism. That is, "Salwa and Jassim move from being invisible citizens who, however, feel they belong, and re-emerge as visible migrants unsure as to where they belong" (Valassopoulos 598). Their status as American citizens uncertain, the two come to resemble unwelcome migrants more than viable citizens. Salwa internalizes the messages of backlash, "like the cars sprouting American flags from their windows, antennas to God, electric fences willing her to leave" (54), like "American flags waving, pale hands willing them to go home or agree" (185). Finding themselves marginalized and threatened, Jassim and Salwa suddenly see and interact with "equally marginalized American citizens who are limited by poverty, drug abuse and the lack of education" (Valassopoulos 598). Through his relationship with Penny, Jassim comes to realize that working-class America had escaped him: "He'd seen the edges of it but had been buffered by a [white-collar] job [. . .] Jassim's eyes, for the first time in his life, singled out pickup trucks and pink faces, shaved heads and snotty-nosed children, food stamps, tattered smiles, ill-fitting false teeth, tobacco-stained fingers, and fourteen-hour-shift bloodshot eyes" (275). These revelations offer Jassim and Salwa little consolation in the end, as they join others in their troubled lives.

Once in a Promised Land's anagram-like structure makes visible the lives and humanity of both Arab Americans and disenfranchised or troubled Americans. Each chapter offers a set of untitled character-based sections. For example, the first two chapters put forward the same set of character-based sections: Jassim, Salwa, and Hassan in that order. Chapter 3, however, removes the Hassan section, adds a section for an unnamed young man (Jake), and gives Salwa two sections: Jassim, Salwa, (Jake), Salwa. This anagram-like recombination begins to render Jake visible, just as an anagram can change the audibility of letters in different combinations, allowing us to hear and perceive them differently. For example, Salwa's partial anagram for "Welcome," *cow*, changes the audibility of the "o" letter from an "uh" sound to an "ow" sound. The "o" letter gains another sound in the partial anagram, another layer of identification. Jake remains unidentified in his debut section in chapter 3, as he is yet to meet Salwa and have an affair with her. But the chapter signals this young man's importance to the plot by opening his section in storytelling mode: "Once upon a time, under a bright and sunny sky, a bright and sunny young man saw himself too clearly: each flaw floated to the surface, each criticism was a thickened wrinkle in the unforgiving sun" (50). The (Jake) section is flanked by two Salwa sections, suggesting his future relationship with her. The storytelling opening, with its poetic language, reminds us of the storyteller's opening in the "Before" and "After" frames, which are anagram-like in their metaphorizing/transposing of the main narrative. Halaby organizes the entire novel around an anagrammatic poetics, as if in solidarity with Jassim's (and, to a lesser extent, Salwa's) wordplay. When the novel introduces Penny in chapter 8, the storyteller's voice reminds us that *"Behind (and sometimes in front of) every story there is another (and sometimes another and another)"* (137). Visibility is mutually constitutive, and the combinations of stories allow for complex forms of visibility. In the anagram-like (re)combinations of character-based sections from chapter to chapter, Halaby renders the lives of Arab

American and otherwise-troubled American characters visible, not despite their human flaws, but because of them.

Realizing that there is something sinister about her lover Jake, Salwa decides to seek her friend Randa's advice. Upon reaching Randa's doorstep, "Salwa stood on the straw welcome mat trying to rearrange the letters, the way Jassim would, but all she could find was *cow*" (282). Not only does Salwa fail to create a complete anagram, what she constructs, *cow*, lays bare her self-loathing and guilt about her affair. Salwa confesses all to Randa, who advises her to return to Jordan for a while so that she can sort out her life. Salwa takes Randa's advice and buys a ticket to Amman. She tells Jassim that she has not been forthcoming with him, but she does not tell him about Jake. She shows him her e-ticket and says that she needs to go home for a while, that she needs to take a break from the US and be with her family. Jassim "stared [. . .] Read and reread Salwa's name. Did not laugh as he thought of *Haddad* being *dad-dah* backward. Or wonder at the irony of her name containing *laws*. He stared in the hope of finding something to say" (301–2). Jassim's final act of wordplay in the novel organizes his thoughts and helps him to communicate with Salwa. The palindrome "*dad-dah*," which sounds like a child calling "dada," prompts Jassim to tell Salwa that he is ready to start a family if this is still what she wants. This attempt at reconnection comes too late, and Salwa answers, "Jassim, I don't know what I want anymore" (302).

Jassim's incomplete anagram for "Salwa," *laws*, attests to the backlash's role in driving them apart. Indeed, "this backlash granted the U.S. government extended authority and a groundswell of popular support to further promote policies [and laws like the USA PATRIOT Acts I and II] that clash with basic American freedoms and rights" (Jamal 116). Salwa and Jassim's marriage is unstable before 9/11, but the backlash and the consequent laws targeting Arabs in the US after 9/11 forestall any possibility of reconciliation. These policies and laws render the couple hypervisible, a condition that conflates and politicizes their private and public lives. Jack Franks's prying is one example of how profiling extends into their everyday lives. The FBI agents' interview with Jassim reveals that they know more about Salwa's life than he does. Salwa has been paying for her niece's schooling, but she conceals this from Jassim. When one of the agents asks, "Why did she send fourteen thousand dollars to Jordan on September twelfth," Jassim answers, "'to help her family,' [. . .] hoping they couldn't see his surprise" (233). The agents also ask Jassim about the nature of the calls that Salwa has been receiving from Hassan Shaheed, her former love interest. At this news, "Jassim felt he had been kicked in the stomach" (233). These revelations deepen the rift between Jassim and Salwa and cast doubt and suspicion on typically unremarkable actions.

After informing Jassim of her plan to leave for Jordan, Salwa goes to Jake's apartment complex to tell him. As she approaches the stairs, she notices three Mexican workers. She "imagined the miles of desert they must have crossed for the opportunity to trim and mow and prune, the perils they must have endured to have their clear shot at the American Dream"; she wants to shout "it's all a lie! [. . .] A huge lie" (316), but she does not. Just as Jassim's eyes have been opened to the dark realities of the working classes, Salwa's eyes now perceive the struggles of fellow immigrants and migrants. She thinks to herself, "She did not come from a culture of happy endings. That she would have been much better off munching on fava beans from her ceiling basket" (317) just as Nus Nsays does in her grandmother's story. In this sense, Salwa realizes that she is in the wrong story. Inside Jake's apartment, she thinks that its "state of disorder should have been enough to shake any fairy-tale princess back to reality" (317). She tells Jake that she is leaving, effectively ending the affair. In his drugged stupor, Jake insults Salwa and says, "So you're running back to the pigsty [. . .] you came from" (320). Ironically, Jake's apartment is more like a pigsty, its disorder a metaphor for the US's condition post-9/11. Jake attacks Salwa, hitting her repeatedly. Salwa screams for help as Jake strikes her with the heavy silver frame of a painting, slicing her cheek and bloodying her face. He pushes Salwa down the stairs and calls her a "bitch! Goddamn fucking Arab bitch!" (322). Luckily, the Mexican workers intervene and save her life.

"AFTER" AS CONCLUSION

The storyteller of "Before" returns in "After" to transpose, quasi-anagrammatically, the narrative of Salwa, Jassim, and Hassan to a folkloric story in the Arab style. Once again, the storyteller invokes the "*kan / ya ma kan / fee qadeem az-zamaan*" formula and reminds us that the story takes place when "Man walked a frayed tightrope on large, broken feet over an impossible pit of his greatest fears" (331). The frayed tightrope and the broken feet, human weaknesses, precipitate a fall. And fear, as exemplified by the culture of backlash in the main narrative, begets violence. The storyteller then introduces us to a peasant girl born to refugee parents. When the mother gives birth to her baby, a *ghula* secretly visits the infant. Wanting the baby for her own, the *ghula* stitches "a thousand and one [magical] red threads" (331) under her skin so that she can pull her back to her at a future date. The allusion to *A Thousand and One Nights* places the peasant girl as a Shahrazad figure who must survive persecution in the US. The "novel characterizes the [US] as a *ghula* (Arabic for "female monster/sorceress") that tricks immigrants and their children into believing the American Dream. In doing so, this *ghula* leads them to abandon their values, culture, language, and religion and to relinquish any attempt at a permanent return home" (Fadda-Conrey, *Contemporary* 151). A nightingale attempts and fails to save the girl from the *ghula*. Clever Hassan, a folkloric hero in the Arab oral tradition, slays the *ghula*, but only after his knife misses the mark and plunges into the girl. Clever Hassan, the stand-in for Salwa's previous love interest Hassan, flees from the girl's disfigured body. The nightingale rushes to the girl's side and severs the *ghula*'s 1001 threads one by one with its beak. The *ghula*'s magic dissolves, and the nightingale turns into an ordinary man. "*Not a handsome prince?*" asks an unidentified listener. "Not a handsome prince," answers the storyteller, but "years of exercise had left him strong and sound in mind and body" (335). In other words, the nightingale transforms to Jassim. This Jassim carries the girl back home, hoping that with proper care she will eventually recover from her wounds. The unidentified listener asks:

> *The End?*
> The End [the storyteller answers].
> *Wait a sec.*
> What is it?
> *There's no "they lived happily ever after"?*
> "Happily ever after" happens only in American fairy tales.
> *Wasn't this an American fairy tale?*
> It was and it wasn't. (335)

The possibilities within anagrams, their poetics, survive Jassim's decision to stop "this ridiculous wordplay" (235) after the FBI agents interrogate him. They continue in the chapter structures and frames in the novel, and in the last anagram Jassim constructs from the letters of Salwa's name. This seemingly "diminutive art-form" (41), as Howard Bergerson defines it, is capable of producing an "*Ars Magna*" (40), or great art, because anagrams participate in what Samina Najmi calls an "aesthetic of smallness." This aesthetic "exposes the ideology undergirding the sublime of war [and backlash, and] may be defined as an artistic emphasis on small-scale objects and material realities, which include not only the ordinary, unadorned, and everyday, but also the personal and the particular" (156). Jassim's anagrams are inspired by small, ordinary material realities, but they reveal the complexity of an immigrant's mind attempting to come to terms with a country that no longer wants him. His anagrams are personal, but their poetics permeates the entire novel. In that spirit, I offer four contextually apposite anagrams for the title, *Once in a Promised Land,* that expose the ideological sublime of backlash:

> Damned in a necropolis.
> Racial sin penned doom.
> A demonic plan indorse.
> Can imprison? Done deal.

CHAPTER 5

Reframing Infidelity

Diana Abu-Jaber's *Crescent*

INTRODUCTION

In her opening to "A Prophet in Her Own Town: An Interview with Diana Abu-Jaber," Robin E. Field relates that Abu-Jaber "*submitted the manuscript of* Crescent *just before 9/11, only to wonder whether she should set the book aside. For who would want to read a story about Iraq, about Arab Americans, about the beauty of Middle Eastern poetry and music and art, at a time when she herself was receiving flyers under the door of her [. . .] office about rounding up the Arabs?*" (207). Despite these dire circumstances, *Crescent* was published in 2003 and received much acclaim from both American and Arab critics (208). In other words, an Arab American novel about beauty and culture, about shared humanity and vulnerability, proves to be a crucial response to fear, hate, and misunderstanding of Arabs and Muslims before and after 9/11. Abu-Jaber recognizes that "novels are one of the very few forms that we have available to really instruct us in the experiences of others. So I do take that very seriously. But it's not a cultural responsibility [or merely a cultural translation]—it's more about art" (211). Abu-Jaber identifies art as the crux of her writing, and the art of *Crescent* mediates fraught content by crossing and transgressing formal, poetic, cultural, and lingual boundaries. In its multiple infidelities, *Crescent* theorizes/poeticizes its own intervention across time and space, both reimagining and reimaging Arab Americans as complex, transcultural, and transmodal citizens.

The poetics and themes of Shakespeare's *Othello*, *A Thousand and One Nights* (the *Nights* henceforth), and Homer's *The Odyssey* travel and combine in *Crescent* to establish cross-cultural and cross-gender Arab American dialogue. While critics have taken up Moorish/Andalusian influences and storytelling in the style of the *Nights* in *Crescent*, they have not addressed the stakes of combining the three works in Abu-Jaber's novel.[1] This chapter argues that *Othello*, the *Nights*, and *The Odyssey* all overlap in the issues of cultural, translational, and relational fidelities and infidelities. One of *Crescent*'s main characters, Hanif, an Iraqi translator and professor in exile, asks, "What does it mean to call oneself an 'Egyptian writer' or even a 'Middle Eastern writer' anymore. [. . .] The [Arab] media is saturated with the imagery of the West. Is it even possible—or desirable—to have an identity apart from this?" (110). To disentangle Arab and Middle Eastern cultural production from European and North American elements, in other words, is neither remotely possible nor necessarily desirable. The long histories of orientalist and neo-orientalist cultural production, moreover, suggest that the inverse formula is equally valid. Cultural translation, like all exchanges, is subject to the inequalities of power, and *Crescent*'s art intervenes as a poetics of justice.

Chapter 5 posits that *Crescent* counters essentialist notions of authenticity, which often render Arabs in the US as alien and undecipherable, by taking up issues of cultural translation and fidelity in *Othello*, the *Nights*, and *The Odyssey*. In terms of the realistic (as opposed to the fabular) characters in *Crescent*, Hanif is initially placed allegorically in relation to Othello and Odysseus. His love interest, Arab American Sirine, is correspondingly related to Desdemona as well as to Calypso, Penelope, and a Siren. *Crescent* presents Sirine's uncle as a Shahrazadian figure who tells stories/fables in the style of the *Nights* for Sirine's (and the readers') benefit and instruction. Both Hanif and Sirine enter the condition of infidelity personally and culturally. While the allegories set the plot in motion, Sirine and Hanif soon diverge from their assigned roles to inhabit, faithfully or otherwise, a series of culturally overdetermined figures from literary history. In this way, Abu-Jaber paradoxically creates characters that defy simplistic conceptions of Arabs and Arab Americans. Infidelity as such counters essentialist and stereotypical formulations, producing complex and surprising combinations that work to forestall moralistic and exoticizing interpretations of *Crescent*'s characters.

---

1. For these, please see Nouri Gana and Magali Cornier Michael.

The form and poetics of *Crescent* follow suit. In addition to combining elements of three antecedent texts, *Crescent*, like *Once in a Promised Land*, offers both a storyteller and a narrator. In *Crescent*, however, the storyteller (Sirine's uncle) and the third-person narrator are made to share the space of every chapter, with the exception of chapter 20. The novel initially places the elements of storytelling and the novel form in culturally specific modes of representation (almost every chapter begins in Arabic storytelling mode). Next it moves to a realistic mode of representation, and it then provides the framework for cross-cultural translation by provoking readers (real, perceived, and characterized) to participate actively in reconciling the storytelling and realistic narratives in the hope of initiating a rewarding cross-cultural, cross-genre dialogue. Furthermore, *Crescent* improvises strategically on certain English words by using accentual play (English spoken with a thick Arabic accent) in order to create words that resonate in both Arabic and English: Arablish. This is not to mention the novel's ubiquitous food metaphors (Sirine is a chef in a Lebanese restaurant), which counterpoint the aforementioned combinational and *infidelious* (a colloquial adjective for the noun "infidelity") modalities.[2]

Crescent's form and poetics, then, provide us with layered and complex models for cultural translation. As Sarah Maitland reminds us, the "act of translation [lingual and cultural], by necessity, broadens our horizons; it means living *with* difference and living with *failure*. It means acknowledging the co-equal incommensurables that separate us. But because it also enables us to envisage and embrace that which we did not previously imagine, translation is about self-transformation" (8). *Crescent*'s mode of cultural translation, which pressures the concepts and practices of fidelity and infidelity, allows for a cross-cultural dialogue across texts and languages in the Arab American experience. The concept of fidelity in translation is unstable. Initially, it was "dismissed as literal word-for-word translation by Horace. Indeed, it was not until the end of the seventeenth century that fidelity really came to be identified with faithfulness to the meaning rather than the words of the author" (Munday 24). If the focus of fidelity has shifted from the words to the author's meaning in lingual translation, what transpositions might fidelity undergo in cross-cultural and relational registers? *Crescent* asks its readers to become cultural translators, who can recognize the transcultural and transpoetic infidelities of its Arab American characters. *Crescent* itself is a crossover text. Written

---

2. I do not investigate the role of food in *Crescent*, except to highlight certain points pertaining to my argument. For more on food and cooking in *Crescent*, please consult Lorraine Mercer and Linda Strom, and Brinda Mehta. Additionally, please see Arlene Avakian's "Baklava as Home: Exile and Arab Cooking in Diana Abu-Jaber's Novel *Crescent*" in *Food, Feminisms, Rhetorics*.

in its entirety before 9/11 and often interpreted as a post-9/11 novel (since it was published in 2003), *Crescent* maps pre-9/11 possibilities onto post-9/11 failures. It is for this reason that I choose to end *Poetics of Visibility* with it. How, then, does the poetics of in/fidelity (the moralless process and interplay between fidelity and infidelity) intervene in the multiplex that is *Crescent*?

ENTER *OTHELLO*

In a 2003 interview with Andrea Shalal-Esa titled "Diana Abu-Jaber: The Only Response to Silencing . . . Is to Keep Speaking," Abu-Jaber reveals:

> When I started writing [*Crescent*], I had the idea of working from the *Othello* story. I wanted to sort of retell *Othello*, where instead of having Othello be the Moor, he's Arab [. . .] The Iraqi professor [Hanif] I described as being very dark. However, I rewrote it and I took all of the direct allusions to *Othello* out.

Yet the traces of *Othello* are not effaced from Abu-Jaber's *Crescent*. Abu-Jaber did not take "all of the direct allusions to *Othello* out" as she claims. Indeed, one finds both direct and indirect resonances of the play throughout the novel. Shalal-Esa follows up by asking Abu-Jaber about her decision to rewrite the novel, and she responds that she did not want to rely on dramatic ideas of villainy and heroism; Abu-Jaber adds, "Freud wrecked it for everybody. After Freud there are no more villains. We understand each other too much—unless of course, you're Arab." Freudian analysis notwithstanding, Abu-Jaber's answer (in context of the backlash against Arabs and Muslims in the US after 9/11) points to the risk that an Arab Othello would be interpellated as a villain rather than a tragic hero, one whose pathology falls outside the scope of Western psychological analysis. Othello's confession to Lodovico that he is an "honourable murderer, if you will, / For naught I did in hate, but all in honour" (5.2.292–93) is likely to solicit a very different reaction in relation to an Arab Othello; a post-9/11 US readership might interpret an Arab Othello who murders his significant other as a misogynist terrorist bent on honor killing.

As if taking their cue from Abu-Jaber, Arab and Arab American critics have avoided comparing *Othello* and *Crescent*. At least two critics refer to *Othello* or to Moors in relation to *Crescent*. In note 6 from his essay "Politics of the Exotic in Diana Abu-Jaber's *Crescent*," Atef Laouyene alludes to the character Hanif's exotic lure, which "characterizes Sirine's initial attraction to

[him] as well as Desdemona's to Othello" (599). Laouyene does not, however, take up this allegory beyond the occasional allusion to the play and the character of Othello. Nouri Gana investigates *Crescent*'s reconfiguration of Arabness in Andalusian terms, considering the Moorish possibilities in Abu-Jaber's novel, including the concept of Moorish conviviality ("In Search of Andalusia"). Yet his interpretation does not touch on the figure of Othello. While neither Laouyene nor Gana deals explicitly with the play, their interventions nonetheless reverberate around the specter of Othello in *Crescent*. This periphrasis renders Othello absent/present, a liminal figure who gestures at once to the possibilities and impossibilities concerning Arab immigration to the US post-9/11. What is at stake here is the way in which Arab Americans experience the condition of Othello in its transposition into the present day. If Othello's experience as an immigrant in Shakespeare's play ends in failure and death, might his intermixed body, history, and cultural experiences find success in the poetics of liminality, transposition, and slippage? Kim Hall observes that while what she terms "race-thinking" in early modern England differs significantly from twentieth-century conceptions of race, race was nevertheless "an emergent category, one with shifting and paradoxical contours." Hall argues, moreover, that "*Othello*'s recurring importance in the growth of modern race-thinking makes it critical to see the significance of race for *Othello*'s modern audiences" (171). I would like to posit here that Abu-Jaber employs the figure of Othello as a nexus of the translational, cultural, ethnic, and relational infidelities in Shakespeare's play, the *Nights,* and *The Odyssey*. That is, Abu-Jaber utilizes a series of cross-cultural slippages that allow her to reinvent Othello by problematizing the concept of fidelity in its multiple valences.

In order to offer some possibilities for the poetics at work in *Crescent*, I begin by pointing to Arab reactions to *Othello*. In her essay "The Arabization of *Othello*," Ferial Ghazoul states, "[No] work of Shakespeare touches chords of Arab sensibility and identity so much as the tragedy of *Othello*. For one thing, the hero is a Moor and therefore an 'Arab'" (1). For Arab inhabitants of southwest Asia, North African Arabs (Moors) *are* Arabs—Maghrebi Arabs, but Arabs nonetheless. The Moors of North Africa are part of the pastiche of Arab regions that have their own flavors and subcultures; these regions, however, all share in collective Arabness. But the Moor has more to offer Arabness. The word "Moor" refers to the mixed Arab-Berber North Africans who conquered Spain in the eighth century. While Arabs might view the character of Othello as a combination of Islam and Christianity, of Arab and Berber, of East and West, they still consider Othello as one of their own. They do so because the Moor's traveling and combinational possibilities stand to benefit Arab culture and polity in a manner that recalls the sociocultural and political advantages of Al-Andalus (Arabic for *Andalusia*): "an exemplum of a cherished cultural poetics of conviviality" (Gana, "In Search" 234). The question is can this recognition migrate to the US, where the lure of a traveling Arab Othello—an "extravagant and wheeling stranger" (1.1.135) as Roderigo puts it—is recognized as a result of his transculturality, not despite it?

Othello's name, in its Western and Arabic resonances, is a site of contestation that relates to the issue of recognition. Khalil Mutran, the first translator of the play into Arabic (which was performed in the Cairo Opera House in 1912), saw in the name Othello a deformation of a possible Arabic name. Mutran identified two plausible Arabic origins for Othello: "'Atallah (literally, 'gift of God') or 'Utayl (the diminutive form of 'Atil, which means 'he who is unadorned by jewelry')" (Ghazoul 3). In the case of 'Atallah, the mixed aspects of Othello gain divine sanction, as he becomes God's gift to humanity. In this sense, 'Atallah seems to align with verse 13 of Surat Al Hujurat (The Walls) in the Qur'an: "O people, we created you from the same male and female, and rendered you distinct peoples and tribes, that you may recognize [or know] one another. The best among you in the sight of GOD is the most righteous. GOD is Omniscient, Cognizant" (Khalifa translation, *QuranBrowser.org*). Moorish "'Atallah" combines "distinct peoples and tribes" as the embodiment of mutual recognition. 'Atallah's combinatory quality deemphasizes physical and political difference in favor of righteousness, the only measure by which God distinguishes people. As such, 'Atallah gains a utopian dimension, a state of being to which one might aspire.

The second possible Arabic name that Mutran identifies for Othello is "'Utayl," which is the diminutive of "'Atil" in Arabic. The diminutive requires a deformation of the original letters. More is less (or, more aptly perhaps, Moor is less); the more the word looks like a motley, the less its sociocultural significance and standing. The mixing of letters in the diminutive creates a negative counterpoint to the ideal mixing of peoples and cultures that produces the Moor. Ghazoul proffers "he who is unadorned by jewelry" as a translation for 'Atil. While plausible, this translation is complicated by the fact that it is inaccurately gendered; furthermore, another definition for 'Atil exists in Arabic. The root of 'Atil is 'utl, and 'Atil translates as

> of women, one devoid of or unadorned by jewelry [...] of men, one devoid of wealth and ethics.
>
> العاطل من النساء التي لا حليَ عليها [...] ورجلٌ عاطلٌ اي خالٍ من المال والادب
>
> (my translation, *Muhit-Ul-Muhit Arabic-Arabic Dictionary* 611).

'Atil itself thus yields two gendered meanings: For men, a lack of wealth seems to engender a lack of ethics, and for women, lack of jewelry signifies a lack of social standing. This definition holds no clear relation to Othello, who, while flawed, is arguably devoid of neither wealth nor ethics, or to Hanif, the absent/present Arab Othello in *Crescent*. Hanif, an exile from Saddam Hussein's Iraq, is a visiting professor and translator at an unnamed university in Los Angeles. Hanif is certainly not wealthy, but he is an ethical character. The correlation of wealth and ethics in this definition of 'Atil does not readily resonate with the characters of Othello and Hanif.

The other definition of "'Utl" (the root for 'Atil) translates as "failure, breakdown (in operation or function), trouble, disorder, a condition of being out of order; defect(iveness)" (*Al-Mawrid: A Modern Arabic-English Dictionary* 767). In this definition, 'Atil produces many relevant meanings. Othello brings trouble and disorder by his very presence in Venetian society. Consequently, he triggers a breakdown "in operation or function" in both the Venetian state and, eventually, himself. So does Hanif, whose history and struggles in exile cause his love interest, American-born Sirine, who feels exiled from her deceased Iraqi American father and American mother, to confront the Iraqi part of her identity. Sirine lost her parents, who were on a relief mission to an unnamed location in Africa, when she was a child. In *Crescent*, the attributes of 'Atil find their way to both Hanif and Sirine, who share together the troubles of Othello. The diminutive 'Utayl serves to highlight these traveling and comparative implications. Mutran eventually chose 'Utayl as the title for his translation of *Othello*, because "the Arabic nominative declension of the name is "Utaylu,' which phonetically echoes 'Othello,'" and because the name 'Atalla is not found in North Africa (Ghazoul 3). In combination, the two Arabizations of Othello's name ('Atallah and 'Utayl or 'Utaylu) transpose the possibilities and failures in Shakespeare's *Othello* to an American setting after the First Gulf War, which constitutes the time frame of *Crescent*. What, then, are some of the pertinent traces and variations of *Othello* in *Crescent*, and how do they employ poetics of liminality, transposition, and slippage to redirect Othello's tragic fate?

For the moment, let us examine the translation of Hanif's name in allegorical relation to *Othello*. "Hanif" translates as "true believer" and "true, upright" (*Almaany.com*). Iago says of Othello: "The Moor, (howbeit that I endure him not) / Is of a constant, loving, noble nature" (2.1.279–80). Hanif's name carries within it the constant nature of Othello, for Hanif is true and upright. Indeed, Hanif exhibits many of Othello's "constant, loving, and noble" traits throughout *Crescent* as his fictional biography unfolds. This is echoed in one of *Othello*'s main sources: John Leo's (Leo Africanus's) *A Geographical Historie of Africa,* translated by John Pory in 1600.³ On describing the Moors of Barbary, John Leo states, "Most honest people they are, and destitute of all fraud and guile; not onely imbracing all simplicitie and truth, but also practising the same throughout the whole course of their liues" (40). Hanif's name becomes clearer with John Leo's description. The phrase "imbracing all simplicitie and truth" resonates exceptionally in Hanif's name. The "simplicitie" of being a "true believer" and the truth of being true and upright are closely related. As John Leo, Othello, and Hanif travel from East to West, so do their names in translation and transliteration.

Hanif's name, however, often appears in *Crescent* as Han. The curtailing of Hanif's name to Han, which echoes the diminutive form, reveals a complex character negotiating his presence between Iraq and the US. The truth of Hanif's name is unable to contend with the infidelity of its opaque synecdoche, Han. Thus, the translation of Hanif's name at once reveals a translational/allegorical meaning of a proper name and subverts it by exposing its untranslatability as Han, which does not resonate in either Arabic or English—unless of course we think of Han Solo, in which case Han becomes a rebel fighter, a traitor translator, who challenges the US empire. There is a sense of wholeness in Hanif's name because it is "true"; it is "upright" in its authoritative undeviation. And yet when Hanif first meets Sirine, he asks her "Please, just call me Han" (33). Hanif's self-curtailing of his name clearly speaks to his crisis of identity in translation between the US and Iraq. Han is a fragment of his former self, and the pre-Saddam Iraq of his childhood that he longs for no longer exists. Hanif's name in motion, as Han, enters the condition of migrant meanings, of a sojourn in meaning on a perpetual journey of meaning making. This is not unlike Othello's name, which possibly derives from the Italian Otello or imaginatively travels from the Arabic 'Atallah and/ or 'Utaylu. In either case, the names overlap phonetically, creating an affinity that both derives from and transcends translingual audibility. This mixability parallels the Moor's cross-cultural and cross-ethnic makeup; it makes possible an Arabization of Othello's name, replete with Arabic meanings that echo the character's qualities.

Apart from the relationship of Hanif's name to the character of Othello, Hanif, like Othello, has to contend with having dark skin.⁴ Instead of falling

---

3. Honigmann agrees with Geoffrey Bullough's assertion that "Shakespeare almost certainly consulted" (Honigmann 4) John Pory's translation of John Leo's *A Geographical Historie of Africa*. In terms of jealousy, John Leo describes the Moors as such: "No nation in the world is so subiect vnto iealousie; for they will rather leese [loose] their liues, then put vp any disgrace in the behalfe of their women" (40).

4. The issue of darker skin as a negative form of visibility comes up in both *Koolaids: The Art of War* and *Arabian Jazz*. In *Koolaids,* Mohammad's friend Samir states that Mohammad "was what we would call cursed. He was dark, looked like an Arab. In Lebanon, that's a curse"

in love with an American woman of European descent, however, Hanif connects with ethnically mixed, American-born Iraqi American Sirine. Abu-Jaber initially positions Sirine, who is fair skinned, as a Desdemona mesmerized by Hanif's exilic travels. The layering and mixing (allegorizing and mythologizing) of Hanif's and Sirine's identities in *Crescent* is far from incidental. Indeed, Nathan Green, an American friend to both Sirine and Hanif who later plays the role of an accidental Iago, tells her, "There's people like you and Han. There's more to you. Layers, surprises" (62). Notice that Nathan calls Hanif by his curtailed nickname "Han." Nathan's observation regarding layers finds resonance in one of the novel's food metaphors a few pages later. The layering of identity manifests while Sirine is preparing baklava with the help of Hanif. Sirine

> considers this [metaphysical quality of baklava], surprised by the memories that start to come to her—the way her mother's small lessons felt like larger secrets when Sirine was a girl: how instructions in the fine dicing of walnuts and the way to clarify butter were also meditations on hope and devotion. (68)

The making of baklava becomes a way for Sirine to reconnect with her dead mother. As such, Sirine's cross-generational ritual of making baklava is a meditation with transcendent qualities. And yet this Arabic cooking ritual is mediated to Sirine by her American mother, which complicates issues of lineage and cultural transmission. Although Sirine's "mother was American, her father always said his wife thought about food like an Arab. Sirine's mother strained the salted yogurt through cheesecloth to make creamy labneh" (56). As the filter through which "leben" (yogurt) becomes labneh, the cheesecloth acts as a metaphor for cross-cultural transmission. In this case, the skill of making labneh and Arabic baklava is mediated through an American setting. While Sirine's mother can never become an Arab, she can transmit food skills to her daughter "like an Arab." Sirine's "parents taught her the value of food as a conduit of human connectedness, a crucible in which religious, linguistic, and racial boundaries are dissolved" (Laouyene 592). This generosity of spirit which allows Americans to share in Arab food cultures is closely related to Matussem's memorializing his deceased Irish American wife through John Coltrane's "Naima" in *Arabian Jazz*. In Abu-Jaber's fiction, culture is never

---

(101). In *Arabian Jazz*, Jem's boss Portia says, "Oh, sure, you're tainted, your skin that color [. . .] Now, if you were to change your name, make it Italian maybe, or even Greek, that might help some [. . .] I'm telling you, Jemorah Ramoud, your father and all his kind aren't any better than Negroes" (294). It is not difficult to imagine how the dark skin of an Arab Othello plays into these formulations.

pure, and it is precisely impurity and infidelity that give her fiction its radiance and potency.

As they make baklava together, Sirine asks Hanif whether he would like to go back to Iraq. Hanif answers

> "Not the way things are now, of course. It's very dangerous—it was terribly difficult for me to get out of the country in the first place." He tries to patch the last broken layer of dough together. "But even so, it's like there's some part of me that can't quite grasp the thought of never returning. I have to keep reminding myself. It's so hard to imagine. So I just tell myself: not yet." (70)

Hanif is an Iraqi living in exile, a condition Edward Said describes as an "unhealable rift," the condition of having been "torn [. . .] from the nourishment of tradition, family, and geography" ("Reflections" 173, 174). A professor of linguistics, Hanif has translated Whitman, Poe, Dickinson, and Hemingway into Arabic. For all of his translations, Hanif is unable to retransmit himself into an Arabic setting, namely, Iraq. Hanif later explains to Sirine that Saddam Hussein actively condemns translators to death, so to return would be perilous. Moreover, Hanif's love relationship with Sirine complicates his desire to return to Iraq. Sirine-as-Desdemona is hungry for Han's stories, and Han loves her for understanding his pain. As Othello states to the duke and the senators, "She loved me for the dangers I had passed, / And I loved her that she did pity them" (1.3.167–68). As we find out later, however, Sirine-as-Calypso worries about the possibility of Han's departure. Stuck in the realm of the "not yet," Han joins Sirine in trying to find solace in the baklava making by attempting "to patch the last broken layer of dough together." By "adding a nonverbal dimension, food can register the parts of cultural experience, tradition, and identity that cannot be readily translated [or voiced]" (Mercer and Strom 39).

After Han relates the pain of exile to Sirine, she "has the feeling of missing something and not quite understanding what it is that she's missing. At the same time, she's not sure what Han means about the dangers [of returning to Iraq] or why it was so difficult to leave—but she also feels embarrassed to ask him and reveal her ignorance" (70). Their variation in skin color and access to Iraqi culture not only points to the heterogeneity of Arabs and Arab Americans, it also asks *Crescent*'s readership to accept Sirine as an American mediator of Iraqi culture. Like most Americans, Sirine does not speak Arabic and knows little about Iraq (except what her Iraqi uncle shares with her, which is not much). What is more, Sirine can pass as white. The novel, however, strategically mythologizes and exoticizes her whiteness, "with her skin so pale it has the bluish cast of skim milk, her wild blond head of hair, and her sea-green eyes" (20). Apart from comparing her skin to skim milk, thereby adding Sirine's whiteness to the novel's catalogue of food metaphors, the narrator's description of her eyes as "sea-green" alludes both to her marine qualities and to her potential for jealousy (when she turns into an Othello figure later in the novel), which Iago identifies as "the green-eyed monster" (Shakespeare 3.3.169). For the moment, the narrator recasts Sirine as a mythical sea creature with wild hair and sea-green eyes. It is no surprise that Han calls Sirine a "sea nymph" (49), as she comes to play Calypso to his Odysseus. Of course, Sirine's name evokes the Sirens of Greek mythology (I will return to *The Odyssey* allegory later in the chapter). Here, *Crescent* begins to trouble race and ethnicity as points of reference and recognition, calling into question the issue of ocular fidelity.

As Sirine and Hanif take a walk, "a little boy [. . .] says, 'Look at them, Mommy.' His mother hushes him, grabbing his hand. Sirine glances at Han's hand, the perfect, coffee-colored skin against her own whiteness" (128). To the boy and his mother, Sirine and Hanif are an interracial couple, a perception complicated, of course, by their shared Arab Iraqi background. This is not to say that Sirine-as-Desdemona does not herself exoticize Hanif's coffee-colored skin, which she later describes as "sleek and African" (84); it "excites her" (126). Yet a shared cultural affiliation binds Sirine and Hanif, one that goes beyond the thrill of mixing skim-milk and coffee-colored skin. The novel's ocular example evokes both the consequences of Othello's metaphoric blindness to Desdemona's innocence and the long history of racial discrimination in the US. Specifically, it recalls the racial-prerequisite cases under successive Naturalization Acts from 1790 to 1952 that limited US citizenship to free white persons (Bayoumi, *This Muslim* 48). Within that time frame Christian and Muslim Arabs appeared in court to prove that they were white, and therefore eligible for US citizenship. Some applicants were granted white status and others denied this privilege. The judges, predictably, relied mostly "on ocular proof to determine race" (61). This process was arbitrary at best, and in a 1913 case,

> the judge aknowledge[d] the limitations of phenotypical race. "One Syrian may be of pure or almost pure Jewish, Turkish, or Greek blood, and another the pure-blooded descendant of an Egyptian, an Abyssinian, or a Sudanese. How is the court to decide? It would be most unfortunate if the matter were to be left to the conclusions of a judge based on ocular inspection." (62)

The judge's naive conception of "pure blood" notwithstanding, his calling into question the validity of ocular inspection reveals the illusory nature of the dominant culture's belief that Arabs are identifiable visually.

Crescent takes up this issue on the translational and cultural levels as well. It is worth repeating Hanif's question, which I quote in the introduction of this chapter, here. Hanif asks, "What does it mean to call oneself an 'Egyptian writer' or even a 'Middle Eastern writer' anymore. [. . .] The [Arab] media is saturated with the imagery of the West. Is it even possible—or desirable to have an identity apart from this?" (110). Hanif's question points to transcultural forms of citizenship and belonging, in which apparently irreconcilable differences between Arab and American cultural production are challenged by the tangible Western and American influence on Arab cultures. This is no simple matter, however. As a translator, Hanif understands that lingual and cultural translations require effort and careful consideration: "When I translate, I deal with words as conscious things. You stare at the pages and you know what everything means, in both languages, and you wonder how on earth to make both languages—with all their history and innuendos—mean the same thing" (131). Transculturality is serious work, and a translator like Hanif, who is able to navigate the cultural productions of the US and the Middle East, understands the gravity of mediating cultures. Unfortunately, the complexity of Hanif's character is often lost to racialized considerations that have to do with the color of his skin.

As in *Othello*, the issue of skin color is intertwined with that of religion in *Crescent*. Hall notes that although the term "*Moor* in the Jacobean period referred to a profusion of identities" (181), it most commonly referred to black or brown Muslims. Um-Nadia (the owner of the café in which Sirine works) and her daughter Mireille are Lebanese American Christians who pass as white and do not identify as Arab. In the storytelling section of every chapter, Sirine's uncle tells her tales in the style of the *Nights* that correspond to her experiences. In one, the uncle relates,

> no one ever wants to be the Arab—it's too old and too tragic and too mysterious and too exasperating and too lonely for anyone but an actual Arab to put up with for very long. Essentially, it's an image problem. Ask anyone, Persians, Turks, even Lebanese and Egyptians—none of them want to be the Arab. They say things like, well, really we're Indo-Russian-Asian-European-Chaldeans. So in the end, the only one who gets to be the Arab is the same little old Bedouin with his goats and his sheep and his poetry about his goats and his sheep, because he doesn't know that he's the Arab, and what he doesn't know won't hurt him. (54–55)

The Arabs are a heterogeneous people. The mix of Indo-Russian-Asian-European-Chaldeans and being Arab should not be mutually exclusive. Arabness yields many possibilities and even more problems that surface as a result of these possibilities. After all, there are many Arab cultures and identities, all of which fall under the category of "Arab." Certainly, the term "Arab" should not be easy to define. But it is so often simplified, racialized, essentialized, and insidiously demonized within many discourses in the US that it almost loses meaning for many Arab Americans. Just as the term "Moor" conflated race and religion in early modern England, the term "Arab" has become almost synonymous with "Muslim terrorist," which gives some Arabs and Arab Americans reason to distance themselves from it and others to embrace it with resistant pride. The image problem is not merely discursive; it is also ocular—the ability to identify Arabs and Muslims by sight.

Arab and Muslim visibility seems to hinge on darker skin color in addition to other visual markers such as veils, beards, and turbans. The Arabs are a mix of races and ethnicities, and Muslims are not a race. While "the majority of Arab Americans descend from the first wave of mostly Christian immigrants, Arab American Muslims represent the fastest-growing segment of the Arab American community" ("Demographics"). *Crescent* does not identify Sirine's religion, but it does reveal that Hanif comes from a Muslim background. Um-Nadia warns Sirine against falling in love with Hanif: "'He's a *Muslim*, you know.' Um-Nadia's voice is half-warning and half-laughter. 'Dark as an Egyptian [. . .] And here is our beautiful Sirine, whiter than this.' She takes a bite out of a whole peeled onion as if it were an apple" (41). Mireille, Um-Nadia's daughter and an Emilia figure in the novel, also joins the chorus with a warning that "'all these guys really want is to get us back into veils, making babies, and I don't know what, nursing goats or something'" (43). *Crescent*'s critique of ocular fallacies cuts both ways, and it includes Arab American prejudices in addition to those of the dominant culture in the US. Both Um-Nadia and Mireille subscribe to the myth that Muslims are dark-skinned and Christians are fair-skinned. In this myth, dark Muslims lust after and try to enslave fair Christian women, recalling the Turk plays of Renaissance England.

This passage in *Crescent* resonates with the confluence of religion and race in *Othello*. Brabantio's lines condemning Othello's marriage to Desdemona, "For if such actions may have passage free / Bondslaves and pagans shall our statemen be" (1.2.98–99), reveal that some Venetians doubt Othello's Christianity because of his race and inside/outsider status. While Othello often adopts a militantly Christian tone (perhaps to quell suspicions about his religious affiliation), Shakespeare offers no conclusive evidence that Othello is a convert. And his gift of a handkerchief to Desdemona suggests some pagan influence. Othello tells Desdemona, "That handkerchief / Did an Egyptian to my mother give, / She was a charmer and could almost read / The thoughts of people" (3.4.54–57). He adds, "'Tis true, there's magic in the web of it. / A sibyl, that had numbered in the world / The sun to course two hundred compasses, / In her prophetic fury sewed the work" (3.4.68–71). The history of the handkerchief, as Othello recounts it, demonstrates that his Christianity does not exist in a vacuum. The influence of other religions, paganism or Islam, is not alien to the intermixed peoples of the Maghreb. Caryl Phillips, in "A Black European Success," argues that Othello's success is also his downfall: Forgetting his status as an outsider, Othello is "confident enough to use the Christianity he has assumed as a measure of 'their' Venetian superiority [. . .] He had fallen for a white girl, married her, and tried to achieve equity in the society through her. Society wreaked a horrible vengeance on them both" (48–50). In Phillips's reading, Othello gives up parts of his identity for the oneness of an "assumed" Christianity. That is to say, his mimicry of Venetian superiority on Christian grounds does not transfer superiority to Othello in this racialized religious context.

The magic in the handkerchief reveals that Othello's cultural inheritance is religiously complex and that it travels with him to Venice and Cyprus. Once Othello divulges the history of the handkerchief's production and the dangers of losing it, Desdemona responds, "Then would to God that I had never seen't" (3.4.76). Apart from the fact the she is worried about losing Othello's love, Desdemona's reaction reveals a hesitancy in adhering to Moorish, here magical, cultural standards that she does not comprehend. It is worth noting that she confirms sight as the primary mode for recognition and reception. What her eyes fail to see, however, is that her acceptance of the handkerchief is also a certain acceptance of the cultural norms that have produced it. This failure in recognition parallels Othello's misrecognition of Desdemona's fidelity and places the handkerchief at the center of ocular determinations. In *Crescent*, the handkerchief transmutes to a headscarf. Hanif gives Sirine a silk scarf. Sirine takes the scarf: "The material is so soft between her fingers it feels like dipping her hand into water. The material floats and gleams in her lap. She's a little afraid of it and she doesn't unfold it" (159). The headscarf is almost magical in its ontological indeterminacy. Seeming to come alive in Sirine's lap, it beckons to her to plunge into its water, to unfold its layers of history and culture. Sirine feels out of her depth, and Mireille's earlier warning that all Muslim men want is to put women in veils has taken root in her mind.

She tells Hanif that she really cannot accept the scarf, but relents when he appeals to her to take it. He then discloses that his family had sent the scarf to him after his escape from Iraq: "This was from my mother. I kept it on my bed in England [. . .] My mother was wearing this when my father fell in love with her" (160–61). The headscarf's relationship to Othello's handkerchief begins to become clear here. Furthermore, the narrator's description of Sirine's visual assessment of the scarf, which is "embroidered along the borders with a precise, intricate design that makes her think of red berries" (160), aligns with Iago's description of the "handkerchief / Spotted with strawberries" (3.3.435–36). *Crescent* adds another ingredient, red berries, to the food metaphor that permeates the entire novel. The design, which reminds Sirine of red berries, entices her to accept the scarf. As Michael Neill points out in his introduction to *Othello*, "The strawberries [. . .] are capable of a remarkably contradictory set of meanings" (155). A strawberry could stand for love or for sensuality and voluptuousness. In "Renaissance emblem books it frequently appeared with a serpent concealed in its leaves as a figure for deceit" (155). As it turns out, Hanif gives the scarf to Sirine as a gesture of love, and he drapes it over her shoulders, not her head. This gesture of love, however, does not stop them from exploring the scarf's sensual possibilities as Han kisses Sirine through its silky material.

Unbidden, Sirine drapes the scarf over her head as she has seen Muslim women do. To that, Hanif exclaims, "Now I see an Arab woman in you—an aristocrat, ancient royalty" (161). Sirine is happy to hear this, as she fears that she is not Arab enough for Hanif. Without the scarf as a visible marker of her Arabness, however, no one perceives her as half-Arab. Her white skin is "all anyone can see: when people ask her nationality they react with astonishment when she says she's half Arab [. . .] You sure don't look it [. . .] She thinks that she may have somehow inherited her mother on the outside and her father on the inside" (231). Like Hanif, Sirine finds that she must negotiate her identity in exteriors (although the stakes are much higher for Hanif). If there is magic in the headscarf, it has to do with its ability to make visible Sirine's Arabness. When Han's veiled student, Rana, sees Sirine with Hanif's scarf wrapped around her neck, she says, "You look so . . . almost Arab in it. You're Iraqi, aren't you?" (187). Rana's half-recognition, half-taunt reminds Sirine of the precarity of her Arabness. Losing the headscarf would not only jeopardize Hanif's love for her: it would also symbolize the loss of the Arab part of her identity. As such, the headscarf's magic also brings out Sirine's jealousy of Rana (whom Sirine perceives as the quintessential Arab woman) and begins the process of transmuting Sirine into a jealous Othello figure.

That Hanif sees an aristocratic Arab woman and not necessarily a Muslim woman in veiled Sirine is far from accidental. In his comment, Hanif is recalling that "Islam did not invent veiling, nor is veiling a practice specific to Muslims. Rather, veiling is a tradition that has existed for thousands of years, both in and far beyond the Middle East, and well before Islam came into being in the early seventh century" (Amer 1). Furthermore, as "during

Assyrian rule, veiling under the Sassanids distinguished upper-class women. A veiled woman signaled an aristocratic lady who did not need to go out to work, unlike peasant women or slaves" (6). As the veil travels through time and space, the meanings attached to it change and overlap, at times in contradictory ways. This is readily apparent in the movement of the veil from a symbol of high class status to that of oppression and backwardness in the West and the US. As the site of cultural, political, and gendered contestation, the headscarf (much like the magical handkerchief with its pagan resonances in *Othello*) accrues divergent meanings in *Crescent*. The headscarf is a visual marker that solicits strong reactions, making it an important symbol for transcultural and ocular negotiations in the novel.

The issue of ocular fidelity and ocular proof plays out in *Crescent* on allegorical registers. *Crescent* puts *Othello* in dialogue with the *Nights* and *The Odyssey*. All these works share the themes of fidelity and gendered violence, which find their way into the novel. In terms of *Othello* and the *Nights*, both Othello and King Shahrayar demand visual proof of their wives' infidelity. Enraged yet half-believing Iago's slander of Desdemona, Othello threatens Iago: "Villain, be sure thou prove my love a whore! / Be sure of it; give me the ocular proof; / Or, by the worth of mine eternal soul, / Thou hadst been better have been born a dog / Than answer my waked wrath!" (3.3.361–65). In a similar vein, King Shahrayar's "blood boiled" (*The Arabian Nights* 7) on hearing his brother Shahzaman's account of the queen's infidelity. He says to Shahzaman, "Brother, I can't believe what you say unless I see it with my own eyes" (7). Seeing his brother "in a rage," Shahzaman says, "If you do not believe me, unless you see your misfortune with your own eyes [. . .] the next morning you can see with your own eyes" (7). Interestingly enough, Iago raises a similar concern about Othello's demand to see his misfortune with his own eyes: "And may—but how? How 'satisfied,' my lord? / Would you the supervisor grossly gape on? / Behold her tupped?" (3.3.396–98). The main difference between the two works is that Shahzaman's account is true, while Iago's report is a fabrication. Nonetheless, both King Shahrayar's wife and Desdemona pay with their lives for actual or perceived infidelity.

In the *Nights,* the queen's unfaithfulness is complicated by two mitigating factors: First, the queen's sexual betrayal takes place in King Shahrayar's pleasure garden, which is frequented by his slave girls or concubines; second, the queen chooses one of the king's black slaves, Mas'ud (whose name translates as "happy or lucky"), as her sexual partner. In this context, the queen exposes King Shahrayar's moral hypocrisy, his blindness to his own infidelity with enslaved women, who cannot refuse him. Furthermore, her choice of a black man for a lover serves to undermine Shahrayar's authority and power over his subjects and slaves. The queen's infidelity is a political act of defiance and subversion even while it involves bodily pleasure. Shahzaman's warning to Shahrayar about seeing his misfortune with his own eyes is perhaps a reminder that all power has its limitations. Once Shahrayar visually confirms the queen's unfaithfulness, his sense of self and power alter irrevocably. Othello experiences a similar alteration: "I had been happy if the general camp, / Pioneers and all, had tasted her sweet body, / So I had nothing known. O, now for ever / Farewell the tranquil mind; farewell content" (3.3.347–50). It is not mere jealousy that operates here, but the male characters' deriving their sense of power and honor from their successful control of women's bodies. Hanif does not exhibit any such tendencies, however, and this marks the beginning of *Crescent*'s departure from *Othello*'s plot line.

As we expect, however, Sirine-as-Desdemona loses the headscarf during the Arab American Thanksgiving—replete with mixed Arab and American ingredients—at her uncle's home. As Sirine is about to pick up her scarf from the kitchen counter, Nathan walks in. He seems dumbfounded by the scarf. Sirine explains, "It's very old. It belonged to Han's mother" (223). On hearing this, Nathan's face darkens. He says, "[Han] told you that?" (223). Sirine slips the scarf from her shoulders, and opens her mouth to speak, but Nathan interjects, "I—can't—I—forgive me. I'm sorry" (223). He quickly leaves the room. Before Sirine can go after him, Um-Nadia and Mireille come into the kitchen to prepare the pies and make coffee. Sirine focuses on the task at hand, and Nathan's reaction slips her mind. We find out later in the novel that the headscarf belonged to Han's dead sister, Leila, and that Nathan was in love with Leila, whom he had met during his stay in Iraq. As the evening passes, Sirine realizes that she has misplaced the scarf. Um-Nadia tries to help Sirine find the scarf by sending Victor and Cristobal, who work at Nadia's Café, to look for it. At one point, Um-Nadia asks Nathan if he has seen the scarf. He answers the question while looking at Sirine: "You didn't lose it? [. . .] I saw you with it right there in the kitchen. I remember. Where did you put it?" (233). The scarf seemingly lost, Sirine "makes everyone swear they won't breathe a word of this to Han" (233).

At Nathan's photography exhibit, which takes place days later, Han blows up at Nathan for taking pictures of his family members in Iraq without asking their permission: "It's not bad enough that your country is bent on systematically destroying mine? Must you also use my family for your personal amusement as well? Or is this strictly about advancing your career?" (285–86). At this point, Han does not know about Nathan's history with Leila and his family, as he was already abroad when Nathan visited Iraq. He makes assumptions, justifiably, based on the ocular proof before him. He understands all too well that the Middle East is an easy ticket to launch a white American's career. Nathan's intention is to honor Han's family, but his photographs (in the context of the US's intervention in Iraq) miss the mark. Han storms out, and Sirine follows him. Outside, Han looks at Sirine with "a metallic glint in his eyes" (286) and asks about the scarf: "What did you do with the scarf I gave you? Why don't you ever wear it?" (286). Sirine stammers, unable to give Han a straightforward answer. Han continues, "Did you lose my scarf? [. . .] I trusted you with that one thing. Just that one small thing, Sirine [. . .] How could I have been such a fool? [. . .] How could I have trusted something so precious with someone like *you*?" (286–87). Han is clearly angry with Nathan in a manner that echoes Othello's anger with Cassio, and his anger spills over to Sirine-as-Desdemona for losing the headscarf. But this recognizable moment from Shakespeare's play serves to propel Sirine into the role of a jealous Othello.

That evening, Sirine imagines "Rana comforting Han in his book-lined office. She sees Rana's hand covering Han's, remembers the way the couple's faces seemed to flicker toward each other under the streetlights [. . .] He had never explicitly denied being with Rana" (287). Sirine remembers *seeing* a couple that looked like Han and Rana days earlier. She was riding her bicycle to Han's apartment building, evocatively called "Cyprus Gardens" (75), on a drizzly night. She thinks that she sees Han and veiled Rana holding hands, but the "water thickens the air, refracting the light; she can't see clearly" (274). Sirine dismounts her bicycle and walks a bit closer to the couple: "He lowers his head. It's hard to see. Are they kissing?" (274). Finding it difficult to breathe, Sirine waits until the couple walks away. At this point, Sirine had already kissed the Syrian poet Aziz (author of a collection of poems titled *Half Moor*), but had not yet slept with him. She clearly projects her guilt onto Han, choosing to see him kissing a woman who looks like Rana. She thinks, "He belongs with this woman" (275). Unsure of what to do next, Sirine lets herself into Han's apartment, only to find him sitting surrounded by his books and translation notes. She notes that his hair is dry and that he is wearing a dry white sweater, not the dark suit that the man on the street was wearing. In reaction, "Sirine is at once both relieved and oddly disappointed" (275). Feeling disarmed, she asks Han directly if he had been kissing a woman outside. Han answers, "You can't be serious [. . .] How could I kiss anybody but you? I'm yours. I'm utterly lost to you" (276). After Han berates her for losing the scarf, however, Sirine returns to this episode. She casts doubt on Han for not explicitly denying being with Rana. Despite so much evidence to the contrary (including her inability to see clearly on that misty night), Sirine-as-Othello convinces herself of Han's guilt.

Sirine's Othello-like self-doubt, and, consequently, her doubt of Han's fidelity, reach their climax under Aziz's influence. Like Iago, Aziz traffics in stereotypes. He is a seasoned womanizer who finds a way to seduce Sirine by playing on her insecurities in relation to Arabness and by stoking her jealousy of Rana. The day after Han scolds Sirine for losing the scarf, Aziz appears at Nadia's Café. Sirine tells him that she is in trouble with Han and asks him if he had seen Rana on campus. Aziz answers, "I don't believe Rana was in [class] today [. . .] So—you think that means exactly . . . what? Han isn't around, Rana is out, hence and so they're having an affair?" (289). As in an earlier conversation with her in which Aziz asks, "Are you sure that Han is so innocent?" (225), Aziz continues to give voice to Sirine's darkest thoughts and insecurities. He tells her that she needs a scenery vacation (a walk), and Sirine leaves the café with him. During their walk Aziz says, "You've simply fallen under his spell. It's natural. You're just an American and you've got no natural defenses" (291).

Not only does Aziz allude to Brabantio's theory that Othello had used magic to seduce Desdemona (1.3.60–65), but his stereotyping of "American" Sirine also places him in the role of Iago, who stereotypes both Venetian women and Othello himself:

> In Venice [women] do let God see the pranks
> They dare not show their husbands; their best conscience
> Is not to leave't undone, but keep't unknown (3.3.205–7)
> [. . .]
> Not to affect many proposèd matches
> of [Desdemona's] own clime, complexion, and degree,
> Whereto we see in all things nature tends—(3.3.233–35)
> [. . .]
> Her will, recoiling to her better judgement,
> May fall to match you with her country forms,
> And happily repent. (3.3.240–42)

Just as Iago claims that licentious Desdemona would repent marrying someone who does not belong to her "clime, complexion, and degree" by finding a lover among her countrymen, Aziz positions Han as an unvirtuous man who will inevitably have an affair with an authentic Arab woman, Rana. In Aziz's formulation, Sirine becomes an American Othello who is rejected by the Los Angeles Arab community, and Hanif turns into an unfaithful Desdemona. Sirine succumbs to Aziz's fiction and allows him to take her back to his studio apartment, where they end up having sex.

The next time Sirine sees Han, he asks her forgiveness for losing his temper. He says, "That scarf was just a thing. If you lost it or not, things are things and that's it. A scarf is a scarf is a scarf, right?" (294). This is a clear departure from *Othello*'s plotline. Here, Hanif uncouples the scarf from its personal and cultural determinants in an attempt to release Sirine from these burdens. In other words, Sirine's misplacement of the scarf should not symbolize a loss of her provisional Arabness or her access to Hanif's history. Hanif's gesture does not have the desired effect, however. Aziz's insinuations have taken hold to such a degree that Sirine ends up believing that Rana had stolen the scarf. This leads to a dramatic scene in which Sirine yanks Rana's scarf off her head only to realize that she has made a grave mistake: Rana's scarf is not the one Hanif had gifted to her. Once more, visual proof fails to convey the truth. After Han leaves for Iraq, Sirine visits Nathan at home. There, she finds him asleep naked with the lost scarf about him. After Sirine wakes him up, Nathan admits that he stole the headscarf. He tells Sirine that Leila was wearing the scarf the last time he saw her alive. He wanted to return the scarf to Sirine, but could not think of how to do so. He also tells her that Han had visited him before he left for Iraq and that Nathan told him about his time with Leila. During their conversation, Han accidentally sees a picture that Nathan had surreptitiously taken of Sirine and Aziz as they were just about to kiss. As a coincidental Iago who offers Han-as-Othello the ocular proof, Nathan reveals that Han "said he felt somehow that it didn't mean anything [. . .] But that he still didn't know if he could forgive you" (380). To this, Sirine responds flatly, "This is why he went back to Iraq [. . .] This picture" (381).

DIALOGUE WITH *THE ODYSSEY*

The third and fourth pages of *Crescent* find Sirine's unnamed uncle extolling Han's qualities. Unlike Desdemona's father Brabantio, Sirine's uncle encourages her romance with Hanif-as-Othello. In addition, he likens Han to Odysseus. "I'm telling you," her uncle teases, "he looks like a hero. Like Ulysses [. . .] If I were a girl, I'd be crazy for Ulysses" (18–19). Sirine retorts,

"What does Ulysses even look like? Some statue-head with no eyes?"
"No," he says, indignant. "He has eyes."
"Still not interested." (19)

Sirine's defensiveness, we find out shortly after, is based on her attraction to Han. Her exchange with her uncle begins the mythologizing of Han and Sirine as allegories of Odysseus and a combination of Calypso/Siren/Penelope. Like Odysseus, Han is a postwar exile (the Iraq-Iran War 1980–88) who is unable to find his way back home. Sirine is mesmerized by Han's dark skin and his travels in exile, both of which overlap with Han as an Othello figure. What is more, Sirine's imaging of Odysseus as a statue with no eyes calls to attention the issue of ocular identification and misidentification early in the novel.

If Han qualifies as an Odysseus figure, Sirine appears first as a Calypso. After all, Han arrives to Los Angeles after arduous travel in a manner not unlike Odysseus's arrival at Ogygia, and Sirine-as-Calypso rapidly falls in love with the traveling hero. As I mention earlier, the narrator recasts Sirine as a mythical sea creature with wild hair and sea-green eyes, and the marine aspect of her identity manifests when she swims with Han at a pool party: "She dives in from the edge of the pool and surfaces near Han. She doesn't feel as shy in the water. It swells around them, and pulls them off their feet. 'Sea nymph,' Han says" (49). Here, Han clearly identifies Sirine as a Calypso figure, whom Odysseus describes as "the seductive nymph with lovely braids—a danger too" (Homer 7.284). As a minor goddess, Calypso can exert some control over natural elements. In this case, Sirine-as-Calypso causes the water to pull Han and Sirine off their feet, allowing them to share an intimate moment.

Moreover, Sirine doubles as a Siren, a dangerous creature (like Calypso) who leads men to madness with her Siren song. Apart from the audible similarity between Sirine's name and the French noun *sirène*, Aziz identifies Sirine as a Siren just before they kiss later in the novel: "Come on, lovely Sirine, my siren, don't you want to know what such a thing tastes like?" (269). Even the forbidden kiss includes a marine quality: The narrator relates that Aziz's "breath rushes against her face and it's like giving way to the force of an ocean current" (269). If Aziz makes the Siren connection abundantly clear here, this revelation comes after many references to Sirine as a Siren earlier in the novel. On page 40, the narrator reveals that Sirine has "always had more men in her life than she's known what to do with. Um-Nadia says that attraction is Sirine's special talent—a sort of magnetism deeper in her cells than basic beauty or charm. She's never broken up with anyone, she just loses track of them, adding new men as she goes." This passage reveals that Sirine's Siren qualities are a part of her makeup on the cellular level. Here as well, Sirine-as-Siren overlaps with Desdemona. Brabantio discloses that Desdemona was "So opposite to marriage that she shunned / The wealthy curlèd darlings of our nation (Shakespeare 1.2.67–68). Like Desdemona, Sirine does not pay any mind to the "three men calling her and coming by the house" (40). All three figures in *Crescent*—Sirine, the Siren, and Desdemona—guard their independence from men initially.

Whether we perceive Sirens as bird-women in the Classical Greek context or as mermaids (half-fish, half-women) as in the story of Sirine's uncle, both are mixed creatures. Sirine is mixed on two levels (setting aside her multiple allegories): She is an Arab American (a second-generation immigrant with Arab Iraqi roots on her father's side) and an Arab/American (the ethnically mixed issue of an Iraqi father and an American-born white mother). As such, Sirine's biological and cultural DNA allow her to function both as a Siren of Greek mythology and as the more contemporary mermaid-Siren. In the realistic sections of *Crescent,* Sirine is "too preoccupied with cooking to return [the men's] calls" (40). She is unconcerned with these men, as she has "an ability to live deeply and purely inside her own body, to stop thinking, to work, and to simply exist in the simplest actions, like chopping an onion or stirring a pot" (22). Ironically, however, Sirine's cooking (along with her striking, mythological appearance) *is* her Siren song. The Arab male students who frequent Nadia's Café try "to talk to Um-Nadia, Mireille, and Sirine. Especially Sirine. They love her food—the flavors that remind them of their homes—but they also love to watch Sirine [. . . with] her wild blond head of hair, and her sea-green eyes" (19–20). If the Sirens of *The Odyssey* call out to Odysseus in "honeyed voices" (Homer 12.203) with the promise of comfort, singing, "We know all the pains that the Greeks and Trojans once endured" (12.205), Sirine calls out to men with her cooking and appearance, as she too seems to know their pain and loneliness in the US. Brinda Mehta asserts, "The seductive authenticity of Sirine's cooking lures [the men] back for more in a ritual of repetitive submission to a woman-centered mode of cultural production" (251). Sirine derives a sense of power and fulfillment from her role as a culinary Siren.

Until she meets Han, Sirine is unable "to lose herself in someone else" or to exchange "the delicious rhythms of work, for the fearful tumult of falling into love" (40). Having lost both parents at an early age, Sirine has a fear of losing a potential loved one that outweighs any desire she might have to find love. When Han appears on her shores, however, Sirine-as-Calypso rapidly falls in love with Han/Odysseus. Sirine comes to realize that unlike other men, Han "looks at her. Even though they barely know each other, she already has the clear, uncanny sense that when he looks, he sees her" (53). Han renders Sirine visible both because he really sees her and because he allows her to see herself from an Arab Iraqi perspective. In a conversation with her uncle, Sirine says that there is something complicated about Han. Her uncle responds:

> "Complicated? [. . .] Well, but he's an exile—they're all messed up inside. But I thought girls are supposed to love that."
>
> "What do you mean, 'exile'? Because he left Iraq?"

"Because he can't go back. Because anything you can't have you want twice as much. Because he needs someone to show him how to live in this country and how to let go of the other."

"Lovely. A project." (53)

Sirine's cynical retort notwithstanding, this exchange allows her to see that Han's exile from Iraq counterpoints her exile from her deceased parents and her father's Iraqi heritage. Both she and Han want what they can't have twice as much, and neither of them can recover their losses. Furthermore, Sirine finds herself attracted both to the fact that Han needs someone to show him how to make a home in the US and to the fact that he may not stay. Sirine's reading of Han as complicated serves to assuage her fear of attachment (Han might continue his journey as an exile) and to place her in a position of power in relation to Han (she would act as his guide in the US).

In a conversation with Sirine, Um-Nadia warns her that Han "is like a fish, you already have him by the tail, but he's slippery, he doesn't want to jump out of your hands but he might not be able to stop himself" (91–92). Acting somewhat like Hermes (sent by Zeus to Ogygia to release Odysseus from Calypso's ensnarement), Um-Nadia delivers the message that Sirine might not be able to hold on to Han, the implication being that Han might find his way back to Iraq. Sirine-as-Calypso already knows that this could happen. Her attraction to him is based in considerable part on this fact, as Sirine too is frightened of commitment. Conversely, finding her match—a flight risk against attachment issues—in Han, Sirine cannot help wanting to keep hold of him. The narrator divulges that Sirine "has never felt this way about a man before— her American boyfriends seemed much easier to possess. Now her desire has spread alarmingly, like a jinn flowing out of its bottle" (140). Sirine's nymph-Siren qualities do not work quite as well on Han, and this makes him all the more desirable to her—so much so that she loses control over her own desires. Furthermore, this passage, like many others in *Crescent*, finds resonance in another register. In this case, *The Odyssey* intersects with the *Nights*. Sirine doubles as a *jinniyyah* (a female genie in Arabic) who seeks to possess Han, only to find that her desire possesses her.

Afraid of losing Han, Sirine begins to project her insecurities onto him. Sirine-as-Calypso dreams that Han has a wife in Iraq: "His wife was a kind of enchantress who had him under a spell—a woman who looked something like Rana [Han's veiled student], passionate and brilliant and capable of anything—someone who would summon him back to the Old Country, to his true identity" (230). Unable to conceive of herself as the goddess-enchantress Calypso who is holding Odysseus captive on her island, Sirine projects her sorcery onto her rival, Han's supposed wife. This Penelope and Rana-like wife would summon Han-as-Odysseus back home and away from her. It seems as if it is scripted that Sirine would lose Han to this dream wife and to Iraq. In *The Odyssey*, Calypso rails against the gods who are responsible for her loss: "Hard-hearted / you are, you gods! You unrivaled lords of jealousy" (5.130–31). Calypso's dubbing the gods "lords of jealousy" identifies the key themes of jealousy and (in)fidelity that permeate *Othello*, *The Odyssey*, and the *Nights* as they combine in *Crescent*. As a goddess, Calypso believes that she has more claim over Odysseus than his wife Penelope. Sirine's dream seems to recall Calypso and Odysseus's exchange on the evening before his departure. Calypso says, "Much as you long to see your wife, / the one you pine for all your days . . . and yet / I just might claim to be nothing less than she, / neither in face nor figure. Hardly right, is it, / for mortal woman to rival immortal goddess?" (Homer 5.231–35). The fact that Calypso must resort to her rights and privileges as a goddess reveals her deep insecurity, one that Sirine shares with her. If it is possible for a goddess to lose Odysseus to a mortal rival, then it is more than possible for Sirine to lose Hanif to a Rana-like wife. Thus does her insecurity about being inadequately Arab cast doubt on Han's fidelity "to his true identity," to his wife, and to Sirine. Han, however, does not have a secret wife in Iraq.

Sirine's insecurity derives in part from Um-Nadia's and Mireille's stereotypical comments about men, and Muslim men in particular. In a conversation with Sirine, Um-Nadia relates the story of her friend Munira (we learn later in the novel that "Munira" is a pseudonym for Um-Nadia's daughter, Nadia): "She's the one who found out her husband had a secret extra family back in Lebanon. It's classic. Men lose track of where they are [. . .] They don't know how to carry their homes inside themselves [. . .] You need to know how to do that" (94). Um-Nadia's story comes shortly after she warns Sirine that Han is a flight risk. Um-Nadia both genders and correlates migration/ exile and infidelity. Since men are unable to carry their homes inside themselves, they attempt to replicate their families in the countries to which they migrate. Um-Nadia's advice that Sirine should learn how to carry her home inside herself contains an implicit message that Sirine should not try to find her home in Han. Gendered discourse notwithstanding, Um-Nadia identifies a pattern of migration-induced infidelity: "Once fidelity to a national identity is broken, it follows that marital and familial obligations might be destabilized as well—and vice versa" (Friedman 71). Natalie Friedman's contention allows us to reinterpret Odysseus's affair with Calypso along the lines of exilic loss, in which Odysseus is as accountable as Calypso for his infidelity to Penelope. In other words, Odysseus's desire for Calypso is not merely a result of her "bewitching" (Homer 1.17) him.

In *Crescent,* however, Han-as-Odysseus is able to cope with his exilic condition, as painful as it is. Sirine's sense of identity, on the other hand, enters into crisis upon meeting Han. When "Sirine falls in love with Han, she realizes how distanced she is from her Arabic roots" (Limpár 254). In a conversation with Han, Sirine reveals, "I guess I'm always looking for my home, a little bit. I mean, even though I live here, I have this feeling that my real home is somewhere else somehow" (132). Han follows up by asking what makes a place feel like home for her. Sirine answers "Work [. . .] Work is home," to which Han comments, "How American of you" (132). Han's presence reminds Sirine of her dead parents, her father's Arab Iraqi culture, and her displacement from both. That is, Han triggers an exilic consciousness in Sirine, which unearths her repressed memories and pain. Sirine had been hiding in her work, convincing herself that work is home. While Han's comment challenges this assertion, it also touches on Sirine's insecurity that she is not Arab enough for him. If Calypso fears that as a nymph she cannot compete with human Penelope for Odysseus's love, Sirine is terrified that she cannot compete with Han's Rana-like Arab wife. Of course, no such wife exists for Han. Sirine, however, proceeds as if in a self-fulfilling prophecy, eventually sabotaging her relationship with Han by sleeping with Aziz.

On her journey to infidelity, Sirine snoops around Han's room for clues in order to ascertain whether it is safe to be in love with him. She finds a letter that is written mostly in English by someone who signs her name as D. After she reads the letter, Sirine "recalls Um-Nadia's stories about women betrayed, their faithless men [. . .] Sirine [also] thinks of the way her parents disappeared" (178). The letter, in addition to Um-Nadia's stories and the memory of the loss of her parents, amplifies Sirine's fears: "What if he's planning to go? Han might be married, she thinks. Perhaps he has children. And perhaps he has killed someone" (178). Under the influence of Um-Nadia's and Mireille's stereotypes, Sirine mis-sees Han. At this point, however, *Crescent*'s readers begin to perceive that the "vulnerability displayed by the men who need the protective care of [. . .] women [. . .] invalidates stereotypes of Arab machismo while simultaneously negating dominant misperceptions of Arab female passivity and subservience" (Mehta 252). Sirine finds out a little too late that the letter was from Han's aunt Dima, who had sent him his dead sister Leila's scarf, the one and the same that Han-as-Othello had gifted to Sirine-as-Desdemona.

Shortly after reading Aunt Dima's letter, Sirine asks Han if it is true that Muslims can have four wives. She feels foolish for asking this question: "'Just something I heard,' she mumbles [. . .] 'Mireille says they do'" (181). Mireille's influence on Sirine is abundantly clear here. What is pressing, however, is *Crescent*'s transposing of the Calypso-Odysseus episode to a Muslim context. If Odysseus's affair with Calypso has to do with the minor goddess's rights and privileges (which serve to overshadow Odysseus's infidelity to Penelope), the Muslim practice of polygyny, as sanctioned infidelity, worries Sirine. Han answers, "I guess technically, if you go by Islamic code, then yes, four wives. But there's a big catch: Muhammad said, if you marry more than one woman you have to treat them all equally. Which lots of religious scholars say is pretty much impossible" (181). While Han's answer is valid, the Qur'an is quite clear about the conditions of polygyny. In the Rashad Khalifa translation of the Qur'an, "Surat An-Nisa' (The Women)" states, "If you deem it best for the orphans, you may marry their mothers—you may marry two, three, or four. If you fear lest you become unfair, then you shall be content with only one, or with what you already have. Additionally, you are thus more likely to avoid financial hardship" (*QuranBrowser.org* 4:3). The Surah continues to clarify polygyny: "You can never be equitable in dealing with more than one wife, no matter how hard you try. Therefore, do not be so biased as to leave one of them hanging (neither enjoying marriage, nor left to marry someone else). If you correct this situation and maintain righteousness, GOD is Forgiver, Most Merciful" (4:129). The Qur'an sanctions limited polygyny, but it does so under exceptional circumstances that pertain to the mothers of orphans, who are unable to provide for their families. Indeed, the Qur'an cautions would-be polygynists that they would never be able to deal equitably with multiple wives, the condition (which Han identifies) that permits polygyny. It is worth noting here that the "vast majority of Muslim men are monogamous in their marriage relationships; those who have more than one wife are very few" (Rizvi).

Sirine presses Han further: "Do you believe that your religion—that Islam—defines who you are?" (181). After remarking that Sirine's question is interesting, Han answers, "I pretty much think I define myself by an absence [. . .] Well, I'm no longer a believer but I still consider myself a Muslim [. . .] I don't believe in a specific notion of God. But I do believe in social constructions, notions of allegiance, cultural identity" (182). For Han-as-Odysseus, exile is all-consuming; it is bigger than anything else in his life. He defines himself by an absence, by seeking echoes of his pre-exilic past. Caught between the past and the hope of return in the future, Han is unable to thoroughly inhabit the present. Islam travels with Han on his exilic journey. In motion, Han's Islam sheds its dogmatic elements and retains its Arab Iraqi cultural resonances. In other words, Iraqi formulations of Islam are culturally located, even while Iraqi culture continues to be suffused by Western and US cultural and media productions. Han is not calling for cultural purity, however; rather, as a translator in exile he is identifying an Iraqi-located transcultural framework that negotiates with transcultural formations in the West and the US. Sirine takes this in and "gazes at him, waiting for him to [. . .] put his arms around her, to say that she's more than made up for all this loss in his life. Instead, however, he closes his eyes, his shoulders lowering heavily, and he clicks through his prayer beads" (183). Although Han had previously assured Sirine of his intention to stay with her—"you are the place I want to be—you're the opposite of exile" (158)—she still fears the day when Iraq calls him back.

Sirine's insecurities get the better of her, and she sabotages her relationship with Han by sleeping with Aziz after she loses the headscarf. Postbetrayal, Sirine avoids having sex with Han. When they begin making love again, she "waits for him to detect her betrayal, to see it in her face. But he closes his eyes, his expression faintly imploring. She is surprised by how easy it is to do this, how available betrayal is" (300–301). Having relapsed into her Siren self, and with Han in an imploring position, Sirine realizes how easily betrayal comes to her. But her sense of power and security rapidly fades when Han receives a phone call that night: "She hears him speaking Arabic [. . .] She hears the words *Iraq* and *Baghdad* and at that moment rising out of the logic of dreams she feels with a startling clarity—the clarity of the obvious and the long-denied—that something is coming to claim him" (301). Sirine's Siren confidence quickly inverts back to Calypso's insecurity. The narrator's repetition of the word "clarity" renders it ironic, as it is in considerable part Sirine's self-fulfilling infidelity to Han that breaks her spell and allows Han to risk returning to Iraq to see his dying mother, not the "obvious and long-denied" clarity that Iraq would eventually reclaim him. That is not to say that Han would not have considered returning to Iraq to see his mother, but that Sirine's one-night stand with Aziz paves the way for his departure.

The next morning finds Sirine ill in Han's apartment. There is a knock at the door, and "for a moment, she wonders if it's Rana knocking" (302). Still unable to fully acknowledge her guilt, Sirine continues to project her betrayal onto Han. It turns out that Sirine's uncle has come to check on her after she called him to say that she was sick. When Sirine's uncle enters the apartment, he looks around and remarks, "Where's the furniture? Habeebti, you're living like a Bedouin in a goat-hair tent" (302). Han's apartment reflects his exilic/nomadic existence. Apart from the bare necessities, the apartment is empty. Embarrassed, Sirine "constructs a chair and table out of stacks of Han's books. Before sitting, her uncle looks at them and says, 'Let's see, *The Iliad* and *The Collected Works of Shakespeare*. That will do nicely'" (303). As if there were any doubt that *Crescent* puts into dialogue *Othello* and *The Odyssey*, this episode refers directly to Homer's and Shakespeare's works. It does so obliquely, however: The references are to *The Iliad* (not *The Odyssey*) and *The*

Collected Works of Shakespeare (not *Othello* specifically). The dialogic overlap carries over nonetheless, as the Trojan War is the precursor to *The Odyssey*, and Shakespeare's collected works would certainly contain *Othello*. The fact that Sirine's uncle makes this comment is not accidental. As I demonstrate in the storytelling section of this chapter, Sirine's uncle synthesizes these two works "nicely" and adds the *Nights* into the mix in his serial story, which spans the entirety of the novel.

Han leaves for Iraq after he sees Nathan's photograph—the ocular proof—of Sirine and Aziz as they are about to kiss, and Sirine is devastated. He leaves her a note on "a piece of paper folded into a sailboat" (334), which corresponds to Odysseus's sailing away from Calypso's island, Ogygia. The note reads, "Things are broken. The world is broken. Hayati, it's time. I've gone. Imagine that I was never here at all" (334). Unsure what exactly "I've gone" means, Sirine searches for Han. She finds out from her uncle shortly afterward that Han has resigned from the university, and she surmises that he has left for Iraq. She attempts to buy an airplane ticket to Iraq, only to find out that no US carriers fly there. A week after Han's departure, Sirine receives a letter that he had written to her between flights at Heathrow airport. In the letter, Han writes: "*There are many reasons why I have to return to Iraq, though I'm afraid to write them here, afraid of seeing the reasons written down* [. . .] *I'm driven by the prospect of return: my country won't let go of me—it's filled me up. You know that. And a certain fear—an emotional fear—has suddenly lifted and freed me*" (352–53). While Han's letter does not refer directly to Sirine's betrayal—she is still unsure as to whether he knows about her night with Aziz—it does complicate the concept of infidelity.

While Sirine's Calypso-like insecurity leads to a self-fulfilling infidelity, her betrayal nonetheless allows Han to return to Iraq, which the letter confirms—"*You know that*"—was his ardent desire. On the one hand, Sirine certainly compromises herself ethically by sleeping with Aziz, and she bears responsibility for her action. On the other hand, her infidelity makes possible a future relationship with Han unburdened by his overwhelming desire to return home. In other words, Sirine's infidelity proves cathartic both to her and to Han. Sirine frees Han from "*an emotional fear*" of losing Sirine if he were to leave for Iraq, and she frees herself from her fear of commitment. In his letter, Han keeps open the possibility of returning to Sirine: "*Sirine, I don't know what's going to happen. Would say that I am coming back to you if I thought I could. I'll contact you if there is any way to do it, but this seems unlikely*" (353). Despite Han's pessimistic outlook—he knows that the agents of Saddam Hussein's regime will be looking for him—he pledges to contact Sirine if there is any chance of returning to her. For the moment, he can only hope for time to see his family and home. Han signs his letter with his full name, "Hanif." Sirine's infidelity gives him the chance to heal the rift between his current curtailed self (as exemplified by his incomplete nickname, Han) and his pre-exilic self. If Han is able to return to Sirine, it would be as Hanif, who is no longer a flight risk. In a highly symbolic moment after Han's departure, Sirine finds Han's coffee cup from their last night together, pours steaming water over the old grounds, and drinks the "thin, grayish brew [. . .] Whatever fate was written in his cup, she thinks, she wants to share it" (354–55). If the magic in the web of the headscarf regenders Sirine as Othello, sharing Han's fate by drinking the old grounds in his coffee cup transforms Sirine from a Calypso/Siren figure to a Penelope waiting for Odysseus to return home. The "grayish brew" in fact creates a gray space for Sirine's infidelity, rendering it a process of in/fidelity: a productive interplay between fidelity and infidelity.

Both Sirine's taking on the role of Othello and her slippage from Calypso/Siren to Penelope reorient the focus of *Othello* and *The Odyssey* to a woman-centered perspective. While *Crescent* pays close attention to Han as Othello and Odysseus, Sirine's experiences remain central as she embodies successive roles. *Crescent* thus asks us to take seriously the layered identities of Arab and Arab American women and to listen to them through Sirine's journey. As Penelope's role in *The Odyssey* is "at once the most necessary and the most mysterious [. . . which] comes near making our *Odysseia* a *Penelopeia*" (Finley 3), so is Sirine's role in *Crescent*. Sirine's mysterious yet necessary infidelity counterpoints Penelope's bow test, which she offers to her relentless suitors: "I set before you the great bow of King Odysseus now! / The hand that can string this bow with greatest ease, / that shoots an arrow clean through all twelve axes— / he is the man I follow, yes, forsaking this house / where I was once a bride" (Homer 21.85–89). The fact that Penelope risks her fidelity to Odysseus by offering the bow test to the suitors has generated much scholarly debate around her character and characterization. Richard Heitman identifies a fundamental assumption that underlies all scholarly approaches that focus on Penelope: "The assumption is that Penelope is to be understood in terms of her sexual fidelity to Odysseus [. . .] The idea has endured. Penelope continues to be praised or blamed principally for her sexual conduct [. . .] The only thing she can do wrong is to embrace a man other than Odysseus" (7–8). And yet, the bow test, which risks compromising Penelope's marital fidelity to Odysseus, is precisely what makes Odysseus's homecoming and revenge against the suitors possible. Penelope's decision makes her "a key to the unity of the poem," as she "is the central figure of home; she both kept it in existence and makes it recoverable" (Finley 2, 4). Sirine's infidelity allows Han to recover his home. But it also doubles as a test for her relationship with him. If her infidelity sends the exile back home, would her emergent fidelity bring him back?

After drinking the old coffee grounds from Han's coffee cup and committing herself to sharing his fate, Sirine exhibits an unconditional loyalty to Han, irrespective of whether he forgives her and returns from Iraq. Penelope-like, Sirine looks for news of her beloved. Nine months after Han's departure, she sees what she thinks is a trace of Han in the *World* newspaper a student has brought in to Nadia's Café: "The newspaper photograph [. . .] of three hooded, barefoot men catches her eye [. . .] one man's head is partially revealed, and she can see the sad slip of his eyes, the way the black shock of hair falls over his forehead; and she knows" (364). As she does not know Arabic, she asks the student to translate the caption. The student translates that Saddam Hussein had executed three men for being Western spies and collaborators. Sirine knows from Han that part of the reason his father allowed him to go to school abroad was that "my father worried over what would happen to a young man like myself, fluent in other languages. I might have been imprisoned" (258). Lest we think that Arab translators are not treated with suspicion in the US, Mireille reveals to Sirine that "some of the students were saying [Han] was a spy [. . . for the] C.I.A., the Iraqis [. . .] Someone else thought he was one of Saddam Hussein's secret sons" (339). Mistakenly thinking that Han is dead, Sirine crosses the café's courtyard and walks into the bougainvillea bushes. There, "she sinks her face into her hands and sobs" (364).

In the same time period, Aziz visits Sirine as a suitor, perhaps as a double for the most villainous suitor in *The Odyssey,* Antinous. Aziz apologizes for not coming to see Sirine after Han left, and he asks her if she would move to Italy with him after the end of the semester:

"Think about it. You don't have to answer right away."
    She shakes her head. "I couldn't leave here. This is my life."
"But perhaps you would care to expand that life?"
    She half-smiles. "Not with you."
    [. . .] "There are some things I've done . . . I am not proud of. I may have done some less-than-noble things in my life. Heaven knows, I'm not Han." (362–63)

No longer conflicted about Han, Sirine-as-Penelope summarily refuses Aziz's suit. She is no longer susceptible to Aziz's suggestions and insinuations. For one, Aziz—feeling guilty about his Iago-like role in undermining Sirine and Han's relationship—does not contact Sirine after Han's departure. Roughly nine months have passed, and this time allows Aziz to resurface as a suitor. After Sirine rejects him, Aziz takes responsibility for his actions. He concedes ironically, "Heaven knows, I'm not Han." Before he takes leave of Sirine, Aziz asks her if Han left "because of what happened between you and me" (363). Sirine answers that she never told Han anything, and Aziz exclaims, "Thank God, thank God. Because I couldn't have forgiven myself" (363). Afraid that Han-as-Odysseus would return to take his revenge, Aziz thanks God twice that Han does not know about the affair (except, of course, he does). Moreover, Aziz's statement that he "couldn't have forgiven himself" is further proof of his compromised ethics. His inability to forgive himself is contingent upon whether Han knows about the one-night stand, and not on the fact that he has betrayed his friend.

As a Penelope, then, Sirine recommits herself to Han, repeatedly seeks out news about him, and rejects Aziz. It is her infidelity that opens the space for her to assume the role of Penelope. Sirine's infidelity, in addition to her assumption of the role of Othello, also saves Han from sharing Othello's fate; it creates a slippage between *Othello* and *The Odyssey*, which in turn propels Han from an Othello figure to an Odysseus figure. Here as well, Han-as-Odysseus does not kill Aziz-as-suitor. Aziz's earlier Iago-like warning (as if Aziz is not an Arab himself) that "probably we shouldn't let Han know about us [. . .] You know these Arab guys. They get jealous and murder people with their bare hands" (292), and Um-Nadia's advice to Sirine not to confess her betrayal to Han, because "if you tell, either it will kill him or he will have to kill someone else" (305), do not come to pass. The slippage between texts, and the resulting infidelity to the plots of both *Othello* and *The Odyssey*, challenge narratives of honor killing and revenge. *Crescent* thus frees Han from the patriarchal constraints of basing his actions on the control of women's bodies and repositions Sirine as an agent in her life rather than a foil within male-centered narratives. Sirine waits for Han as a Penelope because she chooses to do so.

RE-FRAMES

In "Traveling Theory Revisited," Edward Said considered "an alternative mode of traveling theory, one that actually developed *away* from its original formulation" (438) instead of becoming domesticated and assimilated into its new location. Charged with migratory and rebellious tendencies, this theory sets to work in driving neoteric aesthetic and political causes. This section negotiates a third such instance in *Crescent* (following *Othello* and *The Odyssey*): the rearranging of the *Nights*' frames and the rescripting of the figure of Shahrazad.

Abu-Jaber regenders the storyteller's (Shahrazad's) voice and reconfigures the concept of the frame narrative. In so doing, she problematizes Shahrazad's perceived heroism and fidelity to Shahrayar in the *Nights*—one that ultimately capitulates to a traditional role of childbearing and motherhood—and provides models of gendered Arab subjectivity away from the binary of oppressed women and murderous, sex-crazed men.[5]

The *Nights*' most widely remarked-upon formal feature, its frame narrative, "can be considered to be an [. . .] example of the literary genre of mirror-for-princes," says Robert Irwin (103).[6] In this reading, Shahrazad constructs a complex labyrinth of frames (and frames within frames) both to unhinge and gradually instruct King Shahrayar away from tyranny and femicide. In over two centuries of analyses that exoticize and orientalize the work as a whole, however, the *Nights*' framing comes to be treated primarily as a widely emulated aesthetic element whose secondary, thematic function is to entrap the bloodthirsty Shahrayar until such time as his desire for Shahrazad's stories outstrips his desire to kill her. In other words, the frame as commonly understood gradually undergoes a shift of meaning from an allegory of statecraft and rehabilitation to a pathologization of the oriental tyrant. This section considers the aesthetic and political implications of Abu-Jaber's splitting the figure of the storyteller and the female heroine into two characters, regendering the storyteller male and interpolating the storyteller's voice into *Crescent*'s realistic chapters for the heroine's (Sirine's) benefit. Abu-Jaber reframes (in form and content) and regenders the *Nights* to address manifestations of Arabophobia and Islamophobia in the US. This strategy functions as a reflective and deflective set of mirrors that relentlessly pressure pernicious and dehumanizing representations of Arabs and Arab Americans that remain, as Kaldas and Mattawa argue, "one of the few racist images that can still be portrayed with unchecked abandon" (xiii). Indeed, conflating patriotism with anti-Arab racism and Islamophobia is a widespread phenomenon in the US.

Abu-Jaber, then, draws on the Shahrazadian process of storytelling and framing in the *Nights* both to promote a cultural mode of survival, and transform cross-cultural misunderstanding into education and rehabilitation. Much is at stake, and the novel takes up the issue of war and cultural backlash

---

5. I do not engage the relationship of Sirine and Hanif to the characters in the uncle's story, except when they relate to the issue of framing in the *Nights* and *Crescent*. For more on the role of the *Nights* in *Crescent*, including the characters in the uncle's story, please see Magali Cornier Michael.

6. While such works by the Greek philosophers and Renaissance humanists are well known, non-European works also circulated from the medieval period forward. For example, the *Sirr-al-'asrar, an Arabic text on the education of princes*, was translated into Latin at Oxford by Roger Bacon around 1280.

by removing the setting to the first Iraq War—a less fraught but historically leading frame in which the past informs the contingencies of the present—and negotiates its effect on Arab, Arab American, and American characters. To do so, *Crescent* offers both a storyteller and a narrator who must coexist politically and cross-culturally. It is my aim to investigate the cultural connections and disconnections between modes of storytelling and realism (Sirine's Iraqi American uncle as storyteller alongside a third-person narrator, respectively), frames of a literary past, historical past, and the present as they meet, overlap, and challenge one another. The novel places these aspects in culturally specific modes of representation initially and then provides the framework for cross-cultural intervention by provoking readers (real, perceived, and characterized) to participate actively in reconciling the storytelling and realistic narrative as active cultural translators. In other words, Abu-Jaber's infidelity to one mode of narrative (realism or storytelling) produces a necessary dialogic gap between the two.

To begin, one must ask, in addition to the issue of fidelity, why Abu-Jaber chooses the Shahrazadian context and the figure of Shahrazad for her intervention. Obvious, perhaps, is the partial literary inheritance of the *Nights* from which Arab American authors can draw. I say partial not only because I must insist on the dual Arab and American heritage of Arab Americans, but also because the European translations of and additions to the *Nights*, beginning with Antoine Galland, who succeeded "in establishing the work as a classic" (Haddawy xx) in the eighteenth century, have rendered it a collaborative project across time and space. In the *Dialogic Imagination,* Mikhail Bakhtin posits that the "stylistic uniqueness of the novel as a genre consists precisely in the combination of these subordinated, yet still relatively autonomous, [heterogeneous stylistic] unities (even at times comprised of different languages) into the higher unity of the work as a whole" (262). While the *Nights* is not by definition a novel, it is a tale of epic proportions set mostly (but not exclusively) in prose. Not only are the *Nights*' heterogeneous stylistic unities, which, as Husain Haddawy puts it, "modulate between the colloquial and the literary, and even [the] ornate" (xx), examples of pluralistic discourse, they are also dialogic stratifications that manifest in the myriad translations of the work. The *Nights* offers unique sets of both intralingual and interlingual unities (independent and interdependent) that have resulted in East/West dialogue and collaboration, embedded as they are in the inequalities of power.

It is not surprising, then, that the dialogic impetus of the *Nights* informs the poetics and politics of *Crescent*. Indeed, the novel is replete with examples of untranslated transliterated Arabic words and phrases that challenge and participate in the English heteroglot languages of representation, and these are worthy of their own investigation.[7] For the purposes of this chapter, however, the concern lies in the stratification of the modes of representation, storyteller and narrator and their dialectics as weapons of mass novelistic construction. Magali Cornier Michael states, "Abu-Jaber's *Crescent* certainly participates in this tendency within contemporary fiction to reincorporate elements from oral traditions into the novel form as a means of reinvigorating the novel form as socially relevant" (314). In other words, the interplay between oral storytelling and realist narration produces a formal/aesthetic dynamism that extends to the sociocultural and political themes in *Crescent* and beyond. This brings us to Shahrazad and the context of her storytelling. How does Shahrazad fit as an interventional figure in the US? As we know, the frame story of the *Nights* consists of the tale of king Shahrayar, who avenges his wife's adultery by marrying a virgin every day and putting her to death after taking her virginity. In collectively punishing all women for the adultery of one, Shahrayar believes that he is safeguarding his honor. While *Crescent* does not position the US dominant culture and its influence in the role of Shahrayar per se, the dominant culture's fear and suspicion of Arabs and Muslims nonetheless continue to manifest in modes of physical and structural violence and racism. The figure of Shahrazad as storyteller in *Crescent*, then, intervenes to reframe the representations of Arabs and Muslims, on the one hand, and rehabilitate the dominant culture in terms of Sirine's cross-cultural and gender negotiations, on the other. The message is clear: Do not punish or put under perpetual suspicion *all* Arabs, Arab Americans, and Muslims for the crimes of terrorists.

Nor is this intervention without cost. The "literature of representation," states Arab American writer Samia Serageldin,

> is subject to inhibiting considerations. In particular, themes of sexuality and gender relations rarely escape the politics of representation [. . .] The expectations of many publishers favor the portrayal of oppressive, patriarchal fam-

---

7. For example, in the uncle's story, Aunt Camille (Abdelrahman's mother) encounters "auspicious words [. . .] Fil'Imm, Hal-Awud, Dar'Aktr" (214). The uncle later reveals that the words are "Arablish. Dar'Aktr is Arablish for *director* and Hal'Awud is—*Hollywood*" (296). From there, readers are left to deduce that Fil'Imm is Arablish for *film*, since the uncle is talking about Hollywood and directors. The novel does not reveal the Arabic nature of these words, however. Readers get only the English version. If an Arabic speaker looks closely at these words from an Arabic linguistic perspective, "Fil'Imm" could mean *in the mother*, "Hal-Awud" could mean *will I return*, and "Dar'Aktr" could mean *house of more/plenty* or even *house of Moor* if we wish to pun on *more*. As such, these words become symbols of the narrative in which Aunt Camille (Abdelrahman's mother) is searching for her lost/exilic son, who has not returned home and who is perhaps in the land of plenty.

ily dynamics in the writing of Arab or Muslim women. Yet it is interesting to note that [women] writers resist this agenda. ("The Coming Out" 137)

Implicit in the passage above is the charge that publishers have chosen to publish works by Arab, Arab American, and Muslim women writers that champion and uphold the stereotype of the victimized woman under an exceptional Arab form of patriarchy. In *Do Muslim Women Need Saving?* Lila Abu-Lughod states that "after the attacks of September 11, 2001, the images of oppressed Muslim women became connected to a mission to rescue them from their cultures" (6–7). This burden of representation and expectation of victimhood has inhibited, to a considerable degree, sexual and gendered coming-of-age narratives within Arab and Arab American contexts. In an interesting reversal of traditional gender roles, Arab American women writers find themselves defending the honor and humanity of Arab and Arab American men. In *Crescent,* this is certainly the case of the outspoken character Rana, who chooses to wear the veil. Having been married off to an abusive second cousin at the age of thirteen, Rana explains, "I don't like to tell my American friends, it just feeds all the usual stereotypes—you know, the sheikh with the twenty virgins, all that stuff" (316). *Crescent*'s main Arab male characters—Sirine's uncle and Hanif—are quite sympathetic, however, and do not conform to the stereotypes of Arab men. How does *Crescent,* then, move to reframe, reorient, and rehabilitate the dominant culture in the US?

Sirine's uncle begins his story, which intertwines itself with the novel's realistic third-person mode of narration, with "So this is the moralless story of Abdelrahman Salahadin, my favorite cousin, who had an incurable addiction to selling himself and faking his drowning" (17). It is worth remembering here the novel's gender reassignment of storytelling from a Shahrazadian female storyteller to a male one. In *Crescent,* almost every chapter begins in storytelling mode with Sirine's uncle telling her stories in the style of the *Nights*; he does so for her benefit while Sirine, our expected Shahrazadian figure, travels from telling stories to being an active protagonist in the novel. Sirine "thinks of certain heroines from her uncle's stories—warrior women [. . . She] wants to be this sort of woman and she lets them inspire her but then she worries that she does not have their cleverness or stamina" (102–3). The uncle's storytelling thus acts as an opening frame for the realistic events of the novel. But this story also begins as a departure from traditional storytelling inasmuch as it counterpoints the realistic events of the novel. The designation "moralless" skews the expected moral that opens and closes the story in the Arab tradition, and it develops an accompanying metastorytelling, a meditation on the practices of telling and listening to stories. What exactly is a moralless story, though? Is it immoral or simply amoral? Is it a story of experience that perpetually suspends judgment? The listening reader must wait seventy-one pages (after the mention of the moralless story early in the novel) for an interjection by Sirine's storyteller uncle, in which he asks,

> Are you paying attention? The moralless story requires, of course, greater care and general alertness than your run-of-the-mill, everyday story with a moral, which basically gives you the Cliffs Notes version of itself in the end anyway. A moralless story is deep yet takes no longer to tell than it takes to steep a cup of mint tea. (88)

The interjection or self-interruption by the storyteller creates yet another frame, in which a moralless story is described as one that eludes a moral or moralizing. It is a story that refuses to become a synecdoche or "Cliffs Notes version" of itself, the moral being the teleological determinant of the story's process. The suffix *less* in "moralless" is more in actuality a gestalt: The moralless process of telling and listening is more than the sum of its parts. The story's infidelity to morals and its resulting multiplicity and self-reflexivity thus evade moralizing and stereotyping.

As such, the moralless story demands equal parts of silence and receptivity: It demands interactive listening. Sirine initially interrupts and resists *listening* to her uncle's story:

> "It sounds long," Sirine says. "Haven't I already heard this one?"
> "It's a good, short story, Miss Hurry Up American. It's the story of how to love," he says. (17)

Her reluctance is symptomatic of the conditions of a late capitalist culture in which private/familial time is greatly reduced. Indeed, Sirine states that she is "going to be late for work again" (18). Sirine's uncle diagnoses his niece's position as "Miss Hurry Up American" in response to her impatient question. His story of "how to love" ultimately seeks to ameliorate Sirine's inability to love. The uncle insists that his is a "good, short story," a lie that is also true. The story spans the length of the novel, but does so in short increments, which create that Shahrazadian suspension in which readers are made to wait for the resumption of the story after a section of realistic events. Yet the reverse also becomes true. The realistic frame of representation enters the play of suspension, and the result is an interdependence of cross-framing, a partnership of genres and of storyteller and narrator; counterpoint suddenly overlaps harmonically, and the suspended and its other hybridize.

Crescent's cross-cultural and cross-genre oscillations clearly correspond to Sirine's identity negotiations both as an orphan and as an ethnically mixed Arab American woman who does not speak the Arabic language, as someone who is desperately trying to find her place in between cultures. Here as well, Sirine's uncle offers the mermaid character Alieph (the first letter of the Arabic alphabet), who reveals that mermaids are "born without language itself, until the blue whales take pity on us and teach us to sing [. . .] We live in exile from both people and fish" (271). In fact, it is a narwhale who "agreed that I should understand both sides of my nature—the oceanic and the terrestrial [. . .] He was the one who taught me how to speak and read Arabic" (278–79). It is clear that Sirine's uncle creates Alieph as a model for Sirine, so that she can successfully navigate her Arab and American cultural inheritances. The mode of Shahrazadian storytelling, by vicarious displacement, participates in the audience's overall understanding of Crescent, which moves back and forth between Arab and American cultures formally and contextually. In his essay "Framing in Narrative," Lee Haring adds that

> literary scholars conceive [frame stories] as belonging to a genre; performance critics conceive them as manifestations of a process. To conceive the frame story as a genre makes it an entity, a product, a kind of story (Irwin); to conceive "framing" as a device or skill makes it a strategy. (136)

The combinations and hybridizations in Crescent construct the frame as genre and strategy. Crescent's placing of storytelling and realistic frames side by side provokes a dialectics-in-the-making in every Janus-like chapter. Amal Abdelrazek argues that the "uncle's story emphasizes the significance of oral narratives in the Middle East as a means of 'knowing' reality, a fact that traditional and Eurocentric historiography that solely relies on written, objective, 'factual' and 'authentic' documents, disapproves of" (215). What the uncle wants is for his niece to listen for and hear the story's culturally situated reality, which in turn helps mediate her experiential American reality. Since Sirine (like many of Crescent's readers) does not speak Arabic, she can instead learn to decode and translate the stories' cultural truths within her own life.

Cultural translation is key to the storyteller, narrator, and characters, as well as to the readers who must heal the story-narrative rift while navigating Crescent's transcultural contours. As Carol Fadda-Conrey reminds us, the "novel features various intersecting cultures and maps different minority groups (including Arabs, Arab Americans, Turks, Latinos, and Iranians)" ("Arab American Literature" 188).[8] The cross-cultural interpretations, possibilities, complications, and frames are infinite; these construct and reconstruct what Wolfgang Iser terms the "virtual text" (1524) in which "Contact [. . .] depends upon our continually filling in a central gap in our experience [. . .] Interaction is not given by nature but arises out of an interpretative activity, which will contain a view of others, and, unavoidably, an image of ourselves" (1525). I am not advocating a resuscitation of traditional reader response theory here; rather, I am saying that we must consider the often-hostile cultural response in the US to all things Arab or Muslim. Some readers might not be motivated to interact and fill the gap interpretatively and open mindedly. Yet the contrapuntal frames, as political aesthetics, can intervene favorably and create a space for such cross-cultural translation and negotiation as long as the cultural response (hostile or generous) remains dialogic.

Listening closely to the storyteller and his story, the narrator takes up this cross-cultural gap in a conversation between Hanif and Sirine. Reacting to the uncle's storytelling, Hanif tells Sirine that in "Iraq, everyone tells jokes and fables. It's too difficult to say anything directly" (51). Sirine asks, "You mean like fables are secret codes?" (51). Hanif answers that in Saddam Hussein's Iraq everyone must speak in code to survive the brutality of the regime, and jokes and fables, as oral productions, leave no trace except in the memory of the listener. While *Crescent* is partially a post-9/11 novel, it takes place during the first Gulf War. It begins the story again before 9/11 and imagines an alternative dialogic ending. In so doing, the novel removes the present to a perhaps less fraught past, but it also exposes, in its difference, the sad Arabophobic and Islamophobic reality of the present. Must Arab Americans and, more specifically, Arab American women, doubly speak and write in code, as in *Crescent*, in a post-9/11 US, or can they, inclusively American, find their way back to open and productive dialogue?

The penultimate page of the novel finds Sirine thinking about Hanif, who has returned to Iraq to be with his dying mother. In a powerful moment of story-narrative frame overlap, Sirine

> thinks of the story of Abdelrahman Salahadin. Sometimes, in the months after Han left, when she was falling asleep she got confused and couldn't quite remember if it was Han or Abdelrahman who loved her, if it was Han or Abdelrahman who dove into the black page of the open sea. Was it Abdel-

---

8. An at-length investigation of these interconnections is its own project. This book's thesis on the relationship between poetics and visibility necessarily orients this chapter to intertextual and intergenre connections.

rahman who had to leave her, to return to his old home, or Han who was compelled to drown himself, over and over again. (394)

While demonstrably productive, this overlap of Abdelrahman Salahaddin and Han is also disorienting for Sirine. It constitutes a doorway for yet another negotiation, another beginning. At its closing, *Crescent* seems to offer only the possibility of continued and challenging cross-cultural negotiations, a hint at reconciliation embodied by Sirine and Hanif's possible reunion. What it does not do is offer a realization of the dialogic desire, for, as Sirine's uncle puts it, stories "can point you in the right direction but they can't take you all the way there. Stories are crescent moons; they glimmer in the night sky, but they are most exquisite in their incomplete state" (384).

CONCLUSION

The issue of in/fidelity permeates *Crescent*. Sirine sleeps with the poet Aziz while she is dating Hanif, who himself is concerned with issues of fidelity in translation; and Abdelrahman Salahaddin (one of the heroes of Sirine's uncle's tale) roams the world to forget the infidelity of his wife: "Abdelrahman found his wife in bed with another man [. . .] He left their home vowing never to be betrayed again" (55). Unlike Othello and Shahrayar, however, Hanif and Abdelrahman do not murder their significant others, but react by disappearing. Here, *Crescent* slips back into *The Odyssey*, and Sirine-as-Calypso loses her grip on Hanif-as-Odysseus. The loss of the headscarf and Sirine's infidelity release Hanif from his exile, prompting him to risk returning to Iraq. *Crescent* effectively puts these cross-cultural works into dialogue with one another and demonstrates how Arab American stories are not so distant from North African, European, and American ones. Performing cross-cultural dialogism for the listening and reading audience, *Crescent*, then, moves to reframe, reorient, and rehabilitate the US dominant culture while also critiquing the shortcomings of Arab cultures. The realist sections of *Crescent* end with Sirine answering a phone call from Hanif, who is making his way back to the US after escaping Iraq once again. Sirine's uncle's storytelling, which constitutes the beginning of almost every chapter in *Crescent*, ends with Abdelrahman Salahadin (who turns out to be Omar Sharif) leaving Hollywood to star as Othello/'Utayl in Cairo. Abdelrahman's friend Jaipur Al-Rashid "was going to translate [*Othello*] into Arabic with an all-Egyptian cast, and he was going to have [Abdelrahman] powder his face white [for the role]" (384).

Infidelious layers, divisions, and combinations undermine authenticity on the levels of character, form, and aesthetics in *Crescent*. Abu-Jaber's novel is a formidable multiplex of texts, genres, and allegories that follows a long history of cross-cultural mixing and diffusion. The *Nights* contains stories that "may be traced to diverse origins, such as Indian, Persian, Greek as well as Arabic-Islamic [not to mention additions by European translators, namely, Antoine Galland and Richard Burton]" (Ouyang x). *Othello* is influenced by multiple sources, but "only one significant source has been discovered: *Othello* is closely based on Story 7 in the Third Decade of Giovanni Battista Giraldi Cinthio's *Gli Hecatommithi*" (Neill 21). The source itself contained an "uncharacteristically matter-of-fact style [. . .] which suggest[s] that its origins may lie in some sixteenth-century police report" (23). Furthermore, Shakespeare (unfaithfully) developed and added material to Cinthio's story in order to dramatize and further explore Moorish presence in England. *The Odyssey* "joins together separate, smaller types of narrative [. . .] and the genres of myth that comprise the *Odyssey* are also extant in Near Eastern cultures, often in *Gilgamesh*" (Louden 4, 5). In fact, the

> similarities between Greek and Near Eastern myth suggest some form of diffusion [. . .] The likeliest scenario for cultural diffusion is Greek contact with Phoenician culture [. . .] Since the Greeks obtained their alphabet from the Phoenicians [. . .] and Greek myth assigns key roles to Phoenicians (Cadmus, most importantly), it is likely that the two cultures also engaged in *exchanges of narratives*, or specific genres of myth, as well. (10)

The "*exchanges of narratives*" and cross-cultural translations in *Crescent* demonstrate that the *Nights*, *Othello*, and *The Odyssey* are already suffused with one another and other cultures. The power of narrative is that it is never pure. Cultural infidelity allows stories to travel and reenergize cross-cultural dialogue. The characters of *Crescent* do just that as they travel seamlessly from role to role across time and space. They remind the dominant culture in the US that Arabs are transcultural citizens, who, like so many immigrants, participate in productive cultural infidelities.

CONCLUSION

Arab American Polyphonics

In conclusion, I would like to return to Abdelrahman Salahadin, the character conjured by Sirine's uncle in *Crescent*. Her uncle divulges that "Abdelrahman Salahadin may or may not have been the true name of the movie star Omar Sharif. We'll simply never know for sure. But who really knows anything for sure in this strange and notorious world?" (296). In addition to the overlap between Salahadin and Han in the novel, Sirine's uncle adds another twist by suggesting that Salahadin is, in fact, Omar Sharif. He does so in part to expose the long history of Hollywood's casting of non-Arabs to play Arab roles. The uncle relates that after landing "a few minor roles here and there" (336), Abdelrahman auditions for the lead role in *The Sheik*: "A plum role. Arab incarnate. But they'd given the part to an Italian! [. . .] because no one in Hollywood wanted anything to do with an actual Arab" (336). Rudolph Valentino stars in *The Sheik*, the actor and his role almost synonymous for film aficionados. In one sense, Salahadin is correct to assume that the role would be perfect for him: an Arab playing an Arab. Hollywood, however, has long had an altogether different agenda of representation. The Arabian sheikh that Salahadin would have portrayed becomes infatuated with a modern-thinking Englishwoman and abducts her to his home in the desert. In other words, Salahadin would have stepped into a stereotype with no power to modify it.[1]

---

1. For films such as *The Sheik*, Jack Shaheen identifies a widespread formula: "Desert dramas display Arabs living in an 'old' world. Bellydancers appear as exotic maidens. Producers

Salahadin's trials in Hollywood do not end there, however. He auditions for the lead role in *Lawrence of Arabia*. When he reads the line "a small, barbaric people," "his voice split open the air of the theater like a spear and everyone knew that he would be the star of the movie. Except, of course, how could he be the star, this Jordanian, Syrian, Lebanese, Egyptian, Iraqi, Palestinian, drowned Bedouin of an Arab?" (337). Clearly qualified for the role, Salahadin does not land it precisely because he is an Arab, a combination of six Arab nationalities that are reduced to one. In Hollywood, it is unthinkable for an Arab to play a British character, much less an agent of the British Empire. An "Irishman" (357), a second-class European in this pernicious formulation, proves acceptable, however. Salahadin/Omar Sharif's "failure to land any major Arab role during his forty-year career in Hollywood speaks volumes about the history of Orientalist representations in the American film industry" (Laouyene 589). And this failure extends to other professions in the US that would give Arabs and Arab Americans a podium to speak truth to power. This situation is in part due to the US's multiple interventions (military, economic, and cultural) and interests in the Middle East. More to the point, state foreign policy becomes here a regulatory and coercive force that no hiring committee or human resources department can ignore. Furthermore, these instances of intellectual imperialism within professions are certainly influenced by the Arabophobic and Islamophobic hysteria sweeping much of the US. Constructing a national identity "in opposition to a phantasm of Muslim malfeasance," Moustafa Bayoumi contends, "help[s] to produce a perilous politics, one that buttresses conflict both at home [in the US] and abroad and has the further ability to render [Arabs and] Muslims essentially mute to speak about and represent their own experiences" ("Major Problems" 33). It is worth reiterating that such representations and constructions of the Middle East, which reinforce and promote the designs of US foreign policy, find material resonance on the ground and affect human lives both inside the US and abroad.

Things end well for Abdelrahman Salahadin, however. Sirine's uncle relates:

> And so he *stole* the movie [*Lawrence of Arabia*], just like that. Just like the real Lawrence stole the trust of the Arab tribes and just like the gringos stole

---

present an Arabian stallion, 'Jahad.' (Note the resemblance to Jihad [Holy War].) Arab slavers auction off Arab women to the 'Lords of Harems.' Sheikhs romance Western heroines; saber-wielding desert Arabs furiously fight fellow Arabs to secure the light-complexioned heroines. Should the woman be abducted and whisked off to a lecherous sheikh's enclave, no problem. At the last minute, the dashing Western hero will rescue her. In preparation for amour, mute Arab women attend, bathe, and dress the kidnapped civilized woman of the West" (422–23).

California from the Mexicans, Peter O'Toole stole the movie from Omar Sharif [... who] was actually the true brilliance and beauty and intelligence of the story. (357)

Despite this theft, Sirine's uncle suggests that Salahadin ultimately steals the movie back from Peter O'Toole through his astounding performance. The uncle justifies this stealing back as a form of resistance to a history of injustices, which include the US's winning of the Mexican-American War and annexing Mexican territory (including the province of Alta California), and white actors' appropriation of Arab roles. In a final move of performative justice, Salahadin returns to Cairo to play Othello in whiteface. At stake here is the issue of cross-cultural representation, of who has the power to represent whom. One of the main lessons in this segment of the uncle's story is that art, in its "true brilliance and beauty," has the capacity to creatively and symbolically (and sometimes materially) ameliorate the inequalities of power and representation. The poetics of visibility in the Arab American novels I engage open a space for the reimagining and reimaging of Arab Americans along transcultural and transpoetic lines. Each novel offers its unique intervention and formal and aesthetic combinations; together they create a polyphonic multiplex of Arab American self-expression and art.

As "music combining several lines, each of which retains its identity as a line to some degree [... polyphony] can be synonymous with counterpoint and contrapuntal" ("Polyphony," *New Harvard Dictionary* 645). What makes polyphonic music a particularly apt metaphor or lens for Arab American heterogeneity as exemplified by complex poetics is that the word "music" derives from "*mousike*—but this Greek word doesn't mean 'music.' It is related to the word for Muse and means anything pertinent to the Muses" (Albright 1). In this context, *Poetics of Visibility* explores the capacious, polyphonic Arab American identities and poetics in the selected novels. Its analyses highlight the cultural and ethnic diversities in Arab countries and consider the relationship of Arab American poetics and identities to the multicultural fabric of the US polyphonically. Mikhail Bakhtin finds in Dostoevsky's novels a "*plurality of independent and unmerged voices and consciousnesses, a genuine polyphony of fully valid voices* [...] *a plurality of consciousnesses, with equal rights and each with its own world*" (*Problems* 6). This plurality extends to the voices (or voicings) in Arab American novels, as they give expression to a multitude of Arab American experiences. But it permeates the novels' forms and poetics as well, as they counterpoint the polyphony of voices. In these relationships, poetics and identities retain their specificities while allowing for protean combinations, harmonizations, and even dissonances among Arab Americans themselves and between Arab Americans and fellow minorities and people of color in the US.

These polyphonies do not occur haphazardly, however. Individual Arab American writers compose and orchestrate them in their novels to produce specific effects and affects. The "Orchestration" entry in the glossary of Bakhtin's *The Dialogic Imagination* states,

> Music is the metaphor for moving from seeing [...] to *hearing* [...] Within a novel perceived as a musical score, a single "horizontal" message (melody) can be harmonized vertically in a number of ways, and each of these scores with its fixed pitches can be further altered by giving the notes to different instruments. The possibilities of orchestration make any segment of text almost infinitely variable. (430–31)

It is these possibilities of orchestration (combination) that counteract stereotypical and simplistic representations of Arab Americans. Polyphony in the contemporary Arab American novel operates as an interplay between music and *mousike* (related to the Muses), between combinational possibility (hearing) and parallactic modification (seeing). In the blue notes and accented rhythms in Diana Abu-Jaber's *Arabian Jazz,* and in the oral storytelling sections in Abu-Jaber's *Crescent* and Laila Halaby's *Once in a Promised Land,* in music and in orality/aurality, a shift from seeing to hearing occurs. The illusion of identifying Arabs by sight (with attendant stereotypes and demonizations) is disrupted by jazz-inspired improvisation of language and by the audibility of Arab and Arab American storytellers. These sonic interventions, however, also produce a shift in the seeing of Arabs and Arab Americans, a parallactic modification in which readers are positioned to (re)see the dynamic of the encounter from Arab American perspectives. In Rabih Alammedine's *Koolaids* and Mohja Kahf's *The Girl in the Tangerine Scarf,* the horizontal, vertical, and diagonal combinational possibilities of vignettes and epigraph signs offer visual/conceptual analogues for polyphonic music. The visual/conceptual composites counterpoint (and thus highlight) the sonic components.

The chiastic interplay—hearing to seeing and seeing to hearing—evinces an

> illusion of being able to use the same language for phenomena which are mutually untranslatable and can be grasped only in a kind of parallax view, constantly shifting perspective between two points between which no synthesis or mediation is possible. Thus there is no rapport between the two levels, no shared space—although they are closely connected, even identical in a way. (Žižek 4)

If the orchestration of polyphonic compositions constitutes an illusion, it is a productive one. Not only do these shifts of perspective expose the illogic of anti-Arab racism; they also compose complex, polyphonic art in the process, a poetics of visibility that crosses visual, cultural, aesthetic, and political registers. Polyphony as such is the means for achieving strategic modes of visibility in the contemporary Arab American novel. The task of Arab and Muslim American writing, then, is "to wager more programmatically on formal adventurousness in order to wrest the universal humanity of Muslim and Arab suffering from the grinding machinery of the war on terror" (Gana, Introduction 1580). *Poetics of Visibility* not only demonstrates the heterogeneity of Arab America and Arab American experiences, it also places Arab Americans as transcultural and transpoetic citizens as effectuated by the heterogeneous combinations (polyphonies) in their artistic expressions. Arab American polyphonics (or the art of strategic polyphonic composition as I identify it) is formal adventurousness par excellence, one that produces surprising and unlikely combinations across multiple registers. As such, Arab American polyphonics are a crucial poetics for both individual and collective visibilities on Arab American transcultural and transpoetic terms.

BIBLIOGRAPHY

Abdelrazek, Amal Talaat. *Contemporary Arab American Women Writers: Hyphenated Identities and Border Crossings.* Cambria P, 2007.

Abdulrahim, Sawsan. "'Whiteness' and the Arab Immigrant Experience." *Race and Arab Americans before and after 9/11: From Invisible Citizens to Visible Subjects,* edited by Amaney Jamal and Nadine Naber, Syracuse UP, 2008, pp. 131–46.

Abuelezam, Nadia. "As an Arab Woman, I Feel Equally Visible and Invisible in the U.S." *The Huffington Post,* 9 May 2017, www.huffpost.com/entry/visibly-invisibly-arab_b_5911e4e7e4b0 e3bb894d5ac5. Accessed 3 Feb. 2019.

Abu-Jaber, Diana. *Arabian Jazz.* 1993. W. W. Norton, 2003.

———. *Crescent.* W. W. Norton, 2003.

Abu-Lughod, Lila. *Do Muslim Women Need Saving?* Harvard UP, 2013.

Adorno, Theodor W. *Essays on Music.* Translated by Susan H. Gillespie, U of California P, 2002.

Ahmed, Leila. "The Discourse of the Veil." *Women and Gender in Islam: Historical Roots of a Modern Debate,* Yale UP, 1992, pp. 144–68.

———. *A Quiet Revolution: The Veil's Resurgence, from the Middle East to America.* Yale UP, 2011.

"AIDS Dementia Complex." *HIV InSite,* June 1998, hivinsite.ucsf.edu/InSite? page=kb-04-01-03. Accessed 26 March 2017.

Ajrouch, Kristine J., and Toni C. Antonucci. "Social Relations and Health: Comparing 'Invisible' Arab Americans to Blacks and Whites." *Society and Mental Health,* vol. 8, no. 1, 2018, pp. 84–92.

Alameddine, Rabih. *The Hakawati.* Alfred A. Knopf, 2008.

———. *Koolaids: The Art of War.* Picador, 1998.

———. "Sacred Semantics: Using English to Separate 'Allah' from 'God' Has Become a Dangerous Practice." *Los Angeles Times,* 6 April 2008, www.latimes.com/archives/la-xpm-2008-apr-06 -2-story.html. Accessed 21 June 2017.

Albright, Daniel. *Panaesthetics: On the Unity and Diversity of the Arts.* Yale UP, 2014.

"Al-Khidr, The Green Man." *Khidr.org,* Living Heritage Trust, 2018, khidr.org. Accessed 25 June 2017.

Alsultany, Evelyn. *Arabs and Muslims in the Media: Race and Representation after 9/11.* New York UP, 2012.

Amer, Sahar. *What Is Veiling?* U of North Carolina P, 2014.

An-Na'im, Abdullahi Ahmed. *What Is an American Muslim?: Embracing Faith and Citizenship.* Oxford UP, 2014.

The Arabian Nights. Translated by Husain Haddawy, Everyman's Library, 1992.

Ashcroft, Bill et al. *The Empire Writes Back: Theory and Practice in Post-Colonial Literatures.* 2nd ed., Routledge, 2002.

"'Atil.'" *Arabic-Arabic Dictionary,* edited by Butrus Al-Bustani, 1998 ed., Beirut: Maktabat Lubnan Nashiroun, 1998, p. 611.

Avakian, Arlene. "Baklava as Home: Exile and Arab Cooking in Diana Abu-Jaber's Novel *Crescent.*" *Food, Feminisms, Rhetorics,* edited by Melissa A. Goldthwaite, Southern Illinois UP, 2017, pp. 132–41.

Axelrod, Mark. *The Poetics of Novels: Fiction and Its Execution.* St. Martin's P, 1999.

Bakhtin, M. M. *The Dialogic Imagination.* Translated by Caryl Emerson and Michael Holquist, U of Texas P, 1981.

———. *Problems of Dostoevsky's Poetics.* Translated by Caryl Emerson, U of Minnesota P, 1984.

Banita, Georgiana. "Race, Risk, and Fiction in the War on Terror: Laila Halaby, Gayle Brandeis, and Michael Cunningham." *Lit: Literature Interpretation Theory,* vol. 21, no. 4, 2010, pp. 242–68.

Bayoumi, Moustafa. "East of the Sun (West of the Moon): Islam, the Ahmadis, and African America." *Journal of Asian American Studies,* vol. 4, no. 3, 2001, pp. 251–63.

———. "Major Problems, Minor Solutions: Violence, Identity, and Two Contradictions." *Identity and Conflict in the Middle East and Its Diasporic Cultures,* edited by Mazen Naous, Balamand, Lebanon: Publications of the U of Balamand, 2016, pp. 29–49.

———. "The Race Is On: Muslims and Arabs in the American Imagination." *Middle East Report Online,* 10 March 2010, merip.org/2010/03/the-race-is-on/. Accessed 9 July 2018.

———. *This Muslim American Life: Dispatches from the War on Terror.* New York UP, 2015.

Beckman, Karen. "Nothing to Say: The War on Terror and the Mad Photography of Roland Barthes." *Grey Room,* vol. 34, 2008, pp. 104–34.

Bergerson, Howard W. *Palindromes and Anagrams.* Dover, 1973.

Berlatsky, Eric. "Lost in the Gutter: Within and Between Frames in Narrative and Narrative Theory." *Narrative,* vol. 17, no. 2, 2009, pp. 162–87.

Beydoun, Khaled A. *American Islamophobia: Understanding the Roots and Rise of Fear.* U of California P, 2018.

———. "Viewpoint: Islamophobia has a Long History in the US." *BBC,* 29 Sept. 2015, www.bbc.com/news/magazine-34385051. Accessed 29 June 2017.

Bhabha, Homi K. *The Location of Culture.* Routledge, 1994.

"Blue note." *The New Harvard Dictionary of Music,* edited by Don Michael Randel, Belknap P of Harvard UP, 1986, p. 98.

"Break." *The New Harvard Dictionary of Music,* edited by Don Michael Randel, Belknap P of Harvard UP, 1986, p. 113.

Cainkar, Louise. "No Longer Invisible: Arab and Muslim Exclusion after September 11." *Middle East Report Online,* vol. 32, no. 224, 2002, pp. 22–29, merip.org/2002/09/no-longer-invisible/. Accessed 20 May 2018.

Chan-Malik, Sylvia. *Being Muslim: A Cultural History of Women of Color in American Islam.* New York UP, 2018.

Cherif, Salwa Essayah. "Arab American Literature: Gendered Memory in Abinader and Abu-Jaber." *MELUS*, vol. 28, no. 4, 2003, pp. 207–28.

Clingman, Stephen. *The Grammar of Identity: Transnational Fiction and the Nature of the Boundary.* Oxford UP, 2009.

Cordesman, Anthony H. "Terrorism and Hate Crimes: Dealing with All of the Threats from Extremism." *CSIS: Center for Strategic & International Studies*, 5 July 2017, www.csis.org/analysis/terrorism-and-hate-crimes-dealing-all-threats-extremism. Accessed 9 Sept. 2018.

"Counterpoint." *The New Harvard Dictionary of Music*, edited by Don Michael Randel, Belknap P of Harvard UP, 1986, pp. 205–8.

Crenshaw, Kimberlé. "Why intersectionality can't wait." *Washington Post*, 24 Sept. 2015, www.washingtonpost.com/news/in-theory/wp/2015/09/24/why-intersectionality-cant-wait/?noredirect=on&utm_term=.4c3f07d4a4b5. Accessed 28 June 2018.

Cuddon, J. A. "Anagram." *The Penguin Dictionary of Literary Terms and Literary Theory.* 4th ed., revised by C. E. Preston, Penguin, 1998, p. 35.

———. "Anaphora." *The Penguin Dictionary of Literary Terms and Literary Theory.* 4th ed., revised by C. E. Preston, Penguin, 1998, p. 37.

———. "Repetition." *The Penguin Dictionary of Literary Terms and Literary Theory.* 4th ed., revised by C. E. Preston, Penguin, 1998, pp. 742–43.

Darraj, Susan Muaddi. "Abu-Jaber, Diana (1960–)." *The Greenwood Encyclopedia of Multiethnic American Literature*, edited by Emmanuel S. Nelson, vol. 1, Greenwood P, 2005, pp. 9–11.

———. "Arab American Novel." *The Greenwood Encyclopedia of Multiethnic American Literature*. Edited by Emmanuel S. Nelson, vol. 1, Greenwood P, 2005, pp. 179–82.

"Dawah." *The Oxford Dictionary of Islam.* Edited by John L. Esposito, Oxford Islamic Studies Online, www.oxfordislamicstudies.com/article/opr/t125/e511. Accessed 30 July 2018.

Dawood, Ibrahim et al. "The Arabic Frame Tradition." *PMLA*, vol. 99, no. 1, 1984, pp. 109–12.

Deleuze, Gilles, and Félix Guattari. *A Thousand Plateaus: Capitalism and Schizophrenia.* Translated by Brian Massumi, U of Minnesota P, 1987.

"Demographics." *Arab American Institute*, www.aaiusa.org/demographics. Accessed 29 Dec. 2018.

Derrida, Jacques. *The Ear of the Other: Otobiography, Transference, Translation: Texts and Discussions with Jacques Derrida*, edited by Christie McDonald. Translated by Peggy Kamuf, U of Nebraska P, 1985.

"Devotional Music." *The Oxford Dictionary of Islam.* Edited by John L. Esposito, Oxford Islamic Studies Online, www.oxfordislamicstudies.com/article/opr/t125/e528. Accessed 3 Aug. 2018.

"Dhikr" *Al-Mawrid: A Modern Arabic-English Dictionary*, edited by Rohi Baalbaki, 10th ed., Beirut: Dar El-Ilm Lil Malayin, 1997, p. 563.

Duda, Sebastian. *A Revolving Door of Language: Repetition in American Experimental Writing.* Heidelberg, Germany: Universitätsverlag Winter GmbH Heidelberg, 2011.

Edwards, Brent Hayes. *Epistrophies: Jazz and the Literary Imagination.* Harvard UP, 2017.

El-Hajj, Hind, and Sirène Harb. "Straddling the Personal and the Political: Gendered Memory in Diana Abu-Jaber's *Arabian Jazz*." *MELUS*, vol. 36, no. 3, 2011, pp. 137–58.

Elia, Nada. "A Woman's Place Is in the Struggle: A Personal Viewpoint on Feminism, Pacifism, and the Gulf War." *Food for Our Grandmothers: Writings by Arab-American and Arab-Canadian Feminists*, edited by Joanna Kadi, South End, 1994, pp. 114–19.

Ellison, Ralph. *Invisible Man.* Random House, 1952.

Fadda-Conrey, Carol. "Alameddine, Rabih (1959–)." *The Greenwood Encyclopedia of Multiethnic American Literature*, edited by Emmanuel S. Nelson, vol. 1, Greenwood P, 2005, pp. 121–23.

———. "Arab American Literature in the Ethnic Borderland: Cultural Intersections in Diana Abu-Jaber's *Crescent*." *MELUS*, vol. 31, no. 4, 2006, pp. 187–205.

———. *Contemporary Arab-American Literature: Transnational Reconfigurations of Citizenship and Belonging*. New York UP, 2014.

"Fajr." *Arabic-English Dictionary. Almaany.com*, www.almaany.com/ar/dict/ar-en/%D9%81%D8%AC%D8%B1/. Accessed 9 July 2018.

Fayad, Mona. "The Arab Woman and I." *Food for Our Grandmothers: Writings by Arab-American and Arab-Canadian Feminists*, edited by Joanna Kadi, South End, 1994, pp. 170–72.

Field, Robin E. "A Prophet in Her Own Town: An Interview with Diana Abu-Jaber." *MELUS*, vol. 31, no. 4, 2006, pp. 207–25.

Finley, John H. *Homer's Odyssey*. Harvard UP, 1978.

Foucault, Michel. *Discipline and Punish: The Birth of the Prison*. Translated by Alan Sheridan, Vintage, 1977.

"Four Horsemen of the Apocalypse." *Encyclopædia Britannica*, edited by Adam Augustyn et al., 22 Nov. 2018, www.britannica.com/topic/four-horsemen-of-the-Apocalypse. Accessed 3 May 2019.

Franklin, Anderson J. "Invisibility Syndrome and Racial Identity Development in Psychotherapy and Counseling African American Men." *The Counseling Psychologist*, vol. 27, no. 6, 1999, pp. 761–93.

Friedman, Natalie J. "Adultery and the Immigrant Narrative." *MELUS*, vol. 34, no. 3, 2009, pp. 71–91.

"Fugue." *The New Harvard Dictionary of Music*, edited by Don Michael Randel, Belknap P of Harvard UP, 1986, pp. 327–29.

Gana, Nouri. "In Search of Andalusia: Reconfiguring Arabness in Diana Abu-Jaber's *Crescent*." *Comparative Literature Studies*, vol. 45, no. 2, 2008, pp. 228–46.

———. "Introduction: Race, Islam, and the Task of Muslim and Arab American Writing." *PMLA*, vol. 123, no. 5, 2008, pp. 1573–80.

Gerhardt, Mia I. *The Art of Story-Telling: A Literary Study of* The Thousand and One Nights. Leiden, Netherlands: E. J. Brill, 1963.

Ghazoul, Ferial J. "The Arabization of Othello." *Comparative Literature*, vol. 50, no. 1, 1998, pp. 1–31.

Haddawy, Husain. Introduction. *The Arabian Nights*. Translated by Husain Haddawy, Everyman's Library, 1992, pp. xiii–xxxiii.

Halaby, Laila. *Once in a Promised Land*. Beacon, 2007.

Hall, Kim F. "Race and Religion." *Othello*, by William Shakespeare, edited by Kim F. Hall, Bedford/St. Martin's P, 2007, pp. 171–85.

"Hanif." *Arabic-English Dictionary. Almaany.com*, www.almaany.com/ar/dict/ar-en/%D8%AD%D9%86%D9%8A%D9%81/. Accessed 9 July 2018.

Hanks, Patrick, and Flavia Hodges. "Melville." *A Dictionary of First Names*, Oxford UP, 1990, p. 234.

———. "Melvin." *A Dictionary of First Names*, Oxford UP, 1990, p. 234.

Harb, Sirène. "Arab American Women's Writing and September 11: Contrapuntality and Associative Remembering." *MELUS*, vol. 37, no. 3, 2012, pp. 13–41.

Haring, Lee. "Framing in Narrative." *The Arabian Nights in Transnational Perspective*, edited by Ulrich Marzolph, Wayne State UP, 2007, pp. 135–53.

Hartman, Michelle. "'this sweet / sweet music': Jazz, Sam Cooke, and Reading Arab American Literary Identities." *MELUS*, vol. 31, no. 4, 2006, pp. 145–65.

Hassan, Salah. "UnStated: Narrating War in Lebanon." *PMLA*, vol. 123, no. 5, 2008, pp. 1621–29.

Hassan, Salah, and Marcy Jane Knopf-Newman. Introduction. *MELUS*, vol. 31. no. 4, 2006, pp. 3–13.

Hatem, Mervat F. "The Invisible American Half: Arab American Hybridity and Feminist Discourses in the 1990s." *Talking Visions: Multicultural Feminism in a Transnational Age*, edited by Ella Shohat, MIT P, 1998, pp. 369–90.

Heitman, Richard. *Taking Her Seriously: Penelope and the Plot of Homer's Odyssey*. U of Michigan P, 2005.

"Heterophony." *The New Harvard Dictionary of Music*, edited by Don Michael Randel, Belknap P of Harvard UP, 1986, p. 377.

Hill, Scott. "Elijah and the Green Man." *Chedmyers.org*, 6 Sept. 2014, chedmyers.org/blog/2014/09/06/elijah-and-green-man-scott-hill. Accessed 8 Aug. 2018.

Homer. *The Odyssey*. Translated by Robert Fagles, Penguin, 1996.

Honigmann, E. A. J. Introduction. *Othello*, by William Shakespeare, edited by E. A. J. Honigmann, Arden Shakespeare, 2006, pp. 1–111.

Hout, Syrine. "Of Fathers and the Fatherland in the Post-1995 Lebanese Exilic Novel." *World Literature Today*, vol. 75, no. 2, 2001, pp. 285–93.

———. *Post-War Anglophone Lebanese Fiction: Home Matters in the Diaspora*. Edinburgh UP, 2012.

Irwin, Robert. "Political Thought in the *Thousand and One Nights*." *The Arabian Nights in Transnational Perspective*, edited by Ulrich Marzolph, Wayne State UP, 2007, pp. 103–15.

Iser, Wolfgang. "Interaction between Text and Reader." *The Norton Anthology of Theory and Criticism*, edited by Vincent B. Leitch et al., W. W. Norton, 2010, pp. 1524–32.

"Ittesema." *Al-Mawrid: A Modern Arabic-English Dictionary*, edited by Rohi Baalbaki, 10th ed., Beirut: Dar El-Ilm Lil Malayin, 1997, p. 30.

"I'tussema." *Al-Mawrid: A Modern Arabic-English Dictionary*, edited by Rohi Baalbaki, 10th ed., Beirut: Dar El-Ilm Lil Malayin, 1997, p. 128.

Jamal, Amaney. "Civil Liberties and the Otherization of Arab and Muslim Americans." *Race and Arab Americans before and after 9/11: From Invisible Citizens to Visible Subjects*, edited by Amaney Jamal and Nadine Naber, Syracuse UP, 2008, pp. 114–30.

Jarrar, Randa. *A Map of Home*. Penguin, 2008.

"Jemrah." *Al-Mawrid: A Modern Arabic-English Dictionary*, edited by Rohi Baalbaki, 10th ed., Beirut: Dar El-Ilm Lil Malayin, 1997, p. 430.

Jensen, Kim. "Viruses and Epidemics of Futility." *Al Jadid.com*, vol. 5. no. 28, 1999, www.aljadid.com/content/viruses-and-epidemics-futility. Accessed 20 May 2018.

Jimoh, A. Yemisi. *Spiritual, Blues, and Jazz People in African American Fiction: Living in a Paradox*. U of Tennessee P, 2002.

Kahf, Mohja. *The Girl in the Tangerine Scarf*. PublicAffairs, 2007.

———. "The Pity Committee and the Careful Reader: How Not to Buy Stereotypes about Muslim Women." *Arab and Arab American Feminisms: Gender, Violence, and Belonging*, edited by Rabab Abdulhadi et al., Syracuse UP, 2011, pp. 111–23.

Kaldas, Pauline, and Khaled Mattawa. Introduction. *Dinarzad's Children: An Anthology of Contemporary Arab American Fiction*, edited by Pauline Kaldas and Khaled Mattawa, U of Arkansas P, 2004, pp. ix–xiv.

Kayyali, Randa A. *The Arab Americans*. Greenwood, 2006.

"Khadra." *Al-Mawrid: A Modern Arabic-English Dictionary*, edited by Rohi Baalbaki, 10th ed., Beirut: Dar El-Ilm Lil Malayin, 1997, p. 513.

Khater, Akram Fouad. "'Flying While Arab': The Experiences of Arab Americans in the Wake of 9/11." Review of *Citizenship and Crisis: Arab Detroit after 9/11*, by Detroit Arab American Study Team; and review of *Homeland Insecurity: The Arab American and Muslim American Experience after 9/11*, by Louise A. Cainkar. *Journal of American Ethnic History*, vol. 31, no. 4, 2012, pp. 74–79.

Kidd, Sue Monk. *The Dance of the Dissident Daughter: A Woman's Journey from Christian Tradition to the Sacred Feminine*. HarperCollins, 2016.

King James Version (KJV) Bible. *BibleGateway*, www.biblegateway.com/versions/King-James-Version-KJV-Bible/#booklist. Accessed 17 June 2017.

Kinsella, James. *Covering the Plague: AIDS and the American Media*. Rutgers UP, 1989.

Kostka, Stefan, and Dorothy Payne. *Tonal Harmony: With an Introduction to Twentieth-Century Music*. 3rd ed., McGraw-Hill, 1995.

Laouyene, Atef. "Politics of the Exotic in Diana Abu-Jaber's *Crescent*." *Critique: Studies in Contemporary Fiction*, vol. 56, no. 5, 2015, pp. 586–601.

Leo, John (Al-Hassan ibn Mohammed al-Wezaz al-Fasi or Giovanni Leone, known as Leo Africanus). *A Geographical Historie of Africa*. Translated by John Pory, Londini [Printed by Eliot's Court Press] impensis Georg. Bishop, 1600. *Early English Books Online*, quod.lib.umich.edu/cgi/t/text/text-idx?c=eebo;idno=A05331.0001.001. Accessed 29 Dec. 2018.

Limpár, Ildikó. "Narratives of Misplacement in Diana Abu-Jaber's *Arabian Jazz*, *Crescent*, and *Origin*." *HJEAS*, vol. 15, no. 2, 2009, pp. 249–68.

Louden, Bruce. *Homer's* Odyssey *and the Near East*. Cambridge UP, 2011.

MacFarquhar, Neil. "She Carries Weapons; They Are Called Words." *New York Times*, 12 May 2007, www.nytimes.com/2007/05/12/books/12veil.html. Accessed 22 Sept. 2018.

"Madonnas of the Trail." *Roadsideamerica.com*, www.roadsideamerica.com/story/28991. Accessed 9 July 2018.

Mahnkopf, Claus-Steffen. "Theory of Polyphony." *Polyphony and Complexity*, vol. 1, edited by Claus-Steffen Mahnkopf et al., Hofheim, Germany: Wolke Verlag, 2002, pp. 38–53.

Maitland, Sarah. *What Is Cultural Translation?* Bloomsbury, 2017.

Majaj, Lisa Suhair. "Beyond Silence." *Homemaking: Women Writers and the Politics and Poetics of Home*, edited by Catherine Wiley and Fiona R. Barnes, Garland, 1996, pp. 43–51.

———. "New Directions: Arab-American Writing at Century's End." *Post-Gibran: Anthology of New Arab American Writing*, edited by Munir Akash and Khaled Mattawa, Syracuse UP, 1999, pp. 67–77.

Makdisi, Saree. "'Postcolonial' Literature in a Neocolonial World: Modern Arabic Culture at the End of Modernity." *boundary 2*, vol. 22, no. 1, 1995, pp. 85–115.

Malek, Alia. "Invisible Arab-Americans." *The Nation*, 23 Sept. 2010, www.thenation.com/article/invisible-arab-americans/. Accessed 3 Feb. 2019.

"Maqam." *Al-Mawrid: A Modern Arabic-English Dictionary*, edited by Rohi Baalbaki, 10th ed., Beirut: Dar El-Ilm Lil Malayin, 1997, p. 1086.

"Maqam." *Arabic-English Dictionary*. Almaany.com, www.almaany.com/ar/dict/ar-en/%D9%85%D9%82%D8%A7%D9%85/. Accessed 9 July 2018.

"Maqam." *The New Harvard Dictionary of Music*, edited by Don Michael Randel, Belknap P of Harvard UP, 1986, p. 468.

"Masdar." *Al-Mawrid: A Modern Arabic-English Dictionary,* edited by Rohi Baalbaki, 10th ed., Beirut: Dar El-Ilm Lil Malayin, 1997, p. 1052.

Matar, Dina, and Zahera Harb. "Approaches to Narrating Conflict in Palestine and Lebanon: Practices, Discourses, and Memories." *Narrating Conflict in the Middle East: Discourse, Image and Communications Practices in Lebanon and Palestine,* edited by Dina Matar and Zahera Harb, I. B. Tauris, 2013, pp. 1–14.

Mathes, Carter. *Imagine the Sound: Experimental African American Literature after Civil Rights.* U of Minnesota P, 2015.

McClennen, Sophia A. "America's Real Muslim Problem Is Islamophobia." *Salon.com,* 7 July 2018, www.salon.com/2018/07/07/americas-real-muslim-problem-is-islamophobia. Accessed 22 Aug. 2108.

McCullough, Kate. "Displacement as Narrative Structure: Refugee Time/Space in Diana Abu-Jaber's *Arabian Jazz.*" *American Literature,* vol. 83, no. 4, 2011, pp. 803–29.

Mehta, Brinda. "The Semiology of Food: Diana Abu-Jaber's *Crescent.*" *Rituals of Memory in Contemporary Women's Writing,* Syracuse UP, 2007, pp. 228–62.

Mercer, Lorraine, and Linda Strom. "Counter Narratives: Cooking Up Stories of Love and Loss in Naomi Shihab Nye's Poetry and Diana Abu-Jaber's *Crescent.*" *MELUS,* vol. 32, no. 4, 2007, pp. 33–46.

Michael, Magali Cornier. "*Arabian Nights* in America: Hybrid Form and Identity in Diana Abu-Jaber's *Crescent.*" *Critique,* vol. 52, no. 3, 2011, pp. 313–31.

Mohamed, Basheer. "New Estimates Show U.S. Muslim Population Continues to Grow." *Pew Research Center,* 3 Jan. 2018, www.pewresearch.org/fact-tank/2018/01/03/new-estimates-show-u-s-muslim- population-continues-to-grow/. Accessed 22 Aug. 2018.

Morrison, Toni. *Playing in the Dark: Whiteness and the Literary Imagination.* Vintage, 1993.

Munday, Jeremy. *Introducing Translation Studies: Theories and Applications.* Routledge, 2001.

Naber, Nadine. "Ambiguous Insiders: An Investigation of Arab American Invisibility." *Ethnic and Racial Studies,* vol. 23, no. 1, 2000, pp. 37–61.

———. "Introduction: Arab Americans and U.S. Racial Formations." *Race and Arab Americans before and after 9/11: From Invisible Citizens to Visible Subjects,* edited by Amaney Jamal and Nadine Naber, Syracuse UP, 2008, pp. 1–45.

———. "'Look, Mohammed the Terrorist Is Coming!': Cultural Racism, Nation-Based Racism, and the Intersectionality of Oppression after 9/11." *Race and Arab Americans before and after 9/11: From Invisible Citizens to Visible Subjects,* edited by Amaney Jamal and Nadine Naber, Syracuse UP, 2008, pp. 276–304.

"Nai'm." *Al-Mawrid: A Modern Arabic-English Dictionary,* edited by Rohi Baalbaki, 10th ed., Beirut: Dar El-Ilm Lil Malayin, 1997, p. 1148.

"Nai'm." *Al-Mawrid: A Modern Arabic-English Dictionary,* edited by Rohi Baalbaki, 10th ed., Beirut: Dar El-Ilm Lil Malayin, 1997, p. 1181.

Najmi, Samina. "Naomi Shihab Nye's Aesthetic of Smallness and the Military Sublime." *MELUS,* vol. 35, no. 2, 2010, pp. 151–71.

Neill, Michael. Introduction. *Othello,* by William Shakespeare, edited by Michael Neill, Oxford UP, 2006, pp. 1–179.

Nettl, Bruno. "Introduction: An Art Neglected in Scholarship." *In the Course of Performance: Studies in the World of Musical Improvisation,* edited by Bruno Nettl and Melinda Russell, U of Chicago P, 1998, pp. 1–23.

New International Version (NIV) Bible. Biblica. *BibleGateway.com,* www.biblegateway.com/versions/New-International-Version-NIV-Bible/#booklist. Accessed 15 June 2017.

Oldroyd, George. *The Technique and Spirit of Fugue: An Historical Study.* Oxford UP, 1974.

Oliver, Mary. *A Poetry Handbook.* Harvest Original, 1994.

Ouyang, Wen-chin. "Foreword: Genres, Ideologies, Genre Ideologies and Narrative Transformation." *New Perspectives on Arabian Nights: Ideological Variations and Narrative Horizons,* edited by Wen-chin Ouyang and Geert Jan van Gelder, Routledge, 2005, pp. ix–xv.

Pflitsch, Andreas. "'So We Are Called Lebanese': Rabih Alameddine on the Unbearable Lightness of Being Nowhere at Home." *Arabic Literature: Postmodern Perspectives,* edited by Angelika Neuwirth et al., SAQI, 2010, pp. 321–30.

Phillips, Caryl. "A Black European Success." *The European Tribe,* Farrar, Straus and Giroux, 1987, pp. 45–51.

Pickens, Therí. "Feeling Embodied and Being Displaced: A Phenomenological Exploration of Hospital Scenes in Rabih Alameddine's Fiction." *MELUS,* vol. 38. no. 3, 2013, pp. 67–85.

———. *New Body Politics: Narrating Arab and Black Identity in the Contemporary United States.* Routledge, 2014.

"Polyphony." *The New Harvard Dictionary of Music,* edited by Don Michael Randel, Belknap P of Harvard UP, 1986, pp. 645–46.

Porter, Lewis. *John Coltrane: His Life and Music.* U of Michigan P, 1998.

The Qur'an. Translated by Abdullah Yusuf Ali, *QuranBrowser.org,* 2007. Accessed 12 July 2018.

The Qur'an. Translated by A. J. Arberry. *Archive.org,* 2014, archive.org/details/QuranAJArberry. Accessed 15 June 2017.

The Qur'an. Translated by Rashad Khalifa. *QuranBrowser.org,* 2007. Accessed 15 June 2017.

The Qur'an. Translated by Muhammad Habib Shakir. *QuranBrowser.org,* 2007. Accessed 15 June 2017.

Rabassa, Gregory. "No Two Snowflakes Are Alike: Translation as Metaphor." *The Craft of Translation,* edited by John Biguenet and Rainer Schulte, U of Chicago P, 1989, pp. 1–12.

"Race." US Census Bureau, 23 Jan. 2018, www.census.gov/topics/population/race/about.html. Accessed 10 Feb. 2019.

Rana, Junaid. "The 9/11 of Our Imaginations: Islam, the Figure of the Muslim, and the Failed Liberalism of the Racial Present." *The Cambridge History of Asian American Literature,* edited by Rajini Srikanth and Min Hyoung Song, Cambridge UP, 2016, pp. 503–18.

Rancière, Jacques. *The Politics of Aesthetics.* Translated by Gabriel Rockhill, Continuum, 2004.

Revised Standard Version Catholic Edition (RSVCE). National Council of the Churches of Christ. *BibleGateway.com,* www.biblegateway.com/versions/New-Revised-Standard-Version-Catholic-Edition-NRSVCE-Bible/#booklist. Accessed 15 June 2017.

"Rew." *Merriam-Webster.com,* 2019, https://www.merriam-webster.com/dictionary/rew. Accessed 15 Jan. 2019.

Rihani, Ameen. *The Book of Khalid.* Melville House Publishing, 2012.

Rizvi, Sayyid Muhammad. "The Concept of Polygamy and the Prophet's Marriages." *Al-Islam.org,* 2006, www.al-islam.org/articles/concept-polygamy-and-prophets-marriages-sayyid-muhammad-rizvi. Accessed 25 Aug. 2016.

Rogers, Lynne. "Hypocrisy and Homosexuality in the Middle East: Selim Nassib's *Oum* and Rabih Alameddine's *Koolaids.*" *Journal of Commonwealth and Postcolonial Studies,* vol. 10, no. 1, 2003, pp. 145–63.

Rushdie, Salman. *The Moor's Last Sigh.* Pantheon, 1995.

Said, Edward. *Culture and Imperialism.* Vintage, 1994.

———. Preface to the Twenty-Fifth Anniversary Edition. *Orientalism*, Vintage, 2003, pp. xv–xxx.

———. "Reflections on Exile." *Reflections on Exile and Other Essays*, Harvard UP, 2003, pp. 173–86.

———. "Traveling Theory Reconsidered." *Reflections on Exile and Other Essays*, Harvard UP, 2003, pp. 436–52.

Salaita, Steven. *Arab American Literary Fictions, Cultures, and Politics*. Palgrave, 2007.

———. *Modern Arab American Fiction: A Reader's Guide*. Syracuse UP, 2011.

———. "Sand Niggers, Small Shops, and Uncle Sam: Cultural Negotiation in the Fiction of Joseph Geha and Diana Abu-Jaber." *Criticism*, vol. 43, no. 4, 2001, pp. 423–44.

Saliba, Therese. "Resisting Invisibility: Arab Americans in Academia and Activism." *Arabs in America: Building a New Future*, edited by Michael W. Suleiman, Temple UP, 1999, pp. 304–19.

"Salwa." *Arabic-English Dictionary*. Almaany.com, www.almaany.com/ar/dict/ar-en/%D8%B3%D9%84%D9%88%D9%89/. Accessed 9 July 2018.

Sartwell, Crispin. *Political Aesthetics*. Cornell UP, 2010.

"Scale degrees." *The New Harvard Dictionary of Music*, edited by Don Michael Randel, Belknap P of Harvard UP, 1986, p. 729.

Schulze-Engler, Frank. Introduction. *Transcultural English Studies: Theories, Fictions, Realities*, edited by Frank Schulze-Engler and Sissy Helff, Rodopi, 2008, pp. ix–xvi.

Schuman, Joan. "Pick." *Tucson Weekly*, 22 May 2003, www.tucsonweekly.com/tucson/pick/Content?oid=1072358. Accessed 7 Nov. 2018.

"Sequence." *The New Harvard Dictionary of Music*, edited by Don Michael Randel, Belknap P of Harvard UP, 1986, pp. 739–41.

Serageldin, Samia. "The Coming Out of the Chameleon." *Scheherazade's Legacy: Arab and Arab American Women on Writing*, edited by Susan Muaddi Darraj, Praeger, 2004, pp. 133–42.

———. "Perils and Pitfalls of Marketing the Arab Novel in English." *The Edinburgh Companion to the Novel in English: The Politics of Anglo Arab and Arab American Literature and Culture*, edited by Nouri Gana, Edinburgh UP, 2015, pp. 426–46.

Shaheen, Jack G. *Reel Bad Arabs: How Hollywood Vilifies a People*. Olive Branch P, 2001.

Shakespeare, William. *Othello*, edited by Michael Neill. Oxford UP, 2006.

———. *Macbeth*. *The Norton Shakespeare: Based on the Oxford Edition*, edited by Stephen Greenblatt et al., W. W. Norton, 1997.

———. "Romeo and Juliet." *The Norton Shakespeare*, edited by Walter Cohen et al., W. W. Norton, 1997.

Shakir, Evelyn. *Bint Arab: Arab and Arab American Women in the United States*. Praeger, 1997.

Shalal-Esa, Andrea. "Diana Abu-Jaber: The Only Response to Silencing . . . Is to Keep Speaking." *Al Jadid*, vol. 8, no. 39, 2002, www.aljadid.com/content/diana-abu-jaber-only-response-silencing-keep-speaking. Accessed 7 Nov. 2018.

Shams, Tahseen. "Visibility as Resistance by Muslim Americans in a Surveillance and Security Atmosphere." *Sociological Forum*, vol. 33, no. 1, 2018, pp. 73–94.

Shannahan, Dervla. "Reading Queer A/theology into Rabih Alameddine's *Koolaids*." *Feminist Theology*, vol. 19, no. 2, 2011, pp. 129–42.

Sinno, Nadine. "'Dammit, Jim, I'm a Muslim Woman, Not a Klingon!': Mediating the Immigrant Body in Mohja Kahf's Poetry." *MELUS*, vol. 42, no. 1, 2017, pp. 116–38.

Smith, Giles. "BOOKS / Lives of the rich and famous: Judith Krantz doesn't at all resemble the characters in her novels. As Giles Smith found when he was invited into her lovely Bel Air home." *Independent,* 17 Aug. 1994, www.independent.co.uk/arts-entertainment/books-lives-of-the-rich-and-famous-judith-krantz-doesnt-at-all-resemble-the-characters-in-her-novels-1376972.html. Accessed 15 June 2018.

Stewart, Susan. *Nonsense: Aspects of Intertextuality in Folklore and Literature.* Johns Hopkins UP, 1978.

"Takwir." *Al-Mawrid: A Modern Arabic-English Dictionary,* edited by Rohi Baalbaki, 10th ed., Beirut: Dar El-Ilm Lil Malayin, 1997, p. 362.

"Taqsim." *Al-Mawrid: A Modern Arabic-English Dictionary,* edited by Rohi Baalbaki, 10th ed., Beirut: Dar El-Ilm Lil Malayin, 1997, p. 354.

"Tarjama." *Al-Mawrid: A Modern Arabic-English Dictionary,* edited by Rohi Baalbaki, 10th ed., Beirut: Dar El-Ilm Lil Malayin, 1997, p. 307.

"Tarjama." *Muhit-Ul-Muhit Arabic-Arabic Dictionary,* edited by Butrus Al-Bustani, 1998 ed., Beirut: Maktabat Lubnan Nashiroun, 1998, p. 69.

Taylor, Mark C. "Erring: A Postmodern A/theology." *From Modernism to Postmodernism: An Anthology,* edited by Lawrence E. Cahoone, Blackwell, 1996, pp. 514–33.

Tehranian, John. *Whitewashed: America's Invisible Middle Eastern Minority.* New York UP, 2009.

Todorov, Tzvetan. *The Poetics of Prose.* Translated by Richard Howard, Cornell UP, 1977.

Toossi, Katayoun Zarei. "The Conundrum of the Veil and Mohja Kahf's Literary Representations of Hijab." *Interventions,* vol. 17, no. 5, 2014, pp. 640–56.

"Trent Lott Fast Facts." *CNN,* 20 Sept. 2017, www.cnn.com/2013/09/02 /us/trent-lott-fast-facts/index.html. Accessed 9 Aug. 2018.

"Triplet." *The New Harvard Dictionary of Music,* edited by Don Michael Randel, Belknap P of Harvard UP, 1986, p. 873.

"United States: 'WE ARE NOT THE ENEMY': Hate Crimes against Arabs, Muslims, and Those Perceived to Be Arab or Muslim after September 11." *Human Rights Watch,* vol. 14, no. 6, 2002, pp. 3–41.

"'Utl." *Al-Mawrid: A Modern Arabic-English Dictionary,* edited by Rohi Baalbaki, 10th ed., Beirut: Dar El-Ilm Lil Malayin, 1997, p. 767.

Valassopoulos, Anastasia. "Negotiating Un-Belonging in Arab-American Writing: Laila Halaby's *Once in a Promised Land.*" *Journal of Postcolonial Writing,* vol. 50, no. 5, 2014, pp. 596–608.

"Violence against Women in the United States: Statistics." *NOW.org,* now.org/resource/violence-against-women-in-the-united-states-statistic/. Accessed 26 July 2018.

Wolfson, Elliot. "Flesh Become Word: Textual Embodiment and Poetic Incarnation." *Words: Religious Language Matters,* edited by Ernst van den Hemel and Asja Szafraniec, Fordham UP, 2016, pp. 84–160.

Yaffe, David. *Fascinating Rhythm: Reading Jazz in American Writing.* Princeton UP, 2006.

Yip, Andrew K. T. "Queering Religious Texts: An Exploration of British Non-heterosexual Christians' and Muslims' Strategy of Constructing Sexuality-Affirming Hermeneutics." *Sociology,* vol. 39, no. 1, 2005, pp. 47–65.

Young's Literal Translation (YLT) Bible. *BibleGateway,* www.biblegateway.com/versions/Youngs-Literal-Translation-YLT-Bible/. Accessed 17 June 2017.

Žižek, Slavoj. *The Parallax View.* MIT P, 2006.

INDEX

Abu-Jaber, Diana, 149, 152. See also *Arabian Jazz* (Abu-Jaber); *Crescent* (Abu-Jaber)

Abu-Lughod, Lila, 183

actors, non-Arab, in Arab roles, 189–91

Adnan, Etel, 55

African Americans, 1n1, 3n6, 8, 55–56, 56n1, 64, 69, 75, 82, 85, 87, 93, 95–96, 104, 106, 107, 117

Ahmed, Leila, 97, 107, 109, 118

AIDS, 10–11, 13–17, 19–22, 26, 29–34, 48–50, 52

Alameddine, Rabih. See *Hakawati, The* (Alameddine); *Koolaids* (Alameddine)

al-Khidr, 28, 106, 106n5

Allah: in *Arabian Jazz*, 57–58, 71, 80; in *The Girl in the Tangerine Scarf,* 117; in *Koolaids,* 41–42; in *Once in a Promised Land,* 123, 132

alliteration, 21, 35, 38, 43, 68–70, 74, 115, 126

"Ambiguous Insiders: An Investigation of Arab American Invisibility" (Naber), 1

anagram, 122, 124–25, 127

anagrammatics, 5n8, 128–48

Arab Americans: and "flying while Arab," 125n3; as immigrants, 8–9; invisibility of, 1–3; as Muslims, 83; racial classifications of, 1–2; as term, 2; as white, 1–2, 2n2

Arabian Jazz (Abu-Jaber), 8, 10; alliteration in, 68–70; Arab American in, 75–76; blue note in, 57, 64, 70, 85; improvisation in, 56–58, 62, 65–68, 70, 84; invisibility in, 56; names in, 60–64, 71–72; racial identities in, 81–82; religious stereotypes in, 83–84; rhythm in, 59–60, 66–70; skin color in, 156n4; translation in, 58–59, 61–62, 71–74; transliteration in, 58–59, 61–62; triplets in, 59–60; visibility in, 55, 60, 62, 69, 75, 85

Arabian Nights, The 126–27, 164

Arjuna, in *Koolaids,* 14n1, 14–16

Asian Americans, 1n1, 75–76, 79, 85

"associative remembering," 10

Axelrod, Mark, 6

Bach, Johann Sebastian, 42–45, 47

Bakhtin, Mikhail, 181, 191–92

Bayoumi, Moustafa, 24, 63n3, 77–80, 109, 126, 159, 190

Bergerson, Howard, 129, 147

Beydoun, Khaled, 41, 98, 111

"Beyond Silence" (Majaj), 73

Bhabha, Homi K., 76

Bible, 23–24, 31, 34–36, 39, 41–42, 51, 98

blue note, 55, 57, 61, 64, 64n4, 70, 85, 87, 130n6, 192

Book of Khalid, The (Rihani), 11

Bullough, Geoffrey, 156n3

Caucasian, as term, 76, 76n11

census, 2n2

chords, musical, 64, 64n5, 78–79

Christianity, whiteness and, 76–77. See also Bible

citizenship, 2, 4, 7, 9, 12, 32, 134, 140–43, 159–60
Clever Hassan, 147
Clingman, Stephen, 3, 3n7, 10
Coltrane, John, 79–80. See also *Arabian Jazz* (Abu-Jaber)
Cordesman, Anthony H., 109n7
Cortázar, Julio, 14, 14n1
counterpoint, 25–26, 43–44, 53, 56–58
Covering the Plague (Kinsella), 48–49
Crescent (Abu-Jaber), 11; Arab Americans in, 150; betrayal in, 141n8; exile in, 158–59, 172–75; food in, 151n2, 157, 163; headscarf in, 163–64; identity negotiations in, 185; infidelity in, 150–52, 166–67, 171–78, 187; movies in, 190–91; names in, 156; narration in, 151; *The Odyssey* and, 168–79; *Othello* and, 152–68, 177, 187–88; race in, 159–61; September 11 attacks and, 149, 152; skin color in, 156–57; and *A Thousand and One Nights*, 150, 179–83; translation in, 151, 158, 160, 185–86; visibility in, 163, 170
cross-cultural, 7, 26, 81, 92, 102–3, 119, 151, 157, 180–82, 185–88
cross-signification, 89–90, 92, 97–101, 119–20

Darraj, Susan Muaddi, 16, 57
death: in *Koolaids*, 18, 20–22, 28–30, 43
Deleuze, Gilles, 10
dementia, in AIDS, 15, 17–18, 22, 26, 32–34, 43, 52–53
Derrida, Jacques, 71
Dialogic Imagination, The (Bakhtin), 181, 192
diminutive versions, of names, in Arabic, 140, 140n7, 154–56
Do Muslim Women Need Saving? (Abu-Lughod), 183

Ear of the Other, The (Derrida), 71
Elia, Nada, 76–77
erasure, in *Koolaids*, 30–34
ethnicity, 2, 142, 159. See also race
exile, 18–19, 25, 98, 155, 158–59, 169–75

Fadda-Conrey, Carol, 2, 4, 12, 16, 92, 140–41, 147, 185–86

fajr, 90–91
"Family of Imran" Surah, 91, 103, 123, 132
Faulkner, William, 14–15
faux mémoire, 17–18
Fayad, Mona, 75
Field, Robin E., 149
"flying while Arab," 125–27, 125n3
Foucault, Michel, 3
Franklin, Anderson J., 2, 3n6
Friedman, Natalie, 141, 172
fugue (music), 25–26, 53

Gana, Nouri, 153–54, 193
Geographical Historic of Africa, A (Leo), 156n3
Gerhardt, Mia, 126, 126n4
Ghazoul, Ferial, 153–55
Girl in the Tangerine Scarf, The (Kahf): cross-signification in, 89, 119–20; headscarves in, 101–7, 114–15, 118; identity negotiations in, 116–17; intersectionality and, 111–12; Islamophobia and, 87, 90, 93, 95–98, 105–13; jihad in, 100; *Madonna of the Trail* in, 91–92; music in, 94, 104, 104n4; Qur'an in, 91, 99, 103–4; race in, 111–12; selective lexical fidelity in, 90–91; signs in, 88–89, 92–97, 108, 110–11; success of, 88; synecdoche in, 90–98; visibility in, 87–89, 95, 99, 101, 105, 108, 111–12, 118–19
green: in *Koolaids*, 27–28; in Qur'an, 28n5; in *Girl in the Tangerine Scarf*, 88, 105–7; in *Crescent*, 158–59
Guattari, Félix, 10
Gulf War, 93, 105, 155, 186

Haddawy, Husain, 127, 181
Hakawati, The (Alameddine), 36n7
Halaby, Laila. See *Once in a Promised Land* (Halaby)
Harb, Sirène, 10
Hassan, Salah, 7, 27
headscarves, 101–7, 114–15, 118, 119n11, 133–34, 162–65
hijab, 101–7, 114–15, 118, 119n11, 133–34, 162–65
HIV/AIDS, 13, 15, 17–18, 22, 26, 30–34, 48–49, 52–53

Homer, 150, 168–79
homophobia, 24, 31, 34
homosexuality. See *Koolaids* (Alameddine)
Hout, Syrine, 17–18, 17n3, 25, 50
Huntington, Samuel, 104
hyper-in-visibility, 3–5, 8

identity negotiations, 47, 81, 84, 116–17, 120, 124, 133, 185
Iliad, The (Homer), 175–76
improvisation, 56–58, 62, 65–68, 70, 84
infidelity, 83, 150–52, 164–67, 171–79, 187
interart, 14–15, 47, 52–53
intersectionality, 111–12
invisibility, 1–3, 1n1, 3n6; in *Arabian Jazz*, 56, 60, 69; in *The Girl in the Tangerine Scarf*, 89; in *Once in a Promised Land*, 126, 131, 134, 136, 138, 143–44; silencing and, 8. See also hyper-in-visibility; visibility
invisibility syndrome, 2–3
Iranian hostage crisis, 105, 107, 114
ISIS. *See* Islamic State (ISIS)
Islamic State (ISIS), 41, 108–109, 124
Islamophobia, 3, 9, 41, 87, 90, 93, 95–98, 105–13, 116, 118–19, 121, 127, 137, 180, 186, 190

jazz. See *Arabian Jazz* (Abu-Jaber); music
Jesus Christ, in *Koolaids*, 21–24, 28–29
jihad, 42, 99–100, 102–4, 107, 190n1

Kahf, Mohja. See *Girl in the Tangerine Scarf, The* (Kahf)
Kayyali, Randa A., 76
Khater, Akram Fouad, 125n3
Kidd, Sue Monk, 90, 114
Kinsella, James, 48
Knopf-Newman, Marcy Jane, 7
Koolaids (Alameddine), 10–11; AIDS in, 17–18, 22, 26, 30–34, 43, 48–49, 52–53; Allah in, 41–42; art in, 18–20; Bach in, 42–45; death in, 18, 20–22, 28–30, 43; erasure in, 30–34; as *faux mémoire*, 17–18; God in, 41; green in, 27–28; Lebanese Civil War in, 13, 17, 31, 49–50; narrators in, 18; pastiche form of, 15–16; Qur'an in, 23–24, 41, 51–52; repetition in, 15–17, 20–30, 32, 43–44; skin color in, 156n4; Sodom and Gomorrah in, 34–42; straightness in, 30–34, 38, 45–46; as vignettes, 13–14; visibility in, 156n4
Krishnamurti, Jiddu, 14, 14n1
Krsna, in *Koolaids*, 14–16, 20

Latinx Americans, 1n1
Lawrence of Arabia (film), 190
Lebanese Americans, 2n4, 22, 32, 48, 160
Lebanese Civil War, 13, 17, 31, 48–51
Lebanon, 9, 18–20, 27
Leo, John, 155–56, 156n3
Love Supreme, A (Coltrane), 79–80

Macbeth (Shakespeare), 14, 14n2
Madonna of the Trail, 91–92, 100, 102
Maitland, Sarah, 151
Majaj, Lisa Suhair, 4, 73
maqam, 79–80, 106
Mary (religious figure), 91, 102–4
McKnight, Brian, 104, 108, 112–13
metonymy, 3, 76, 131
Michael, Magali Cornier, 182
microtone, 64–65, 70
Mondrian, Piet, 27–28
Moor's Last Sigh, The (Rushdie), 11
movies, 189–91
music, 25–26, 42–45, 53, 94, 104, 104n4, 191–93. See also *Arabian Jazz* (Abu-Jaber); blue note; *maqam*
Muslims, Arab Americans as, 83. See also Islamophobia
Mutran, Khalil, 154–55

Naber, Nadine, 1, 133, 135
names: in Arab American novels, 74n9; in *Arabian Jazz*, 60–64, 71–72; in *Crescent*, 156; in *Once in a Promised Land*, 129–31, 139–40; in *Othello*, 154–56
Native Americans, 1n1, 55, 73, 81, 84–85, 87, 94

O'Toole, Peter, 191
Odyssey, The (Homer), 150, 168–79, 188
Oklahoma City bombing (1995), 49

Oliver, Mary, 133
Once in a Promised Land (Halaby), 7–8, 11; "After" section in, 127, 146–48; anagrammatics in, 128–48; "Before" section in, 122–27; "flying while Arab" in, 125–27; invisibility in, 143–44; names in, 129–31, 139–40; Qur'an in, 123–24, 132; September 11 attacks in, 121, 125, 129, 135; Shahrazadian mode of storytelling in, 121–22, 126–27, 146–47; thirst in, 124–25; *A Thousand and One Nights* in, 146–47; visibility in, 124, 126–27, 129, 135–36, 143–45; water in, 123–25, 131–32, 136–37
"One Last Cry" (McKnight), 104, 108, 112–13
orientalism, 110–11
Orientalism (Said), 3
Othello (Shakespeare), 150, 152–68, 177, 187–88
Ottoman Empire, 1, 9

pastiche form, of *Koolaids*, 15–16, 31
Pflitsch, Andreas, 33
Pickens, Therí, 22, 33, 40, 51
poetics: defined, 6–7
poetics of visibility, 5–7, 9, 87–88, 191, 193
Poetry Handbook, A (Oliver), 133
polyphony, 25–26, 191–93
Pory, John, 155–56

Qur'an: in *Crescent*, 154, 174; in *Girl in the Tangerine Scarf*, 91, 99, 103–4; green in, 28n5; in *Koolaids*, 23–24, 31, 41, 51–52; in *Once in a Promised Land*, 123–24, 132

race, in *Arabian Jazz*, 66–67, 81–82; in census, 2n2; citizenship and, 159; in *Crescent*, 159–61; in *The Girl in the Tangerine Scarf*, 94–95, 97, 111–12; improvisation and, 65–66; in *Othello*, 153, 161–62; terrorism and, 109n7. *See also* African Americans; Arab Americans; skin color; white(s)
racial classification, 1–2
racialized visibility, 9
racism, 6, 8–9, 56, 82, 95–97, 101, 114, 180, 182. *See also* Islamophobia
Rana, Junaid, 94–95, 107
Reagan, Ronald, 48–49
"Reflections on Exile" (Said), 25

religion, stereotypes and, 83–84; whiteness and, 76–77. *See also* Islamophobia
repetition, in *Koolaids*, 15–17, 20–30, 32, 43–44
Rihani, Ameen. *See Book of Khalid, The* (Rihani)
Roosevelt, Eleanor, 14, 14n1
Rushdie, Salman. *See Moor's Last Sigh, The* (Rushdie)

Said, Edward, 3, 8, 25, 158, 179
Salaita, Steven, 2n4, 4, 15–16, 55, 67, 88, 116, 121
Sartwell, Crispin, 9, 17
scales, musical, 57, 64, 64n4, 66, 78–79
selective lexical fidelity, 62, 90–91
September 11 attacks, 3–4, 41, 87, 121, 125–26, 125n3, 129, 132, 134–35, 139, 142, 149, 152, 186
Serageldin, Samia, 110, 127, 182–83
Shahrazadian mode of storytelling, 78, 78n12, 121–22, 126–27, 146–47, 150, 179–85
Shakespeare, William, 14, 150, 152–69
Shakir, Evelyn, 75
Shalal-Esa, Andrea, 152
Shams, Tahseen, 6, 143
Shamy, Khadra, 41, 41n9, 88
Sheik, The (film), 189, 189n1
Sikes-Picot Agreement, 9
silencing, 8, 140, 152
Sirr-al-'asrar, 180n6
Sitt Marie Rose (Adnan), 55
skin color, in *Arabian Jazz*, 156n4; in *Crescent*, 156–57; in *Koolaids*, 18, 156n4. *See also* race; white(s)
Sodom and Gomorrah, 34–42
Sound and the Fury, The (Faulkner), 14–15
stereotypes, 6, 13, 20, 65, 69, 74–77, 82–84, 114, 116, 125–27, 167, 173, 183–84
straightness, in *Koolaids*, 30–34, 38, 45–46
Surat At-Takwir, 23–24
Surat Yusuf, 51–52
synecdoche, 3, 50, 90–98, 122, 130n6, 131, 156, 184

Syria, 1, 9, 12, 41, 90, 96, 98–99, 116, 118–19, 159

terrorism, 3–4, 41, 49, 105, 107, 109n7, 119, 124. *See also* September 11 attacks
thirst, 124–25
Thousand and One Nights, A, 11, 58, 78n12, 146–47, 150, 164–65, 179–83, 188
Todorov, Tzvetan, 7, 12
tonality, 64, 64n5
Toossi, Katayoun Zarei, 102, 116
transculturality, 4–9, 53, 68, 73, 79, 85, 88, 121, 150–51, 154, 160, 174–75, 191, 193
translation, 58–59, 61–62, 71–72, 71n7, 72–74, 122–23, 151, 158, 160, 185–86
transliteration, 11, 58–59, 61–63, 71, 122
transpoetic, 5–7, 12, 151, 191, 193
"Traveling Theory Revisited" (Said), 179
triplets, 59–60, 63, 68

Valentino, Rudolph, 189

veiling. *See* hijab
Velázquez, Diego, 26–27
vignette, 13–14
visibility, in *Arabian Jazz*, 55, 60, 62, 69, 74–75, 85; in *Crescent*, 161, 163, 170; in Foucault, 3; in *The Girl in the Tangerine Scarf*, 87–89, 95, 99, 101, 105, 108, 111–12, 118–19; in *Once in a Promised Land*, 124, 126–27, 129, 135–36, 143–45; poetics of, 5–7, 9, 87–88, 191, 193; racialized, 9; September 11 attacks and, 3; skin color and, 156n4. *See also* hyper-in-visibility; invisibility; poetics of visibility

water, 123–25, 128, 131–32, 136–37, 162, 169
white(s): Arab Americans as, 1–2, 2n2; in *Arabian Jazz*, 65–66, 73–77, 81–82, 84–85; Caucasian vs., 76, 76n11; in *Crescent*, 158–63, 166; in *The Girl in the Tangerine Scarf*, 87–89, 92–93, 97–98, 101, 105, 108–12; in *Koolaids*, 32
whiteness, 18, 24, 41, 76–77, 158–59

www.ingramcontent.com/pod-product-compliance
Lightning Source LLC
Chambersburg PA
CBHW030137240426
43672CB00005B/166